THE
FEMININE
SPIRIT

at the
Heart of the Bible

THE
FEMININE
SPIRIT

at the
Heart of the Bible

LYNNE BUNDESEN

ANAMCHARA
BOOKS

Anamchara Books
Vestal, New York 13850
www.AnamcharaBooks.com

Paperback ISBN: 978-1-62524-491-8
Ebook ISBN: 978-1-62524-497-0

Cover design by Ellyn Sanna.
Interior design by Micaela Grace.

INTRODUCTION

I first "met" Lynne while sitting on a beach, reading a book I had just bought at a used bookstore. That book, *So the Women Went Her Way*, Lynne's personal memoir, spoke to me about my identity and my relationship with God in a way I'd never experienced. I grew up in a home where Christianity was central to everything we did, and through my growing-up years and young adulthood, I'd never lost touch with my faith. At that moment, though, alone on the beach, I was questioning who I was as a person of faith, as a woman, and as a human being. My selfhood felt emptied of all the meaning I'd taken for granted up until that point. I was cynical and weary, and God seemed irrelevant.

But Lynne's story, though very different from my own, opened a door in my mind. I would read a few pages, and then look out at the waves, letting the ideas settle and take root. At the end of the day, I was sunburned but refreshed. God and the Bible had come alive to me in a practical, useable way that was not only relevant to my life, but suddenly *essential* to my life.

That was more than two decades ago. Lynne's book remained on the bookshelf by my bed, where I could reread it periodically, each time finding that it spoke to me in new ways. I continued to think of Lynne as a friend I had never met, someone who had changed my life. And so, when Lynne and I began corresponding via e-mail, I was delighted to discover that not only her memoir but also *The Feminine Spirit* were available for republication—and I am honored that Anamchara Books has the opportunity now to make these books available once more.

This version of *The Feminine Spirit* is nearly double in length compared to the original book that was published in 2007 by Jossey-Bass. Lynne and I expanded the text in order to better speak to today's social climate. In the twelve years since the book's original publication, and especially during the past few years, there has been a growing awareness among women regarding their identity and relationship to patriarchy, accompanied by a corresponding new understanding among many men. We seem to be at a crisis point now—a moment in time when our world can turn one way or another—and as is so often the case, the impulse to change and grow is countered by resistance to change and growth. Lynne and I hope this book will add another drop to the ever-increasing tide of positive change.

Women today are forging new identities, ones not defined either by patriarchy or the resistance to patriarchy but rather integral to themselves. As philosopher Tamar Ross has noted, "The very polarization of genders—the tendency to dichotomize all of reality in terms of binary opposite—can be seen as a function of a male way of thinking."[1] In creating this book, we have sought to avoid that polarized thinking. God is She *and* He. Both genders are included within the identity of the Divine. Hebrew professor Wil Gafney expresses this well:

She, the Spirit of God, She-who-is-also-God, at the dawn of creation fluttered over the nest of her creation at the same time as He, the more familiar expression of divinity, created all. They, Two-in-One, are the first articulations, self-articulations, of God in (and the God of) the Scriptures. God is female and male, and when God gets around to creating creatures in the divine image, they will be male and female, as God is.[2]

Finding new ways to speak and think is seldom comfortable, however. As I've talked about this book during its production stages, I've found that people (as many women as men) are particularly uneasy about the use of feminine nouns and pronouns to speak of God. It's okay apparently to say God is *like* a mother—but to refer to God as "our Mother" or speak of Her as "she" is not only uncomfortable for many people but also sacrilegious.

And yet we are not seeking to replace Father God. As theologian Elizabeth Johnson has pointed out, "Men, too, are created, redeemed, and sanctified by the gracious love of God, and images taken from their lives can function in as adequate or inadequate a way as do images taken from the lives of women." But Johnson also points out that we have confined God within the box of patriarchy for far too long—and in doing so, we have limited our understanding of who God is and who we are in relation to God.

> Naming toward God with female metaphors releases diving mystery from its age-old patriarchal cage so that God can be truly God—incomprehensible source, sustaining power, and goal of the world, holy Wisdom, indwelling Spirit, the ground of being, the beyond in our midst, the absolute future, being itself, mother, matrix, lover, friend, infinite love, the holy mystery that surrounds and supports the world.[3]

Yes. *That's* why Lynne and I created this book.

And that door Lynne's words opened in my mind all those years ago has swung wider and wider open as I have worked with her. Each chapter we completed brought me new insights and revelations as we uncovered the Feminine Spirit, hidden beneath layers of men's translations and interpretations.

While much scholarship went into this book, on the part of Lynne, myself, and those referenced and noted, in the final analysis we have relied on the philosophy of Blaise Pascal, who had a statement similar to this one sewn into his coat: "God of Sarah, God of Rachel, God of Ruth—not of the philosophers and scholars." Like the Bible itself, this is a book that relies on stories—the experiences of living women and men—more than it does on intellectual or academic proof.

In addition, this book asks us to go one step further. As Rabbi Sandy Eisenberg Sasso has pointed out, "Customarily, when we read the Bible we listen to its ancient words, allowing it to tell us our ancestors' stories." And then Sasso asks, "What would it mean to read the Bible by allowing it to help us tell the stories of our lives? What if we read our joys, our fears, and our doubts into the biblical narrative?"[4] We encourage you to do just that. Find your own story within the Bible.

— Ellyn Sanna
Anamchara Books, Executive Editor

REFERENCE NOTES

1. Tamar Ross. *Expanding the Palace of Torah: Orthodoxy and Feminism* (Waltham, MA: Brandeis University Press), page 8.

2. Wilda C. Gafney. *Womanist Midrash: A Reintroduction to the Women of the Torah and the Throne* (Louisville, KY: Westminster John Knox Press, 2017), page 20.

3. Elizabeth A. Johnson. *Quest for the Living God: Mapping Frontiers in the Theology of God* (New York, NY: Bloomsbury, 2011).

4. Sandy Eisenberg Sasso. *Midrash: Reading the Bible with Question Marks* (Brewster, MA: Paraclete Press, 2013), page 3.

AUTHOR'S NOTE

Reading the
Bible for Ourselves

One Saturday in 1981, while reading the Los Angeles morning newspapers, I noticed the page devoted to religion—three columns by noted male names in Judaism, Roman Catholicism, and Evangelical Christianity, each of whom was blaming women for one thing or another. What happened to women in religion, I wondered? I set the newspapers aside and took a walk on the beach to clear my head.

Women had entered the ministry, become cantors and rabbis, translated texts, and started churches. We

were no longer living in the land described by Elizabeth
Cady Stanton over a century ago, where "the Bible and
the Church have been the greatest stumbling blocks in
the way of women's emancipation." Women in religion
was a big story—so why was it not being reported?
Brushing the sand from my feet, I went into the house
and made a phone call to the editor of one of the newspapers. I suggested a column on women and religion—
and she agreed.

She asked me to write a few samples to give her
an idea of what would be reported. I'd been living outside the United States for some years, and I assumed
eventually she would assign the column to one of her
reporters. As it turned out, I wrote the column for the
next five years. My interviews with eyewitnesses to this
influx of women into key roles in religion allowed me to
reported the creative new ways women were exploring
spiritual beliefs.

I identified somewhat with what Luke, writing in
his Gospel, says:

*Forasmuch as many have taken in hand to set forth
in order a declaration of those things which are most
surely believed among us, Even as they delivered
them unto us, which from the beginning were eyewitnesses, and ministers of the word; It seemed good
to me also, having had perfect understanding of all*

things from the very first, to write unto thee in order, most excellent Theophilus. (Luke 1:1–3 KJV)

Male historians and biblical scholars over the years have described Theophilus as an important first-century man, but I knew enough Greek to know that the translation from the original text is literally "friend of God." Male or female throughout time, we all can be "Theophilus." That term could be applied to each of the women I interviewed and wrote about fifty-two times a year for those five years. From Africa to Argentina, from Korea to Canada, all of them identified themselves as "friends of God."

During that time, I also studied the original language of the Hebrew Bible, and I pondered what it might mean that in the first chapter of Genesis, the Spirit of God, *ruah*, is a feminine-gendered word. I wondered if there were other places in the scriptures of Judaism and Christianity that also described God, Spirit, in feminine language.

And so, for almost forty years, I have been tracing the Feminine Spirit through the pages of the Bible. I've discovered feminine-gendered nouns and pronouns in the original languages, which had been hidden by both the English translations and my own assumption that the biblical God was male. I found verbs applied to God's action that could only describe women's experiences—and yet centuries of male translators had minimized, obscured, or obliterated that meaning. Finding these clues has been a lifelong treasure hunt, filled with the thrill of discovery. Rising above that, however, and even more important to me, was the consistent conviction that the biblical writers do describe a Divine Feminine Spirit who is present and transformative.

If you are uncomfortable with the concept of the Feminine Spirit existing both in scripture and in the world around you, remember that many things considered normal and obvious today were once thought to be heretical. According to the nineteenth-century geologist Louis Aggassiz, "Every great scientific truth goes through three stages. First, people say it conflicts with the Bible. Next they say it has been discovered before. Lastly, they say they always believed it." I suspect something similar is happening when it comes to the scriptural Feminine Spirit.

Our Acute Need for the Feminine Spirit

Thirty years ago, theologian Susan Brooks Thistlewaite noted:

Following a presentation I gave on the Bible and battered women . . . one member of the audience raised the question, "why deal with the Bible at all?" But as anyone who works with abused women knows, this is not an option. . . . Phone calls to shelters often begin with the phrase, "I'm a Bible-believing Christian, but. . . ." We begin to develop a feminist interpretation because the Bible is part of the fabric of the oppression of battered women. . . . Feminist biblical interpretation thus becomes necessary in order for these women to see that the Bible has messages that do not devalue women, but instead empower women. During the process of healing from the emotional trauma of an abusive relationship with a man, religious women also need to reconcile their relationship with the Bible.[1]

Our world today continues to experience the same painful issue. A 2019 study by the Fawcett Society, a UK nonprofit working for gender equality, found that gender is the most common cause of hate crimes against women. The Society stated:

There are as many gender-based hate crimes as there are race-based hate crimes. As this statistic refers only to violent crime, it is clearly the tip of the iceberg. Women are targeted with harassment on the street and online, on an everyday basis. Accepting this as normal creates an environment in which

1 in 5 women have experienced sexual assault, and each week two women are murdered by a partner or ex-partner.[2]

The numbers are even higher in the United States: according to the National Coalition Against Domestic Violence, one out of every four women have been sexually assaulted at some point in their lives—and the FBI reported in 2016 that each week, on average, more than eighteen women are murdered by a partner or ex-partner. Clearly, gender issues go deep, and interpretations of the Bible have played and continue to play a terrifying role in these ingrained attitudes toward women. Interpretations of other sacred texts have also suppressed women—it's a global issue that involves many religions—but this book concerns itself with the Bible.

Reading into the Bible that God is exclusively male has overturned the full biblical message. This mistaken interpretation of the Bible's words leads to and supports sexism. It encourages the abuse and subjugation of women, and it shapes the way we live our lives, raise our children, and choose our leaders. It warps the masculine-feminine relationship, and it damages the whole of humanity.

I do not seek to replace an exclusively masculine perspective with an exclusively feminine perspective. Instead, I believe all genders are aspects of the

Divine One, the Spirit who creates. The genders can be restored to their God-intended identities when the biblical God is encountered as described in scripture—as both Mother and Father, as Feminine and Masculine, the genders existing in simultaneous harmony.

I am not alone in this conviction. The world has changed since 1981, when I first began to study this topic. This book is now part of the exploration going on in many languages in homes and schools and universities and houses of worship, on social media and in the hearts and minds of women and men worldwide. I've noted some of that exploration in this book.

Reading the Bible in the Present Tense

Throughout the decades-long researching and writing of *The Feminine Spirit*, I continued to be struck by the fact that women's activities and thoughts and actions described in the Bible are not different from those of us today. There really is no need to cloud over those women's lives with the assumption that "women of that time" were somehow different sorts of creatures. Women throughout time have had the same desires and responses and aspirations as women today. If, as I believe, the Bible speaks as powerfully and meaningfully in the twenty-first century as it ever did, we may assume the women of those biblical times speak as we would speak, care as we would care, think as we would think, and respond to the Motherhood of God as we do now. If we distance them from ourselves, picturing them as dim, long-ago, powerless figures wearing strange clothes in a foreign land, we lose the immediacy of their message to us.

After all, chronological time is only one way of perceiving reality. There is also cosmic time, the Eternal Now. The Bible takes place in chronological history—and it also happens in the Now. The Bible should be read in the present tense, as relevant and pertinent as it ever was.

Your Personal Encounter with Scripture

Some people read scripture from a literalistic perspective; some read with self-righteousness and the need to prove themselves right and others wrong; some read with fear and guilt; and some read with hope, looking to find comfort and closeness to God. Do not worry about anyone else's reasons for reading the Bible.

Here's my suggestion: simply begin by reading the Bible as the person you are today, with the sum of all your experience. Don't try to manufacture faith or knowledge you don't currently possess, but instead, encounter scripture without preconceptions. Take a Bible, go into a room alone, and shut the door behind you—or if you prefer, take the Bible outdoors.

Scripture becomes more immediate if you read it alone. No one hears with your ears, sees with your eyes, knows what you need or what you want, in just the way you do. Allow yourself to be alone with the Bible and your own unlimited potential for understanding.

Scripture is a lens that magnifies your spiritual self; it can be a guide to your own consciousness. Each reader in each age is always discovering the Bible— and each discovery is new to that reader. You can learn from the past discoveries of other biblical explorers, but you are on your own voyage of exploration.

NOTE

For the purposes of this book, the Hebrew and Christian portions of the Bible are taken as a whole, which will allow a reading of the themes and repeated words from Genesis to Revelation. I am not looking at the Bible as a denominational text, nor do I intend this book to serve as an argument either for or against any particular form of worship or understanding of God. I recommend reading these scriptures as a whole for their inspiration—to you personally, individually—but not in search of arguments to prove anyone else right or wrong.

Translations

Unless you read Hebrew—the original language of the Jewish Bible—or the biblical Greek language of the Christian New Testament, you will be reading a translation. Translations of the Bible exist not only in almost every spoken language on Earth but often in many styles of just one of those languages. Some Bibles have many different translations all on the same page.[3]

Churches and religions use different translations of the Bible, depending on their traditions—but you are not a church or religion. You are an individual about to begin reading the Bible as the person you are today. So take some time to skim through the various translations that are available to you (either in a bookstore or online)—and pick the one that speaks most clearly to you.

Keep in mind, though, that ever since Martin Luther translated the Bible into German in 1522 and the English language King James Version was published in 1611—and even before, the printing press, as well, when the Bible was read mostly in Latin—most translations have reflected the idea that God is male. That concept has informed literature, language, and national and international policies.[4]

Not only the translation of the Hebrew text but also the tone of the language used in the King James Version contributed to our confusion about the nature of the biblical God. In naming the translation after James

I (1566–1625), king of England and Scotland, the translators were fully aware that James was replacing a female monarch, Queen Elizabeth I. James had earlier written for publication his view of the monarch as spiritual patriarch of the people. Given that, it's easy to understand why a magisterial, legal note crept into the King James Bible texts. This tone has come to represent what some refer to as "male thinking"—irrefutable, linear, lacking in nuance.

Yet the original Hebrew biblical texts do not indicate this quality of meaning. Instead, they point to fluidity and process rather than the fiat that created the world in one single edict, without any further effort or change. In her book *The Grammar of God*, Aviya Kushner writes:

> Translating punctuation from the Hebrew Bible is a problem, since ancient Hebrew has no periods, commas, semicolons, colons, exclamation marks, question marks, or quotation marks. The King James Bible, on the other hand, has a lot of punctuation. It affects tense, sound, and sense, but it also makes everything read slower. Way slower. With a period at the end of the sentence, God is definitely done with creation, instead of breathlessly rushing on and possibly still continuing.[5]

Other aspects of the original languages are also obscured in our English translations. An important difference in Hebrew and Greek is the presence of feminine-gendered nouns, which allow us to see more clearly when feminine imagery is being used. Sometimes, the original languages lack pronouns, but "for smoother reading," English translations insert masculine pronouns. And sometimes a clearly feminine metaphor has been replaced with masculine images because the translators simply didn't see—or didn't want to see—that the original authors intended to indicate that God is Feminine.

Jewish author and scholar Aviya Kushner, who grew up in a home where discussions of Hebrew grammar and meaning were ordinary dinner conversation, notes this difference in approach between reading the original Hebrew versions of the Bible and English translations, and she describes her sorrow and confusion the first time she read an English version of the Bible:

Reading [the Bible] in English left me in a new country entirely. I was lost much of the time, and many times saddened at what had been misrepresented or obscured in moving the Hebrew to the English, from the ancient to the more contemporary. . . . But perhaps the biggest surprise was the lone voice of the Bible I encountered in English. . . . The Hebrew text I grew up with is beautifully unruly, often ambiguous, multiple in meaning, and hard to pin down; many of the English translations are, above all, certain.[6]

I encourage you to look past the "certainty" of English translations and encounter for yourself the "beautifully unruly" Bible.

Useful Tools

You don't need a degree in theology to catch the Bible's nuances, but I do recommend that you use a Bible concordance. A concordance is an alphabetical index to biblical words with a reference to the sentence in which each word appears and usually some part of the context. Strong's *Exhaustive Concordance of the Bible*—the easiest to use and most thorough concordance to the King James Version of the Bible—shows every word of that translation of the Bible in alphabetical order. Each word is assigned a number for cross-reference to the original Hebrew or Greek word. Strong's numbering system is used by most other biblical references that use the original Hebrew or Greek.

NOTE

Many versions of the Bible contain concordances (as well as maps, alternate readings, dictionaries, chain

Using a concordance not only tells you where to find words in the Bible but can also totally transform your understanding of the Book. The Bible often speaks in allegory, simile, and parable, and a concordance takes you into those dimensions of thought. Keep in mind, though, that most concordances were also created by men, with a masculine slant on the Bible. As a result, some meanings may be missing.

Another useful tool is a Hebrew or Greek lexicon. Bible lexicons provide definitions and meaning of biblical words found in the original Hebrew languages and New Testament Greek of the Bible. This resource can deepen your understanding of the possible meanings contained within a passage of scripture by giving you the origins and root meaning of the ancient language. Additionally, lexicons give the context and cultural meaning that may have been intended by the authors. They can help you see past the gendered language in an English translation.

NOTE

Lexicons can be found online. Here are a couple of options:

- *https://www.biblestudytools.com/lexicons/*
- *https://biblehub.com/lexicon/*

Your Personal Journey

The Bible can be yours (no church or denomination can possess it), and as such, it is a passport to the greatest adventure of all—the adventure toward self-realization. As Abraham Maslow wrote about this process, "One can choose to go back toward safety or forward toward growth. Growth must be chosen again and again; fear must be overcome again and again. . . . What is necessary to change a person is to change his [sic] awareness."[7] This journey to the Feminine Spirit's connection to your own being is not a religious task; instead, it is a personal and intimate exploration of your inner self—and as it changes your awareness of yourself and the Divine, you too will be changed. The growth that the Feminine Spirit offers has no limits.

And so I invite you to reread scripture with me, from Genesis through Revelation. You'll find my thoughts in these pages, as well as the ideas of other Bible scholars and theologians, but what really matters is this: What do *you* find when you encounter the original meanings found in the Bible?

Now, without anyone looking over your shoulder, turn to the very beginning of the Bible to catch your first sight of the Feminine Spirit: *In the beginning God creates the heavens and the earth, the land being unformed and empty, with darkness over the face of the deep, and the breath of God hovering over the water, God says, "Let there be light. . . ."*[8]

Your journey is underway.

— Lynne Bundesen
May 26, 2019

REFERENCE NOTES

1. Susan Brooks Thistlewaite. "Every Two Minutes: Battered Women and Feminist Interpretation." In *Feminist Interpretation of the Bible*, Letty M. Russell, ed. (Philadelphia: Westminster, 1985), page 97.

2. Fawcett Society. "New Fawcett Data Reveals Gender Is the Most Common Cause of Hate Crime for Women," January 14, 2019,

https://www.fawcettsociety.org.uk/news/new-fawcett-data-reveals-gender-is-most-common-cause-of-hate-crime-for-women.

3. *Whose Bible Is It? A Short History of the Scriptures* by Jaroslav Pelikan (New York: Penguin, 2005) is one of the best and easiest books to read on the history of the Bible and its translations and compilations.

4. *God's Secretaries: The Making of the King James Bible* by Adam Nicolson (Perennial, 2004) is an exhaustive, entertaining, illustrated account of the translators and translation of the King James Bible.

5. Aviya Kushner. *The Grammar of God: A Journey into the Words and Worlds of the Bible* (New York: Spiegel & Grau, 2015), page 19.

6. Ibid., pages vv–vvi.

7. Abraham Maslow. *Toward a Psychology of Being* (New York: Wiley, 1961), page 37.

8. This is a literal translation from the original Hebrew, using the NASB Lexicon.

ONE

IN THE BEGINNING

*In the beginning God created
heaven and the earth·*

—Genesis 1:1 (KJV)

W hat if the biblical God is not male? What if the biblical Creator, in the original language of the Bible, spoke of Herself as a Feminine Spirit?

Genesis 1:12 through 2:3 describes the Creation of the Universe by an all-good, all-powerful God. This Creation—not just of all objects but also of all ideas—sets the tone for the entire Bible. All else, all the remainder of the pages that make up the text of the Hebrew and Christian holy words, are, I think, commentaries. Backgrounds and foregrounds; highlights and dim places; all politics, history, art, relations between women and men; all of it stands in relation to the first chapter of Genesis.

Let's look at what the opening lines of the Bible say about the Creator:

> *In the beginning God created the heaven and the earth. And the earth was without form, and void; and darkness was upon the face of the deep. And the Spirit of God moved upon the face of the waters.* (Genesis 1:1–2 KJV)

"Spirit of God," in the original Hebrew, is *ruah Elohim. Ruah*, the word meaning "spirit," is a feminine noun. *Elohim* is a plural form of "god," which can include both male and female deities. (Some Hebrew scholars believe that making the word plural is a way to "add majesty" or create a superlative.) Nothing is said here about a bearded old man dressed in flowing white robes. What is said is that the Spirit, denoted by a feminine word, of God, a plural word, is Creator—and He/She moves.

So, as you begin your journey, remember what the Bible tells us at the very beginning: life springs from the Feminine Spirit. With this as your foundation, there is no longer either a fearsome father or an overbearing mother to run from or avoid. In fact, from this most primordial concept of God, there is no absent parent for whom to search at all. There is only Spirit, moving. Remind yourself as often as you need reminding: at the very beginning, the God of the Bible is described as Feminine Spirit.

In reading the Bible for yourself, do not dismiss the Book of Genesis as simplistic mythology—and don't make the reverse mistake of reading it from a purely literal perspective. I encourage you also not to skim over the surface of the Creation story, skipping ahead to stories of women and men that are found later in Genesis. The deeper meaning, the continuity, within those stories is found here, in these first chapters.

The Bible is an intentionally self-referential text; there is hardly a line, book, or story that does not relate to another in its pages. Themes repeat themselves, with significant words and ideas underlined by their repetition. To start with the misconception that God is exclusively male and not, as the text says, a creative force that is both feminine and masculine, is to read the pages of scriptures not in the light of the text but under a foggy shadow of misunderstanding.

I recommend that you read the Creation account for yourself. For now, let's examine just a glimpse of the bounty that lies beneath the surface of a few key words in the first chapter of the Bible.

Time

Things happen in the Bible in two different kinds of time. The opening words in the Bible describe one kind of time: in-the-beginning time is spiritual, synchronous, simultaneous. It is everything good that ever was or will be, all happening in the present moment. We are referring to this kind of time when we speak of immortality or eternal life, or when we say "forever."

Simultaneous time can't be measured or budgeted by a clock (or, for the biblical writers who lived before clocks, the setting and rising of the sun or the tides), but at the same time it's not variable. The message of synchronous time is spiritual, perfect, and unvarying. The first chapter of Genesis describes only simultaneous time, a time that is still real today, at this moment.

Time is a mysterious thing. Although it governs our days, we don't truly understand exactly what it is or how it works. Albert Einstein posited that time is relative to the observer, and current physicists suggest one step further, that time is created by the observer.[1] These ideas are hard to fathom, but the Bible also dips in and out of a concept of time that extends beyond our normal understanding.

The second chapter of Genesis, however, introduces time as measurable, whether in hours, days, and years or by genealogies where the generations are named in linear order. This is historical and chronological time (the kind of time where we can say, "My mother was born in 1924," or, "I'll meet you at eight o'clock").

The distinction between these two kinds of time is important. Among other things, it explains miracles, because what we call miracles are events that happen at the intersection of the two kinds of time—timeless truth meeting the lives of men and women in clock time. The time referred to as being "in the beginning" describes Spirit God appearing and acting through the Cosmos simultaneously. In my experience, this kind of biblical time is freedom and endless, perfect peace. It can reach you, often unpredictably, wherever you are in chronological o'clock time.

These two kinds of time intercept throughout the Bible's pages. Keep that in mind.

Water

Water plays such an important role in the Bible that we cannot possibly consider only its literal meaning. As we read in Genesis 1:2, the Spirit of God moves on the face of the waters. In major events found in the early chapters of the Bible–the Ark and the Flood, the parting of the Red Sea—water is also a metaphor for the physical manifestation of the first main element of Creation. According to Rabbi Lawrence Troster, "In the Hebrew Bible, water, wells, dew, rain, cisterns and fountains serve as metaphors for the divine," or to describe Divine attributes.[2] In the Christian New Testament, the water of baptism symbolizes new birth.

Should you choose to pursue this thread through the Bible, you'll find a lifetime of study—seas, ocean, rivers, fountains, rain, snow, hail, and the mixture of water and light, the rainbow.

Day One

The revelation of Creation comes into focus with the words "and God said." God speaks the Universe into existence.

The first thing God says is, "Let there be light" (Genesis 1:3). The original Hebrew word for light is *or*. Later, in the Bible the word is often translated as "revelation" or "truth" or both, and it can have the same symbolic meanings that light has for us today, such as "happiness" and "clarity." (See Strong's concordance for more on this.) Light, like water, streams through the Bible.

All creation in the first chapter of Genesis takes place in the light. Though there is yet no sun, moon, stars, still there is light. Creation is revealed—or more specifically, the truth of what already exists is revealed.

To get a better idea of what I'm talking about here in reference to the Creation of the world, imagine you're moving through a dark house, groping your way by touch. When you hit the light switch, however, the room floods with light—and in stages, your eyes take in every inch, every nook and cranny in the room, including everything that has been purposefully, carefully, artfully placed there for nourishment, comfort, and rest. In a way, that is how Genesis 1:3 introduces the nuances of Creation. Everything is already there in this in-the-beginning time, but the light makes it visible.

> *And God saw that the light was good: and God separated the light from the darkness. And God called the light day and the darkness night. And there was evening and there was morning, one day.* (Genesis 1:4–5, literal translation of the Hebrew)

Notice the word "and" that an English translation inserts at the beginning of each sentence in this passage, indicating an action that continues to flow between the sentences, rather than pausing.

Something else that is evident in this literal translation of the Hebrew words is that the first day of

Creation is called "one day" rather than the "first day." In other words, the first day of Creation is written in Hebrew with the cardinal number "one," while all the other days are described with ordinal numbers (second, third, fourth, and so on). Jewish Bible scholars have paid attention to this small detail in the Hebrew scripture and believe that it implies a sense of completeness in a "time outside of time" before anything else was yet created. The Hebrew word for "one"—*echad*—can also mean "unique" or "alone," indicating that as yet in the Creation story there is nothing else but this oneness. The thirteenth-century rabbi called Nachmanides, whose work is still studied today, wrote that only "when something is formed, time takes hold," allowing for the linear comparison of second, third, and so on.

God's words throughout the Creation story define and make distinctions. There is one source, but not one big blur. So, in the first verses of Genesis, light is day and not night, and as the story continues, more distinctions appear. Dry land is not water, fruit trees are not grass, the moon is not the sun, birds are not whales. Each and every idea is distinct and individual and moves within the context of *ruah Elohim*, the Spirit of God.

The Second Day

And God said, "Let there be an expanse in the midst of the waters, and let it divide the waters from the waters." And God made the expanse, and divided the waters that were under the expanse from the waters that were above the expanse, and it was so. And God called the expanse Heaven. And there was evening and there was morning, a second day. (Genesis 1:6–8, literal translation)

After the light of the first day and the visibility that comes with the light, there is the second day spoken into being by the Voice that clarifies. And it is all harmony—Heaven—though there is still no Earth.

The Third Day

By the third day, Creation is pregnant with activity and implicate, enfolded order (Genesis 1:9–13). References to the "third day" appear throughout the Bible, and each time it indicates a change between the historical story-in-time and the spiritual in-the-beginning time. As you stay alert to the "third day" wherever it is mentioned in biblical texts, you will see that when that day is mentioned, the story moves into another dimension.

On the original third day, dry land appears and the seas are gathered. This same *ruah Elohim* says:

> *Let the earth sprout vegetation. Seed bearing plants and fruit trees of every kind on earth that bear fruit with the seed unit. And it was so. The earth brought forth in vegetation, seed-bearing plants of every kind, and trees of every kind bearing fruit with the seed in it. And God saw that this was good. And there was evening and morning, third day.* (Genesis 1:11–13 TNK)

The text indicates that every plant, every tree, every thing and idea already exists. The seed is within itself, is how the King James Version puts it. All things already have being, not in an hour or a year but in in-the-beginning time where everything already made is made.

Author Aviya Kushner notes in her book *The Grammar of God* that the original Hebrew indicates that on the third day a feminine earth sprouts forth her grass, alongside the masculine seed that yields a second form of grass.[3] This green and living balance between feminine and masculine is ignored in most translations (or, as in the case of the King James Bible, depicted as exclusively male). At this point in Genesis, however, there is no creation of—nor division of—human males and human females.

NOTE

Later, after gender and sex are introduced into biblical accounts, attacks are made on the seed of the woman. The question we can ask is this: are these attacks on woman only—or are they also attacks on the Spirit of God and Creation? As we trace the word seed in the lives of women through the Bible, the answer seems clear to me: woman in the Bible is a surrogate for the attack on the Creation of ruah Elohim. *Woman and the Earth are intertwined within scriptural symbolism, and both have been assaulted and wounded by men and by a patriarchal society.*

The Fourth Day

On this day, the Voice says, "Let there be two luminaries" (Genesis 1:14). These lights divide the day from the night, in the same way that the expanse (or, in the King James Version, the firmament) of verse six divides the waters from the waters. The lights are "set in the firmament of heaven to give light upon the earth and to rule over the day and over the night, and to divide the light from the darkness" (KJV). The light has already been divided into "night" and "day" on the second day, so these two great lights, the sun and the moon, are given to the Earth not only for light but also for "signs and seasons," as well as for days and years.

Note that in Hebrew, we again have a relationship between masculine and feminine indicated here, for "sun" and "moon" are masculine words, while "earth," which receives the light, is feminine. Further, the two lights are to have "dominion" or "rule" over the day and night, and the Hebrew word for "dominion" is also a feminine-gendered word—*memshalah*—the same word that is used later in the Bible for the "realm of God." The stars also appear on the fourth day, which throughout the Bible will be signs of fertility, abundance, and birth. Everything is in its place, and all is good.

The Fifth Day

The Voice rings out again: "Let the waters teem with swarming creatures that have life, and let flying creatures fly above the Earth in the open expanse of the sky (Genesis 1:20, literal translation). The King James Version uses the word "abundantly" in this verse; the Hebrew word, *sharats*, relates to prolific fertility and reproduction. And again, at the end of the day, God sees that it is all good (verse 21).

Abundance is a feminine concept that threads throughout the Bible, taking on added significance as scripture unfolds. In Isaiah, for example, the prophet promises, "For you will nurse and be satisfied at her comforting breasts; you will drink deeply and delight in her overflowing abundance" (66:11 NIV), while the psalmist writes, "They feast on the abundance of your house; you give them drink from your river of delights" (36:8 NIV). This theme extends into the Christian New Testament (look up the word "abundance" in your concordance to see for yourself), where abundance continues to flow out from God to humankind, with the Greek word for "abundance" a feminine noun that speaks of generosity, potency, bounty, and fruitfulness. In the Bible, no virtue is gained nor points awarded for starvation or privation, either physical or emotional. The biblical Creator, the Feminine Spirit of the first chapter of Genesis, provides abundantly for Her children.

Sixth Day

In this ascendant order of Creation, from light to day and night, from Heaven and Earth to seas and land to plants to fish to fowl to beast, to the sixth day when male and female are revealed, the female is the last, the ultimate manifestation of Creation.

> *And God said, "Let us make humankind in our image, according to our likeness". . . . So God creates humans in the image of God, male and female are created.* (Genesis 1:26–27, literal translation)

The feminine-plural *ruah Elohim* says, in Robert Alter's Hebrew translation of Genesis, "Let us make a human in our image, by our likeness." Alter adds in a note:

> *The term* 'adam *(a human) is a generic term for human beings, not a proper noun (suggesting a person's name). It does not automatically suggest maleness . . . and so the traditional rendering "man" is misleading, and an exclusively male* 'adam *would make nonsense of the last clause of verse 27.*

Whether we read male and female to mean two separate genders or one single image that includes both genders as a compound idea, this account lists the female as the last item of Creation, indicating that she is the highest idea in the revelation of the Spirit's unfolding Creation. "Be abundantly blessed," God says to the male-and-female human. "Be fruitful" (verse 28).

The Seventh Day

The Creation outlined in Genesis 1 is now completed in the repetition of God's words, summarizing all the abundance that has been revealed. The crowning achievement is a seventh day in which to survey, set a stamp on, and reflect on the whole of Creation. Just as the living creatures on the fifth day and the male and female on the sixth day are blessed, so too is the seventh-day state of rest blessed (Genesis 2:3).

There are countless examples of good and blessing throughout the Bible. When they are linked with references to the first Creation story with words and phrases such as "water," "the third day," and "light," they are reminders that the story being told is not taking place merely in historical time or geographical location but also in spiritual territory. To explore and settle into spiritual territory, multiple biblical texts describe the light that shines on the path to the place where the light dwells.

But first the scriptural text goes to Eden, where gullible, victimized, incomplete women and weak, frightened, jealous men pass the days of their lives, young and restless, old and forlorn. The feminine concept of the Divine is overturned in chapter 2 of Genesis, where another Creation account and another name for God is introduced.

Unfortunately, life gets complicated under a masculine-gendered concept of God.

REFERENCE NOTES

1. To read more about this, see the *Science Alert* article, "Time Might Exist Only in Your Head, Say Physicists," September 27, 2016, https://www.sciencealert.com/time-might-only-exist-in-your-head-say-physicists.

2. See the online article, "Jewish Teachings on Water" by Rabbi Lawrence Troster, GreenFaith Rabbinic Scholar in Residence, at https://www.faithinwater.org/uploads/4/4/3/0/44307383/jewish_teachings_on_water-greenfaith.pdf.

3. Aviya Kushner, *The Grammar of God: A Journey into the Words and Worlds of the Bible* (New York: Spiegel & Grau, 2015), page 43.

TWO

THE SECOND CREATION STORY

And the Lord God caused a deep sleep to fall
upon Adam, and he slept; and he took one of
his ribs, and closed up the flesh instead thereof.

—Genesis 2:21 KJV

Where is the *ruah Elohim*, the Spirit of God, in the story of Adam and Eve? It's not in the Garden of Eden, not in the biblical text as it's given to us in chapter 2 of Genesis. Instead, another God with another name takes the stage.

If you are a woman and have ever felt that you do not have your own distinct identity, or that you exist only in relation to a man, or that you are walking around in a dream, blamed for things that are not your fault, then you are in the land of Eve, as it's described in the second account of Creation, in chapter 2 of Genesis.

After the first account of Creation has been spelled out, the Bible presents a second creation, which is in complete contradistinction to the first. It is in this account that evil is introduced. From then on, the unhappy parts of the Bible (in which innocents are slaughtered and cities laid waste) lie side by side with the happy parts (in which lives are long and full, and nations and cities are built up and made whole). Sometimes the two accounts of Creation are mixed together within a sentence, verse, or story. It's not always easy to spot when this is happening, but once your vision is sharpened so that you can detect what's going on, you'll have a new understanding of some of the paradoxes in the Bible.

NOTE

The consensus within modern biblical scholarship is that the first chapters of the Hebrew Bible contain at least two written sources, which were woven together, redacted, and amended over several centuries. The older, original sources were kept alongside the newer (though still ancient) perspectives.

Another God, Another Woman

In the second chapter of Genesis, English translations usually use Lord to indicate YHWH. (Jehovah and Yahweh are also used in some translations.) The Hebrew word did not originally mean "lord," however, but rather something along the lines of "the one who is," "the one ever-coming into manifestation," or "the self-existing one." Bible scholars have put forward many reasons (or excuses) explaining why the name was changed; whatever the reason, Jewish scribes and redactors changed YHWH to "lord," starting around the sixth century BCE, and early Church fathers continued the practice. So a word that was genderless and expansive was made limited and masculine, a word that implied no hierarchy was replaced with one that indicated a relationship of subservience. The feminine *ruah*, Spirit, no longer had a role in this version of God's name. But, as we shall see, the name and idea were not erased.

In the second account, woman is created last, just as she was in the first account. But she is not created good.

No other texts have affected women in the Bible-reading world as much as those found in these opening chapters of Genesis. The variety of interpretations of Hebrew words and the various biblical translations leave the consequences of the second account of Creation and subsequent gender relationships to the dominant culture of the era. Joining the Creation by *ruah Elohim* in Genesis 1 to the Creation described in Genesis 2 has deprived both masculine and feminine of their inherent mutual and individual spiritual birthright. The idea that God had to re-create or add to Creation produces not only a rather convoluted theology but also a second class of human beings.

Conflicting Creations

The story of Adam and Eve in the Garden of Eden is not the story of spiritual Creation. It's not even a continuation of the first account, but rather a second, entirely different, turned-upside-down story set against the backdrop of the spiritual revelation in the first chapter, in which the Spirit (feminine) of *Elohim* (plural God) is visible in a light-filled, spiritual, and complete Universe.

Here is how the stories conflict: The Creation sketched by Genesis 2 posits that instead of Spirit moving on the face of the water and the Word calling forth Light, a mist moves up from the Earth and covers everything, watering the entire face of the ground. Then, instead of a blessed and whole male-and-female human emerging as the penultimate issue of *ruah Elohim*, YHWH makes the first man out of the dust of the ground and breathes life into him through his nose.

The "dust-man" is put into a garden called Eden (the root word of Eden means "pleasure").

If you're familiar with Bible stories, you may recall that there are all kinds of trees in the Garden of Eden. One, in the midst of the Garden, is the tree of life. The other tree, in no specific location, is a tree of the *knowledge of both good and evil.*

NOTE

That which has no life but is based rather on abstract knowledge has no geographical place, no specificity of location.

Next, we are given a fairly detailed description of the river that flows out of the Garden and separates into four rivers. A literal reading of the Bible might use these rivers to attempt to pinpoint the exact geographical location of Eden but some biblical scholars believe that just as Genesis describes two sorts of time, it also describes two sorts of "place," one temporal and one cosmic. They compare the four rivers described in Genesis 2 to ancient Assyrian carvings that portray a god pouring out four streams of water from a vase. From this perspective, these rivers point to the transition where Divine water, life, and blessing permeate from God into the human world.[1]

Then a woman is made out of the rib of the dust-man while he is sleeping. She wakes up next to a man she does not know. Poor Eve.

Here in this second chapter of the Bible is where women's ills begin, and it is this chapter that has shaped the false notion that the entire Bible (not to mention God "Himself") created the genders as separate and unequal (rather than simultaneously complete), with one gender subservient to the other.

Before long, according to this account, Eve has doomed all humanity to sin and death. That belief continues, in some form, to this day. It is the product of a literal, out-of-context reading of the Adam-and-Eve story. But this story does not stand alone; rather it stands in contrast to the first chapter of Genesis, where the genders are united in the image of God.

Good and Not Good

The Lord God tells the man to eat from any tree except the tree of the knowledge of good and evil and warns the man that if he does eat from that tree, he shall surely die. The injunction is to know only good (in other words, to not know evil). But what is good?

Previously, in the first chapter of Genesis, God pronounced that many things were good—in fact, all of Creation, including male and female created simultaneously rather than one at a time. In the second chapter account, God announces that for man to be alone is not good. The man has no helper, no *ezer kenegdo*.

There are many interpretations of the meaning of these Hebrew words. Traditionally, they have been thought to mean "suitable helper," with *ezer* being translated as "helper" and *kenegdo* meaning "suitable, appropriate, fit." *Kenegdo* also has other meanings, such as "in front of," "in the presence of," "against," "opposite," and "under." (If it seems strange that one word could have so many meanings, think about the English word *of* and how many variations of meaning it can have.) As you can see, some interpretations of *kenegdo* imply a relationship not of equality between the man and the woman but one of subordination on the part of the woman.

According to Rabbi David Freedman, however, the word *ezer* is a combination of two roots, *'z-r,* meaning "to rescue and save," and *g-z-r,* meaning "to be strong."[2] Freedman points out that the word *ezer* occurs twenty-one times in the Hebrew scriptures, and in many places it definitely carries the implication of strength, as it does in these verses, where the word is applied to God:

There is no one like the God of Israel. He rides across the heavens to help you, across the skies in majestic splendor. (Deuteronomy 33:26 NLT)

Happy art thou, O Israel . . . O people saved by the Lord, the shield of thy help, and who is the sword of thy excellency! and thine enemies shall be found liars unto thee; and thou shalt tread upon their high places. (Deuteronomy 33:29 KJV)

The case can be made, says Freedman, that a more accurate translation of Genesis 2:18 would be: "I will make a power (or strength) that is equal to and corresponding to man." This is the way in which man's loneliness will be removed; it is the way in which "good" will be restored to Creation. When it comes to the Bible, various translations can change the entire meaning of the text—which is then used to claim Divine authority for human attitudes that are far from "good."

Male Versus Female Translators

As the King James Version of the Bible influenced subsequent thought, as well as subsequent Bible translations, so too, for centuries, the Hellenized Jew Philo of Alexandria (20 BCE to 50 CE) helped shape Jewish and Christian writers who viewed women as inferior to men—and this idea was carried over into their interpretation of scripture. The Church fathers Augustine and Aquinas, the twelfth-century Jewish philosopher Maimonides, the Protestant reformer Martin Luther, author John Milton in his epic *Paradise Lost*, and the Reformation leader John Knox, all brought into their work themes from Philo regarding women. Centuries later, Philo's influence can still be seen in the twentieth-century Danvers Statement, in which the Christian Evangelical Council on Biblical Manhood and Womanhood said, among other things, that "Adam's headship in marriage was established by God before the Fall." Using selected biblical texts, the Council included in its mission the notion that some roles in the Church are restricted to men and that women should not resist their husbands' authority. The Bible does not say that (at least not exclusively), as we shall continue to see in later chapters.

NOTE

The Danvers Statement was drafted in 1987 (by both men and women), but it has not fallen by the wayside in the years since. The Council on Biblical Manhood and Womanhood (CBMW) is still active, and in 2017, it issued the Nashville

Statement, to address the issue of same-sex marriage. According to John Piper, the founder of CBMW, the two statements differ in that the main point of the earlier statement was "that God has called men . . . to bear the special responsibility of authoritative teaching and leadership in the church," while the 2017 statement affirms that God-ordained marriage is between one man and one woman.[3]

For centuries, people relied on a translation of scripture that supports this understanding of men's and women's roles. However, though the hierarchical model of biblical creation has been the majority rule, occasionally—and increasingly, over the past century—voices have been raised, sermons preached, and articles and books written presenting another point of view that sees *both* Creation accounts as propounding gender egalitarianism. In many cases, it's been women who have written about this alternate—but more accurate—interpretation of the Bible.

An egalitarian interpretation of the first and second chapters of Genesis blossomed in the Society of Friends (often referred to as the Quakers), particularly in the writings of the seventeenth-century Englishwoman Margaret Fell, who wrote that in the creation of male and female "God joins them together in his own Image, and makes no such distinctions and differences."[4]

Egalitarian readings of the Genesis accounts of Creation became even more widely known and disseminated in the United States of the nineteenth century. Angelina and Sarah Grimke, converts to Quakerism, were abolitionists who asked, "What then can women do for the slave when she is herself under the feet of man and shamed for silence?"[5] Sarah's 1837 letter, "The Original Equality of Women," was a groundbreaking exegesis on the Creation accounts in Genesis, where she affirmed that male and female had been "both made in the image of God" and were "created in perfect equality."[6]

The Shakers, founded by Ann Lee (1736–1784), also noted the plural nature of the word *Elohim* and considered God to have dual gender. In the early twentieth century, Shaker Eldress Anna White explained:

Shakers believe in One God—not three male beings in one, but Father and Mother. And here the Bible reader turns at once to Genesis 1:26. "And God said"—in the beginning of creative work, whether by fiat or evolution matters not—"let us make man in our image, after our likeness." Did three masculine beings appear, in contradistinction to every form of life heretofore known? Nay! Verse 27 says: "So God created man in His own image, in the image of God created He him, male and female created He them."[7]

"But no one," wrote the editors of the exhaustive and authoritative *Eve and Adam: Jewish, Christian, and Muslim Readings on Genesis and Gender,* "more thoroughly established the priority of the first creation account, with its intimations of gender equality, than Mary Baker Eddy."[8] Eddy, the founder of the Church of Christ, Scientist, noted the evidence of two documents in the early parts of Genesis, pointing to the differences between the "Elohistic" portion and the "Jehovistic" portions. Her study of the first account of Creation led her to conclude:

Man and woman as coexistent and eternal with God forever reflect, in glorified quality, the infinite Father-Mother God. To emphasize this momentous thought, it is repeated that God made man in His own image, to reflect the Ideal man and woman divine Spirit. It follows that man is a generic term. Masculine, feminine, and neuter genders are human concepts. . . . The ideal man corresponds to creation, to intelligence, and to Truth. The Ideal woman corresponds to Life and to Love. In divine Science, we have not as much authority for considering God masculine, as we have for considering Him feminine, for Love imparts the clearest idea of Deity.[9]

Then, late in the nineteenth century, Elizabeth Cady Stanton, with a group of twenty-six other women, produced *The Woman's Bible*. Their goal was to challenge the traditional position of religious orthodoxy that woman should be subservient to men. In the commentary on the second chapter of Genesis, *The Woman's Bible* noted:

"In the beginning," proclaims the simultaneous creation of man and woman, the eternity and equality of sex; and the New Testament echoes back through the centuries the individual sovereignty of woman growing out of this natural fact. . . . With this recognition of the feminine element in the Godhead in the Old Testament, and this declaration of the equality of the sexes in the New, we may well wonder at the contemptible status woman occupies in the Christian Church of to-day. All the commentators and publicists writing on woman's position, go through an immense amount of fine-spun metaphysical speculations, to prove her subordination in harmony with the Creator's original design.[10]

Stanton did not seek to overturn the Bible, but rather she hoped that her commentary would liberate women from a theology that had kept them undeveloped as individuals in their own right. Unfortunately, it scandalized even the feminist women of the day, and led to Stanton being removed from her position of influence in the feminist movement.

Stanton might have been happy to know that almost exactly seventy-five years later, biblical scholar Phyllis Trible would present a paper at Andover Newton Theological Seminary that would change the scholarly reading of the second and third chapters of Genesis. "Accepting centuries of (male) exegesis," wrote Trible, "many feminists interpret this story as legitimating male supremacy and female subordination. They read to reject. My suggestion is that we reread to understand and to appropriate." She went on to argue against the patriarchal assumption that Eve, being created second, was intended to be subordinate to Adam:

> The last may be first, as both the biblical theologian and the literary critic know. Thus the Yahwist account moves to its climax, not its decline, in the creation of woman. She is not an afterthought; she is the culmination. Genesis 1 itself supports this interpretation, for there male and female are indeed the last and truly the crown of all creatures.

Trible also pointed out that in the Eden story, "the man is not dominant; he is not aggressive; he is not a decision-maker."[11]

NOTE

Phyllis Trible went on to write several books, including God and Rhetoric of Sexuality *and* Texts of Terror: Literary-Feminist Readings of Biblical Narratives. *In the decades since Trible's initial work, women theologians have proliferated—and yet their work is still considered controversial in many branches of Christianity, even in the twenty-first century.*

The Fall

After the story of Creation, comes the story of the Fall, which has long been considered to be the original source of humanity's sinfulness. A narrative device occurs here that is repeated again and again throughout the Bible: the story that starts with a man moves to a woman and her situation or condition—and this is where the action takes place. In this case, a talking serpent appears and asks the woman, "Did God really say you couldn't eat from any tree in the garden?" After some discussion, Eve does eat from the tree; she then gives the fruit to Adam, who meekly accepts it without any discussion at all.

When God confronts Adam and Eve with their actions, Adam immediately blames Eve. Or actually, he first blames God for making Eve in the first place, and then he blames Eve. The woman, however, sticks to reporting the facts and makes no excuses for her actions: "The serpent deceived me and I ate" (3:13). Eve admits her actions, blaming neither God nor Adam.

Down through the millennia, men have continued to blame women for their own sinfulness. In the second century, the Church father Tertullian taught that all women are like Eve in that they are "the devil's gateway," "the first deserter of the divine law," who destroyed "God's image, man." This thinking was an underlying force in the Church all through the Middle Ages, when it provided the Inquisition with its theological justification for persecuting women as witches. It showed up yet again in the teachings of Protestant reformers such as Luther, Knox, and Calvin, who all wrote of women's seductiveness and evil. Even today, some Christian denominations point to Genesis 3 to justify men's right to "discipline" their wives—and women who are victims of marital abuse may accept it, believing that it is their biblical duty to be punished.

NOTE

The Malleus Maleficarum *("Hammer Against Witches"), a fifteenth-century document that drew heavily on a male-biased interpretation of Genesis 3, was a bestseller in Europe, second only to the Bible, for two centuries after its publication.*

The result of Adam and Eve's disobedience is that they are expelled from the Garden of Eden. Adam is told, "Because you have listened to the voice of your wife, and have eaten of the tree about which I commanded you, 'You shall not eat of it,' cursed is the ground because of you; in toil you shall eat of it all the days of your life" (Genesis 3:17 NRSV). Men who find it painful to listen to women's voices or accept their insights have sometimes used this verse to justify the notion that they too will be cursed if they, like Adam, give heed to the women in their lives. In sharp contrast to this apparent condemnation of Adam for listening to the voice of Eve, however, the biblical men who do listen to women and act on what they have to say are the ones we remember today. Abraham, Isaac, Jacob, David, Jesus, and Paul are all included in that list.

Meanwhile, in Genesis 3 God says to Eve, "I will greatly multiply your pain in childbirth, in pain you will bring forth children" (3:16 NASB). The Bible says nothing about Eve's female descendants sharing her pain, and yet many generations of women have referred to their monthly menstrual cycle as "the curse." There is no question that women's bodies have become a battlefield for a host of opinions and ills. The "curse" on Eve continues to cast its shadow on how women's bodies are seen today.

Investigations into different standards of medical treatment for women and men reflect layers and layers of assumptions based on this perspective. Researchers and physicians have tended to assume that, with the exception of the sexual organs, men's and women's bodies are the same. Assuming a male body to be the standard for all humans has resulted in research that drew conclusions based solely on male subjects, with repercussions on every area of women's health.

NOTE

In 2001, University of Maryland academics Diane Hoffman and Anita Tarzian published an analysis of the ways gender bias plays out in clinical pain management and concluded that women were more likely to be inadequately treated by health-care providers, which they attributed to "a long history within our culture of regarding women's reasoning capacity as limited." Similarly, a 2016 study from University College London revealed that women with dementia receive worse medical treatment than men with the condition. And a 2017 study by the American Heart Association and the US National Institutes of Health found that if a woman collapses

Not all theologians agree that God's words to Adam and Eve after their disobedience should be viewed as punishment for sin, but rather they might be seen as simply a summary of the consequences of their actions. (Language focusing on sin is not introduced in Genesis until Cain murders his brother Abel in Genesis 4.) According to this interpretation, the story is meant to indicate the origins of work (for the man) and child-bearing (for the woman), while it implies no female subordination but does accept the reality experienced by men and women for millennia to come.[13]

After the Fall

Feminist Bible scholars have often focused on the first three chapters of the Bible, but Jewish theologian Ilana Pardes suggests that these early chapters of Genesis are a part of a "larger unit of primeval history."[14] Pardes further points out that although biblical studies have often considered the Fall to be the conclusion of the story of Creation, the first ten chapters of Genesis do not single out Adam and Eve's transgression as *the* Fall, but instead describe multiple failures on the part of humans—both men and women—and after each of these incidents, the world is reestablished and equilibrium is restored, implying that Creation is ongoing.

Genesis 4 begins with Eve naming her son, and in many of the stories in the Hebrew scriptures, women will be the ones who name their children, indicating that their authority in this area was recognized. Furthermore, in Genesis 4:1, Eve states that with Yahweh, she has acquired a manchild,[15] implying that she considers herself to be an equal co-creator with God (while she makes no mention at all of Adam's role in the process).

Umberto Cassuto, who was one of the first Bible scholars to acknowledge how radical this verse truly is, suggested that "the first woman in her joy at giving birth to her first son, boasts of her generative power, which approximates in her estimation to the Divine creative power," allowing her to "feel the personal nearness of the Divine presence to herself."[16]

For all that patriarchy is described throughout the Bible, again and again, from the very beginning, women in the Bible upend their roles as subordinates—and their voices are heard and recorded. "Through the naming of her sons," concludes Ilana Pardes, "the primordial mother insists upon her own generative powers and attempts to dissociate motherhood from subordination."[17]

The Begats

Despite all our modern-day interest in ancestry, the long genealogies in the Bible can seem monotonous—and meaningless—to a twenty-first century reader. The first genealogy listed in the Bible in the fifth chapter of Genesis, the genealogy of Adam, Seth, Enos, Cainan, Mahaleel, Jared, Enoch, Methuselah, Lamech, and Noah, can make your eyes glaze over. If you read the list literally, skim over it, or dismiss it as an example demonstrating that the Bible is about men long dead, however, you will miss the message. Even the pesky "begats" can take on new meaning when you use a concordance. What on the surface looks like a boring chronological history of patriarchy (notice that contrary to Eve's pronouncements, men do all the begetting in this genealogy) becomes, instead, a spiritual message concealed in the names.

Remember, our English translations only offer one interpretation of the Hebrew words, when there is often more than one meaning to the Hebrew. Using this approach to find the hidden significance in the Hebrew names yields this: human (Adam), places (Seth), incurable sickness (Enos), deplorable (Cainan), the blessed God (Mahaleel), descends (Jared), teaching (Enoch), death sent away (Methuselah), to the distressed (Lamech), and comfort/rest (Noah). If you read this as a narrative, what seemed to be a list of male *begats* is transformed into an encoded message of hope that says, "Humanity placed in incurable sickness is deplorable, and therefore the blessed God descends, teaching that death be sent away and bringing to the distressed comfort and rest."

This may seem a stretch at first glance. But it seems less so if you're familiar with the concordance, those names in Hebrew, the variety of their implications and interpretation, and the fact that the Bible's message is not about patriarchy but about the nondenominational and complete Spirit of God: the creative Mother caring for her children . . . for you

The Flood

Even if you're not familiar with much of the Bible, you've probably heard of Noah, the Ark, and the Flood. Although only the males in the story are given names (Noah and his sons—but not their wives), enfolded in the midst of the Flood story are more glimpses of the first version of Creation: "seven days" is a significant time period that is mentioned more than once; the animals are brought into the Ark as both males and females; and the Ark is lifted above the earth on the waters—the same waters upon which the Feminine Spirit of God moved in Genesis 1. *Ruah Elohim* also moves the Ark and its inhabitants.

The Ark represents safety and security, a place evil and danger cannot reach. It's a feminine word, and the Ark's purpose is much like a woman's womb. Both carry life and keep it safe until conditions are ripe for it to emerge.

When the floods at last subside, Noah sends out a raven to test if it is safe for him, his family, and the animals to leave the Ark. The raven—which in Hebrew is a masculine word—goes out but does not return, so Noah next releases a bird that carries feminine gender in Hebrew—a dove. The dove returns to Noah, indicating that there is not yet enough dry land for her to perch, and Noah brings her back into the Ark with him. Then Noah waits another seven days before he sends the dove out again—and this time she returns to him with a "fresh-plucked olive leaf" in her beak (Genesis 8:11). The faithful dove is an echo of the Feminine Spirit who brings the promise of life, fertility, and fresh abundance to the Earth. Later, in the New Testament, the dove once more appears, this time with an explicit reference to the Spirit, when She descends on Jesus "in the bodily form of a dove" (Luke 3:22).

The Flood comes to give humankind a second chance by wiping away the Adam and Eve story with all its repercussions for men and women. Afterward, God—the Existing One—establishes a new covenant and promise with Noah. This new promise is memorialized in the rainbow (which is feminine in Hebrew). Like the dove, the rainbow reappears later in the Bible, in both the Hebrew scriptures and the Christian New Testament, where it represents Divine splendor and glory, as well as being a reminder that even in apparent destruction, the Feminine Spirit always seeks humanity's salvation and renewal.

According to the biblical account, those of us who are alive today are all descendants of Noah and his family—so why do we continue to hold on to our sense that we carry the "sin" of Adam and Eve? Adam and Eve are dead and gone, and their "curse" has been buried with them, washed away by the Deluge of Creation's waters.

REFERENCE NOTES

1. This perspective is examined nicely by Terje Stordalen in her article "Heaven on Earth: Jerusalem, Temple, and the Cosmography of the Garden of Eden," which can be accessed at https://tidsskrift.dk/cb/article/download/16986/14747.

2. Rabbi David Freedman. "Woman, a Power Equal to Man," *Biblical Archeological Review 9* (1983): 56–58.

3. John Piper. "Precious Clarity on Human Sexuality: Introducing the Nashville Statement," *Desiring God*, August 29, 2017. https://www.desiringgod.org/articles/precious-clarity-on-human-sexuality.

4. Margaret Fell. *Women's Speaking Justified*, location 32.

5. This quote can be found in *The Letters of Theodore Weld, Angelina Grimké Weld and Sarah M. Grimké, 1822–1844* (New York: DeCapo Press, 1970), pages 425–432.

6. Grimke, Sarah. *Letters on the Equality of the Sexes and the Condition of Woman* (1838).

7. From *Shakerism: Its Meaning and Message* by Anna White and Leila S. Taylor (Columbus, OH: F.J. Heer, 1905), page 255.

8. Kristen E. Kvam, Linda S. Schearing, and Valarie H Ziegler, eds. *Eve and Adam: Jewish, Christian, and Muslim Readings on Genesis and Gender* (Bloomington: Indiana University Press, 1999).

9. From Mary Baker Eddy's *Science and Health with Key to the Scriptures* (Boston, MA: Trustees under the Will of Mary Baker G. Eddy, 1906), pages 516–517.

10. *The Woman's Bible* (Edinburgh: Polygon, 1898), pages 20–21. The entire book is available online at https://www.sacred-texts.com/wmn/wb/index.htm.

11. Phyllis Trible's paper, "Eve and Adam: Genesis 2–3 Reread" (Copyright 1973 by Andover Newton Theological School) is available online at https://www.law.csuohio.edu/sites/default/files/shared/eve_and_adam-text_analysis-2.pdf.

12. Fay Shopen. "The Healthcare Gender Bias: Do Men Get Better Medical Treatment?" *The Guardian*, November 20, 2017.

13. To read more about this interpretation, see Carol Meyers' *Rediscovering Eve: Ancient Israelite Women in Context* (New York: Oxford University Press, 2013).

14. Ilana Pardes. *Countertraditions in the Bible* (Cambridge, MA: Harvard University Press, 1993), page 178.

15. Literal translation of the Hebrew.

16. Umberto Cassuto. *A Commentary on the Book of Genesis. Part One: From Adam to Noah* (Jerusalem: Magnes, 1953), pages 201–202.

17. Pardes. *Countertraditions in the Bible*, page 181.

THREE

THE BREASTED ONE

*And Sarah said' God hath made me laugh'
so that all that hear will laugh with me'*

–Genesis 21:6 (KJV)

G od tells husbands to obey their wives.

The God of the Bible, the God of Creation, says to Abraham, "In all that Sarah hath said unto thee, hearken unto her voice" (Genesis 21:12 KJV). But that's a Bible verse the patriarchy has ignored.

Instead, the story of Abraham, Sarah, and Hagar has been read for centuries as a patriarchal text. Now, through new scholarship, revelation, and common sense, it's become obvious that the God revealed in these texts is not a fearsome male God but a Mothering God. The texts also clearly relate a narrative of spiritual power coming to women; women are agents for change, and their rights are acknowledged. Both sexes, without regard to their ethnic background or nationality, hear and speak to God. Descendants are promised to both Hagar and Abraham, and both have children who receive a blessing.

Ruah Elohim, the Creator of the first chapter of Genesis, appears with new names in the lives of the first matriarch, her maid, and her husband. As *ruah Elohim* enters their lives, biblical women and men are no longer myths or abstract concepts but instead appear as real people with whom we can identify. And we see that the Feminine Spirit has intense concerns involving compassion, fertility, life, and identity.

A closer reading of the texts that begin with Genesis 11 and continue on through Genesis 22 has revised what we once thought about God's nature—and what the Bible has to say about women. In these texts:

- God comes to powerless women.
- God works through biological conception.

- Ticking biological clocks are rewound.

- The "curse" in childbirth is reversed.

- Children are a blessing.

- A woman sees God face to face.

- A woman identifies God and gives God a new name.

- God announces for Herself a new name.

- Laughter is introduced as an appropriate reaction to God's revelation.

- A man weeps for a woman.

More Than History

After the Flood, a new story begins in Genesis 11, a family history that still impacts the world even today, thousands of centuries later. It begins with these words:

Now these are the generations of Terah: Terah begat Abram, Nahor, and Haran; and Haran begat Lot. (Genesis 11:27 KJV)

Judging by this verse, you might think that the story that will follow will be about some men who are the descendants of a man named Terah. But the Bible often makes a statement that leaves out the part that will be later revealed to be relevant for the development of the spiritual meaning concealed within the factual narrative. This is what's happening here.

One of the many ways in which the Bible is instructive is in its simple telling of a story. The accounts it gives are often so sparse, even ambiguous, that the reader has to fill in the blanks. This process may raise questions that reach beyond the text. The Bible becomes the background, while the reader's thought moves into the foreground, played out on the canvas of the narrative's desert landscape. Go even deeper, behind the desert background, and there *ruah Elohim* moves, speaks, and appears.

And so we learn that Haran dies, and then the text moves right along, focusing ever more sharply on the main point.

> *And Abram and Nahor took them wives: the name of Abram's wife was Sarai.* (Genesis 11:29 KJV)

And now, in the next verse, we learn what the story is actually about:

> *But Sarai was barren; she had no child.*

And yet this is not merely a story about a child born against the odds to a woman and her husband.

As we read more closely, we find enfolded within it the days of spiritual Creation in Genesis 1 and the continuing displacement of clock time with synchronous time. Another way to think about in-the-beginning, synchronous time is to say that within the framework of this story, we see that God insists on becoming all that exists. What's more, not only does clock time fall beneath spiritual time, but the curses from Eden are also lifted—and Judeo-Islamic-Christian history begins.

The story of Abram and Sarai starts a fascinating progression of biblical women who conceive despite what we know today about the patterns of biology. In fact, Sarai is an example of a breakthrough in conception, although at this point, early in the account, we have no indication that she or Abram want children.

The name "Sarai" means literally "princess," and the Hebrew word carries within it the implication of authority, leadership, and dignity; we're not talking about a Disney princess here! Perhaps Sarai, a strong woman used to her freedom and power, liked being a childless princess, free to travel with Abram. Perhaps he liked it that way too. Or perhaps the culture of the day demanded that they have children, whatever they may have secretly wanted. Whatever was the case, as their story begins we know only that she is married and barren.

And then, with no previous announcement, God speaks to Abram, calling him to "get up and go" (*lekh lekha*) from his father's house to a land that God will show him. For Abram and Sarai, leaving the house of their family and starting over is essential. Their move breaks family patterns, and in the process, God, rather than any biological mother or father, is revealed as benevolent Parent. This loving Mother-Father will be with them throughout their lives.

The Bible: An American Translation (AAT) continues the story with these easy-to-read words:

> *When he was on the point of entering Egypt, he said to his wife Sarai, "See now, I know that you are such a beautiful woman that when the Egyptians see you, they will say, 'This is his wife.' And they will kill me in order to keep you. Please say that you are my sister, so that I may be well treated for your sake, and my life spared through you.* (Genesis 12:11–13)

Interpretations of this passage are mixed. The one heard most often is that Abram is being manipulative and dishonest, while Sarai is silent property with no say in the matter. The text, however, actually indicates that Abram is asking—not telling—his wife, that he treats her as an equal in this journey but he understands possible implications for her and their marriage, as well as himself, and that this may be the wisest thing to do. By entering Egypt, the couple are leaving their own culture and must be prepared to handle the demands of another society. Furthermore, Sarai *is* in fact Abram's half-sister, though the text does not divulge that information until later.

"The Egyptians saw that the woman was very beautiful and she was taken into Pharaoh's household and Abram was well treated for her sake" (Genesis 12:14–16 AAT). Sarai apparently enters Pharaoh's harem, and as a result, Abram owes her his life. Although we hear nothing from Sarai during these events, she is the pivotal figure in the couple's shared journey. The author of the text seems intent on making clear that Sarai's role is critical to everything that unfolds.

Author and Torah teacher Chana Weisberg notes that when the Bible calls Sarai by name, it is underlining her strength and even superiority. When the story enters the territory of Egypt, however, Sarai is referred to only as "the woman," indicating that within the Egyptian culture, women were judged by their physical appearance rather than their spiritual and emotional power.[1]

God, however, remembers Sarai by name, and because of her, the story tells us, plague strikes Pharaoh's household. Pharaoh, angry over the couple's subterfuge, sends the couple on their way, with all Abram's great wealth intact. No mention is made that either Abram or Sarai suffers from this episode.

Echoes of Creation

Abram and Sarai continue on their journey, and eventually, they find a place to settle down. At this point in the story, the Divine Being makes a startling announcement: "I will make thy seed as the dust of the earth: so that if a man can number the dust of the earth, then shall thy seed also be numbered" (Genesis 13:16 KJV).

Within this Divine promise are key words from both the first and second accounts of Creation—*seed* and *dust*: the seed within itself from the third day of Creation in the first chapter of Genesis; and dust, the stuff of which Adam was made, as recounted in the second chapter. What these words together give us is a glimmer that *Elohim* has reformed the Adam story by taking control over "the dust." The Spirit of God is to be in charge of human conception and the multiplication of ideas, as in the first Creation. This is a promise from the Creator that things will evolve—Creation is a continuing process—and that stages of consciousness are involved in the fulfillment of Divine Creation. To go back a bit, to the first verse of chapter 13, the story tells us that Abram "went up from Egypt," which metaphorically indicates that his development is rising to a new height—and ours can as well, as we continue with Abram and Sarai on their journey.

One of the stages of the Divine evolution in their story is a strange meeting with the king of Salem, Melchizedek. The Hebrew word *salem* means "peace," and *melchizedek* means, literally, "my king is justice." Melchizedek brings Abram bread and wine; he blesses him; and he introduces still another name for God—*El Elyon*, "God the Most High" (Genesis 14:18–20). As Abram and Sarai—and we the readers—journey, new views and understandings of the Divine reveal themselves.

One way to read this story is to stop here and use a Bible concordance to look up the words "bread" and "wine," which reveals a richness hidden within simple events. Not only are bread and wine timeless parts of human life, but their spiritual meaning throughout the scriptures indicates the bounty of Divine provision that is available at every stage and state of consciousness.

NOTE

Melchizedek is the first "priest" to appear in the Bible. This mysterious figure is mentioned again later in the Bible, first in the Book of Psalms and then in the Epistle to the Hebrews, where he is linked with Jesus. The author of Hebrews states that this "king of peace" was "without father or mother, without genealogy, without beginning of days or end of life, resembling the Son of God, he remains a priest forever" (7:3 NIV).

Implicit in this encounter in the desert is a sense of a sacred idea being unfurled, for after this exchange of bread and wine, God gives yet another new description of Divinity: "I am a shield to you: Your reward shall be very great" (TNK).

From Seeds to Stars

Any author who tells a story chooses which events to include—as well as which to leave out—and places them in an order that will best express the deeper meaning within the narrative. The ancient author of this account is no different.

In this case, what follows next is Abram's question about his childlessness—and God's reply: "Look up to the heavens, and count the stars, if you can count them. . . . So shall be your seed" (Genesis 15:5 TNK). Adam's seed was like dust—but Abram's will be like the stars.

Biblical thought is seldom a straight-line narrative but instead starts with one idea and then moves beyond that into a broader or deeper concept. Here, for example, we see the third-day reference to the seed, but now we have moved into fourth-day Creation, where the stars and other luminaries are made. Abram's heirs are no longer children of dust; now they are numberless children of light. God's spiritual Creation is revealing itself to human thought as Abram's consciousness continues to climb upward, moving from one phase of spiritual Creation to the next.

If we are meant to learn from this biblical experience, then a meaning we may draw from this is that while Spirit's promises always come true, fulfillment does not always come with the first dawning of an idea. From the standpoint of synchronous time, all that God promises already exists, but the progression of clock time may be required before we see the visible realization.

Women's Decisions

After God's promise to Abram, Sarai says to her husband, "The Lord has kept me from having children. Go, sleep with my maidservant; perhaps I can build a family though her" (Genesis 16:2 NIV).

Though Sarai's offer to send Abram to her slave girl's bed may seem either selfless or stupid, though it may seem clear to us as the readers that trouble is bound to ensue, the Bible passes no judgment on Sarai's actions (contrary to the traditional notion that throughout the Bible's pages, women are judged and found wanting). Scripture simply tells the story, without editorializing: "He slept with Hagar, and she conceived. When she knew she was pregnant, she began to despise her mistress" (Genesis 16:4 NIV).

Now, Sarai tells Abram that he is responsible for the situation—but Abram responds that it's up to Sarai to figure out how to resolve this crisis. Throughout the story, Sarai has been in charge, and she continues to be. She is responsible for her own consciousness of God and Divine expectations, and she asks God (not Abram or any other man) to judge the matter directly (Genesis 16:5–6).

We may be so aware Sarai did something foolish (at least from our Western, twenty-first-century perspective) that we miss the profound biblical point that's being made here: women are in charge of their own decisions and their own understanding of God. Readers of this passage have often projected into it their limited knowledge of the culture of those times and assumed that Sarai had no legal rights or status. As we read the Bible stories as they are written, however, laying aside our preconceptions, we can see that the patriarchs were by no means the rulers of their households. Sarai is the first of a line of woman who make pivotal decisions, while the men obey, follow, and go along.

Hagar's Story

Hagar despises Sarai—and Sarai responds by being hard on Hagar. The Bible narrator feels no need to analyze, explain, excuse, or judge either Hagar or Sarai. It merely states that Hagar ran way.

And now, for the first time in the Bible, an angel appears—and not to a man, but to a woman, a woman who is suffering, alone, foreign, and without societal status. Hagar is the first of a long line of biblical women whose children are announced or named by angelic representatives. The Bible often does not distinguish between God and an angel (a Divine messenger), and so in this story, the "angel of the Life-Giver" (which is one possible interpretation of "Yahweh") is later referred to by Hagar as God, rather than as an angel.

The angel finds Hagar beside a "spring of waters in the wilderness." This is a biblical code for *ruah Elohim*, the Feminine Spirit who moved "on the face of the waters" in the first chapter of Genesis. The angel asks the questions of the ages: "Where have you come from? And where are you going?" (Genesis 16:8).

NOTE

Throughout the Bible, the wilderness is a place where intense experiences occur, both physically and emotionally. The Hebrew word for wilderness, midbar, comes from the same root as "mouth" and "words." Revelation, the word of God, is often given in wild and lonely places.

Hagar answers directly and to the point, as women in the Bible often do: "I flee from the face of my mistress Sarai." The angel tells her to go back to Sarai and accept her authority, but Hagar will not go back unchanged. Instead, she receives the same promise that has been unfolding to Abram—the promise that her descendants will be too numerous to count—as well as the information that she is pregnant with a son. The angel tells Hagar to name her child "Ishmael" (which means "God has heard"), because "Yahweh has heard your affliction" (Genesis 16:10–11).

New Names for the Divine

Hagar, a woman, is the first person in scripture who names God for herself. She calls the Divine One *El-roi*, which means literally "the seeing God who sees" or perhaps "I have seen the God who sees." She indicates the transforming depth of the experience when she asks, "Have I even remained alive here after seeing?" (Genesis 16:13). The spring of waters is also given a new name: *Beer-lahai-roi*, which means "Well of the Living One Who Sees Me." The Hebrew word for "well" is feminine, implying that from this source of life has issued the Spirit of God. The God who both sees and hears—the Feminine Spirit—has entered into a reciprocal relationship with Hagar, allowing Herself to be seen and heard.

Ishmael is born and the years go by. Abram is now ninety-nine years old, and he and Sarai still have no children together. But God comes to him for the seventh time, again promising to "multiply" him abundantly. Note here the appearance again of Divine abundance, as mentioned in the Creation story, as well as the echo of the seventh day, the day of Creation's completion when *Elohim* rested and saw that everything was very good.

During this seventh meeting with Abram, God reveals to him another new name for the Divine—*El Shaddai*. Most English translations (including Strong's concordance) have used the word "Almighty" to translate *Shaddai*, but scholarship over the past century has revealed that the word actually means "Breasted One" or "Double-Breasted One."

Many Christians, and some Jewish scholars, are uncomfortable with this translation. A quick search on Google brings up numerous attempts to refute it, including these arguments:

- Although *shad* is the Hebrew word for "breast," *Shaddai* does not in fact come from the word *shad* but rather from *shadad*, meaning "to deal violently with, despoil, devastate, ruin, destroy, spoil," which is correctly interpreted as "Almighty." Far from being womanly and breasted, the God of Israel is fearsome, powerful, and masculine.

- *Shaddai* does come from the Hebrew word *shad*, meaning "breast"—but the root for *shad* is *shuwd*, which means "to ruin, destroy, spoil, devastate" (perhaps because breasts are temptations and therefore can "ruin a man"), thus bringing us back to the interpretation that God is violent and dangerous.

- Any reference to breasts, particularly multiple breasts, could not possibly be the correct translation, since this would imply a blasphemous connection to the "abominable practices" of ancient fertility cults, which scripture consistently condemns.

- *Shaddai* is actually from an ancient Semitic language, rather than Hebrew, and refers to mountains, not breasts, with the implication that God is high or elevated, hence "almighty." To say that mountains are in fact rather like breasts would be a misunderstanding of how the ancient mind shaped metaphor according to action rather than appearance. Thus, the implied meaning might also have to do with the refreshment, safety, and sustenance to be found wherever the Bible makes reference to mountains—but not breasts.

- To focus on the literal meaning of the Hebrew word *shad*, which is admittedly "breast," as the root for the name *El Shaddai* is a shallow interpretation. Our concept of God should not be limited by one attribute that may encourage us to form an idol-like concept of a female god. A less confusing translation would be "Mighty Sustainer."[2]

Clearly, the notion that God could have breasts, even metaphorical ones, makes many people uncomfortable. This sampling of online theorizing illustrates what lengths people have gone to in order to conceal the Feminine Spirit.

The Divine name *El Shaddai,* as well as simply *Shaddai,* will show up again in the Bible. In almost all cases, it is used alongside a blessing connected with fertility. As Rabbi Arthur Waskow says, "In the Bible all the blessings in which Shaddai is over and over invoked are about fruitfulness and fertility. God is seen as an Infinite Mother, pouring forth blessings from the Breasts Above and the Womb below, from the heavens that pour forth nourishing rain, from the ocean deeps that birth new life."[3]

El Shaddai makes a covenant with Abram that his descendants will become a great nation. God also gives Abram and later Sarai new names: Abraham and Sarah. Names have meaning and power throughout the Bible, and in this case, they signify that Abraham and Sarah have entered yet another new phase of their lives. "I will make you abundantly fruitful," God promises (Genesis 17:6).

After God's promise to Abraham regarding his descendants, Abraham's thoughts turn immediately to his only son at the time, Ishmael, Hagar's son. God replies that yes, Ishmael will also receive the Divine blessing of fruitfulness, but then God makes clear that another promise made to Abraham concerns Sarah, whom God speaks of by name. This covenant has one catch, though—God asks that Abraham and all the other males in his household be circumcised.

By focusing on the male phallus, many feminist Bible scholars believe we are now in the territory of the masculine, patriarchal God first glimpsed in the second Creation story. Although the Bible tells us that the symbolic meaning of the circumcision ceremony has to do with relinquishing pride and submitting to God's authority, circumcision nevertheless became a symbol of male pride and superiority, with the implication that women are incapable of entering into the same relationship with God.

However, the Talmud, Judaism's ancient source of rabbinical law and theology, offers another interpretation, saying that "a woman is considered to be naturally circumcised."[4] Author Rochel Holzkenner writes that circumcision is a way to indicate that the body and the spirit are fused, a reminder that the body's sexual desires should not override the spirit in a way that selfishly dehumanizes or exploits others' bodies. She goes on to say:

> A woman's body was created with an organ that is naturally quite selfless—a womb. For nine months a woman shares her body with another fragile life, often at great expense to her own comfort. . . . Consciously or unconsciously, the female body is built for benevolence in a radical way, in a holy way. . . . perhaps this is part of the Talmud's intended meaning when saying that "a woman is naturally born circumcised.". . . This gift of "natural circumcision"—the perspective of fluidity between the holy and the mundane—empowers (and obligates) women to become leaders.[5]

In any event, Abraham is now a changed man, in more than physicality, and Sarah, in turn, is a changed woman. Their entire story so far has been told in six chapters. They have left their homeland, journeyed to Egypt and back, gained riches, and met with kings and potentates; Hagar has conceived and given birth to Ishmael; God has made seven promises to Abraham; and finally, their names have been changed and so have their perceptions.

This altered dimension is indicated more fully in the seventh chapter of their lives, when El Shaddai comes to Abraham as he sits in an oak grove in the doorway of his tent in the heat of the day (Genesis 18:1). We might read a great deal into this sentence; for example, the reference to the "heat of the day" could be a hint that we're talking about the sun, created on the fourth day of Creation. The "doorway of his tent" might be a symbolic indication that Abraham was in the liminal space of his consciousness—half in and half out of his body—where he could more easily perceive the Divine. A thousand years ago, Maimonides, the great Jewish scholar, suggested that Abraham was having a vision, rather than seeing events with his physical eyes.

NOTE

The fact that the Bible specifies that God appears to Abraham in an oak grove may also be significant. Although later Christian authorities would condemn sacred oak groves as

While Abraham was sitting there in this state of meditation or prayer, the text tells us that "he lifted up his eyes" (Genesis 18:2), and as we've already learned, this phrase is a biblical signal that the story is about to move into another, more spiritual dimension. In Abraham's case, he sees three men coming to visit, unexpectedly and uninvited.

Abraham leaps up and bows himself to the ground. He steps into the role of a good host and begs the men to stay, washes their feet, and bids them rest under a tree while he fetches them bread to eat. Then he goes inside the tent and tells Sarah to quick, prepare three "cakes" of bread, while he runs to kill a calf and get some curds and milk. The entire passage conveys a sense of Abraham's hurried and eager response to his guests: he runs, he hastens, he tells Sarah to *hurry*.

New Testament authors refer back to this event, pointing to it as an example of faith and hospitality. Later, early Christian interpreters of the Bible found important symbolism in each of the details. According to the fifth-century theologian Procopius of Gaza, for example, the heat of the day stands for the fullness of Divine radiance; the three mysterious visitors are actually Father, Son, and Spirit, in physical form; the tent is the abode of the soul receiving God; and the mystery of the Trinity is indicated by the three cakes made by Sarah within the tent.[7] Meanwhile, modern feminist interpretations have focused with disapproval on Abraham's preemptory commands to Sarah, who is not invited to come out and meet the guests.

But once the hurried (but generously extravagant) meal has been served, the first thing the men say is, "Where is Sarah, your wife?" No chit-chat about weather or politics or the economy. Biblical people get right to the point. Perhaps Abraham had thought there was no need to include Sarah in this unexpected gathering, but the three strangers make clear that Sarah is the reason for their visit.

Laughter

Earlier, when Abraham heard God's promise to him regarding his and Sarah's descendants, he fell on his face laughing. He knew that he and Sarah were far, far too old to conceive a child together. Perhaps God laughed too. "Your son will be called 'He Who Laughs'—Isaac," God said to Abraham.

Now, the visitors repeat what *El Shaddai*—the Breasted One—has already told Abraham: there will be a child next year. This time, Sarah is the one who is in the doorway of the tent, where she overhears God's message and laughs. "After I am waxed old shall I have pleasure, my lord being old also?" she says to herself (Genesis 18:12); the King James translation is a rather sedate and coy version of what is meant, for in Hebrew, the word translated as "pleasure" may mean sexual moisture or lust.

God says to Abraham, "Why did Sarah laugh? Is anything too hard for Yahweh?"

Sarah, who has now apparently joined the group, denies that she laughed. Proof that human thoughts are not hidden from God, the Breasted One responds, "No, you did laugh" (Genesis 18:5). Although commentators often say that God chided Sarah for laughing, the text indicates only that God matter-of-factly confronts Sarah with the truth. God, with whom women converse easily and who converses easily with them, knows even our interior thoughts.

Before the visitors leave, they reveal that the cities of Sodom and Gomorrah are about to be destroyed because of their wickedness. The text says that two of the men "turned away and went from there" (Genesis 18:22), but Abraham continues to talk with God, negotiating for the survival of the inhabitants of Sodom and Gomorrah. Abraham refers to himself as a "dust-man," like Adam (verse 27), and yet he has gained so much stature and confidence and is so friendly with his God that he can argue with Her easily.

Sub-Plot

Again, the Bible is interested not merely in chronological time but also in synchronous time, so the narrative often interrupts one story to tell another, the threads of which have already been laid or will be picked up later. The story of the Breasted One's intervention in the fleshly affairs of women and their wombs is interrupted by a story about the wife and daughters of Abraham's cousin Lot, which takes place in and around the cities of Sodom and Gomorrah.

This story begins in Genesis 19, with Lot sitting in the gateway of the city (in contrast to Abraham who sat in the doorway of his tent) as the two Divine messengers approach. Lot, like his cousin, shows the strangers hospitality and invites them into his house. The people of the city, however, surround the house and demand that Lot give them access to the strangers so that they can sexually assault them. Lot refuses—but offers to send out his daughters instead. His visitors prevent the daughters from being gang raped by blinding the crowd outside the door.

The destruction of the cities follows, with Lot's wife looking back and being turned into a pillar of salt. If we are meant to take this as a cautionary tale, then the message is clear: "Don't look back at destruction. Keep going. Looking back can paralyze you." Medical doctor Stephen Luger reads a similar psychological meaning into this passage and connects it to women who suffer post-traumatic stress disorder as a result of trauma.

> Lot's wife . . . sees the world as she knows it destroyed. What is her reaction to this terrible loss of her entire world? She is . . . as immobile and rigid as a pillar of salt. This catatonic reaction, too, has been described in the psychiatric literature as a result of severe psychological trauma.[8]

Lot's daughters, unlike their mother, do not look back. They survive and live with their father in a cave. Apparently, they think they are the only people left on Earth and feel responsible for repopulating the planet, and so they decide to get their father drunk and have sex with him, one on each successive evening. They both become pregnant; the elder sister delivers a son, Moab, and the younger has a son named Benammi. All this is recorded without judgment or moralizing. Finger-pointing is out, as far as Spirit is concerned.

The daughters' actions introduce a matriarchal line we will see picked up later in the Bible. Ruth, a female descendent of Moab, will be the great-grandmother of David, the king and psalmist. Jesus himself will also be born from this line.

The story of Sodom and Gomorrah is a difficult one to understand, but several things are clear: first, looking forward leads to life, but looking back can bring paralysis and death[9]; second, Spirit sweeps up even human errors and what we might call immorality into Her unfolding Creation; and third, biblical women take matters into their own hands.

God and Wombs

The narrative now cuts back to Sarah and Abraham, who have more adventures in a strange land. Once again, Abraham tries to pass Sarah off as his sister. This time, Yahweh steps in and "closed fast all the wombs" of the women in the king's household (Genesis 20:18). The king sends Sarah and Abraham on their way, giving them even more riches to take with them, and God heals the women, in answer to Abraham's prayers, so that they can once more have children.

And now, God "attends" to Sarah, and she conceives (Genesis 21:1–2). She gives birth to Isaac (whose name means "he laughs") just as the Breasted One promised. "God has made laughter for me," she says. "Everyone who hears will laugh with me" (verse 6, literal translation).

At this point, the Genesis account has made clear that conception is unmistakably the province of the Creator *ruah Elohim, El Shaddai*. So too are life, protection, direction, and promises kept. Whereas Eve's experience carried a curse, Sarah is blessed.

After the birth of Isaac, however, Sarah worries that Ishmael will be a threat to her son's inheritance, and so she asks Abraham to get rid of Hagar and her son. This breaks Abraham's heart—but God tells him to "listen to whatever Sarah tells you" (Genesis 21:12). The Spirit, who affirms Sarah's authority, also promises to bless Ishmael and his descendants.

NOTE

Just as Jews claim Abraham as their father through Isaac, Muslims have an equal claim to him through Ishmael. Some Bible commentators see the current conflict in the Mideast as an echo of the broken relationship between Sarah and Hagar. Rabbi Amy Eilberg writes: "What if the women, instead, had helped one another to transcend the unjust rules of the patriarchal society that governed their lives? . . . The resonances of this text for our times are irresistible. Sarah and Hagar, each privileged in a way in which the other is not, descend into mortal conflict, acting out of envy and blame rather than out of justice and compassion. . . . Nonetheless, we must imagine, work and pray our way to a different reality, when the privileged and the underprivileged will join hands for the sake of the land they love and the society of peace and justice they seek to build together."[10]

Wilderness Experience

First, however, Hagar and now her child are back in the wilderness, that feminine place of intense experiences and encounters with God. Hagar's water is gone, and she and her child are thirsting to death. She puts Ishmael under a bush and goes a good distance away, because she does not want to watch her boy die. "And she sat opposite him and lifted up her voice and wept" (Genesis 21:16).

While Hagar weeps, God hears Ishmael crying—and an angel calls out to Hagar, "What, Hagar? Don't be afraid, for God has heard the boy's voice" (verse 17, literal translation). Spirit is once again vocally present with Hagar, as She is with other seemingly powerless and rejected biblical women.

And now, God opens Hagar's eyes, and she sees what was apparently there all along—a well of water. *Ruah Elohim,* who once moved on the face of the waters for the entire Cosmos, now moves in a specific, life-saving way for Hagar and her child.

If Hagar failed to remember her previous encounter with God in the wilderness, where she saw God and God saw her, then perhaps we should not be too hard on ourselves when we too forget past insights and fall apart in current crises. Perhaps we should write the words the angel spoke to Hagar—"Fear not"—on our doorposts and keychains and in our hearts.

The Mountaintop View

Bible scholars have struggled for centuries with the story that follows in Genesis 22.[11] The idea that God would ask Abraham to kill his child is horrifying, and a surface reading of the story yields an image of an angry, vengeful, demanding Father God, who commands that His favorite person on Earth sacrifice Isaac in order to prove his love. Feminist Bible scholars also note that Sarah, who has been at the center of the story so far, now suddenly disappears from the narration, and they interpret that as the patriarchy dismissing the matriarchal role, establishing "father-right" over "mother-right."[12]

This story, however, demands a much, much deeper reading, within the context of what we have already been told about *ruah Elohim*—the Shield, the Breasted One—whose concerns have been conception, life, seeds, water, stars, protection, promises, and blessing. The story of the almost-sacrifice is fraught with symbols and prefigurations, and it must be read through the lens of those symbols rather than from a literal, simplistic perspective. It is not evidence of a bloodthirsty patriarchal God; instead, the idea that God demands human sacrifice is put to death in this story. When God is seen, children are protected.

The scripture tells us that God tells Abraham to take Isaac to Moriah, a name that means "Seen of

God." In the third day of their journey, Abraham raises his eyes and sees the place where God has sent him. Here we have two code references, one to the third day of Creation by *ruah Elohim* and the other when Abraham lifts his eyes, both signaling a shift into another dimension. And this entire process takes place in the land of "Seen of God."

When questioned by his son, Abraham says that God will provide an animal for a burnt offering, which is what does in fact happen. An angel calls to Abraham, telling him not to hurt his son, and when Abraham again looks up, he sees a ram caught in a thicket. Abraham names the place "God Sees," and the text tells us that "it is said to this day, 'In the mountain of the Lord it is seen'" (Genesis 22:14).

This terrifying story ends with promises of blessing, where God again refers to stars and seeds and abundance. "In your seed," God promises, "all the nations shall be blessed" (verse 18); as in the Creation, the seed is within itself, carrying a promise that reaches far beyond the chronological time of Abraham and Sarah, into cosmic, synchronous time.

Not the End of the Story

Years later, when Sarah dies, Abraham weeps and wails for her. The Genesis account describes in great detail the place and circumstances of her burial—and then Sarah's name lives on throughout the pages of the Bible. In the New Testament, Paul writes:

The children of the promise are counted for the seed. For this is the word of promise, At this time will I come, and Sarah shall have a son. (Romans 9:8–9 KJV)

Promises that are seeds and seeds that are promises. Fulfilled promises, both in chronological and cosmic time. New birth, both of flesh and spirit. Nothing is impossible to Spirit. Creation is revealed to complex human consciousness, regardless of gender. That's the story of Sarah, Hagar, and Abraham. It is a story that lives today.

REFERENCE NOTES

1. Chana Weisberg. *Crown of Creation: The Lives of Great Biblical Women Based on Rabbinic & Mystical Sources* (Oakville, ON: Mosaic Press, 2010).

2. All these are paraphrases of actual online discussions of the Hebrew word *Shaddai*. Conservative pastor Owen Strachan, in a 2014 Twitter war with author Rachel Held Evans, summarized the position: "Let's stop pretending it's all OK" [to refer to God as feminine]. "This is heresy straight up."

3. Arthur Ocean Waskow and Phyllis Ocean Berman. *Freedom Journeys: The Tale of Exodus and Wilderness Across Millennia*

(Woodstock, VT: Jewish Lights Publishing, 2011), page 40.

4. Rabbi Yochanan in Avodah Zarah 27.

5. Rochel Holzkenner. "Why Women Don't Need Circumcision," *The Jewish Woman*, https://www.chabad.org/theJewishWoman/article_ cdo/aid/2287938/jewish/Why-Women-Dont-Need-Circumcision.htm.

6. Emil G. Hirsch and I. M. Casanowicz. "Oak and Terebinth," *Jewish Encyclopedia*, online at http://www.jewishencyclopedia.com/ articles/11638-oak-and-terebinth.

7. Procopius of Gaza. *Commentary on Genesis,* discussed in "The Early Christian Reception of Genesis 18: From Theophany to Trinitarian Symbolism" by Bogdan G. Bucor, available online at https://www.academia.edu/13190369/The_Early_Christian_Reception_of_Genesis_18_From_Theophany_to_Trinitarian_Symbolism.

8. Steven Luger. "Flood, Salt, and Sacrifice: Post-Traumatic Stress Disorder in Genesis," *Jewish Bible Quarterly 38* (2010):124–126.

9. Rabbi Sandy Sasso offers another interpretation of Lot's wife. In rabbinic literature, Lot's wife has a name, Idit, which derives from the Hebrew root meaning "witness." Rabbi Sasso suggests that Idit turns out of compassion; she is the only witness to the destruction of the cities, and it is her tears that turn her into a pillar of salt. Twelfth-century rabbi and scholar Nachmanides speaks of her turning in compassion. (Sandy Eisenberg Sasso, personal communication, July 1, 2019.)

10. Amy Eilberg. "A Feminist Lens on the Story of Sarah and Hagar," *T'ruah: The Rabbinic Call for Human Rights*, 2012, https://www.truah.org/resources/a-feminist-lens-on-the-story-of-sarah-and-hagar/.

11. For a good overview of the various ways in which commentators have struggled to make sense of the story of Isaac's almost-sacrifice, see "Akedah," *Jewish Virtual Library*, https://www. jewishvirtuallibrary.org/akedah

12. See Alicia Ostriker's *Feminist Revision and the Bible* (Cambridge, UK: Blackwell, 1993), page 41.

FOUR

A GATHERING OF WOMEN

And Jacob kissed Rachel,
and lifted up his voice and wept,

–Genesis 29:11 KJV

What is it in our own present culture that makes us inclined to think that biblical women are veiled, isolated nonentities, trailing behind their husbands who worshipped a vengeful, male God?

In reality, *ruah Elohim*—the Breasted One, the Existing One, the Feminine Spirit—sweeps through the accounts of the lives of the matriarchs, just as She moves across the face of the waters during Creation. The biblical accounts of the matriarchs' lives show us women who have their own relationships with God and who have legal and spiritual rights.

As we move into these women's stories, the King James Version uses the term *Lord God*, giving the sense that the God in this story is masculine, but remember, the Hebrew word *YWHW* actually means "the Existing One," with additional inherent meanings having to do with being, becoming, and becoming-like. These enfolded implications show us a Divine One who is not static but living and in motion, the inclusive epitome of life itself. In the lives of the matriarchs, we hear again the echo of *ruah Elohim*, who created humans in the male-and-female image of God.

Since we cannot demythologize Eve—and with her the nature of all women—in a single stroke, our journey into scripture take us into the connections, experiences, and histories of a large gathering of biblical women. The lives of these women reveal to us the mothering aspect of the Divine, the Feminine Spirit of the God of Abraham, Isaac, and Jacob—and Sara, Rebekah, and Rachel.

Rebekah

When we first meet Rebekah, the central human player in chapters 24 through 28 of Genesis, she is at a well—a feminine symbol for life and renewal, and also a reminder of the Spirit who moved on the face of the waters in the first chapter of Genesis. These micro-versions of the waters of Creation occur again and again throughout the pages of the Bible, and wells in particular are often the locations for significant transformative meetings. (Recall, for example, that Hagar had her second encounter with God by a well in the wilderness. Later on in the Christian New Testament, in the Gospels, Jesus meets a Samaritan woman by a well, and their conversation is also both significant and transformative.) And yet wells were mundane locations, essential to daily life in a desert world. Drawing water for the household was often a woman's chore—and Spirit moves through this ordinary task, using it to further the Bible's continuing revelation of the Divine One.

In Rebekah's story we will see that she has the right to decide who and when she will marry; she prophesies about her children; and she directs a son's marriage and the futures of both her sons. She is not an isolated, solitary figure in a desert landscape; rather, she appears as part of a prophecy that will reach generations into the future. The ongoing, active process of Creation is the context of her story.

But it starts first with a love story.

After Sarah's death and burial, Abraham sends his servant as an emissary to Mesopotamia, the land of Sarah's sister-in-law, Milcah, to find a wife for Isaac.

Abraham makes clear to his servant that if the woman he finds doesn't want to come back with him, he is not to force her.

When the servant reaches Mesopotamia, he knows that wells are good places to meet women, so he goes there first. He then gives the Existing One detailed instructions as to what the still unknown woman will say and do: "May it be that when I say to a girl, 'Please let down your jar that I may have a drink,' and she says, 'Drink, and I'll water your camels too'—let her be the one you have chosen for your servant Isaac" (Genesis 24:14 NIV).

Before the emissary is even done speaking to God, Rebekah appears—and her actions and her conversation with him are exactly what he just outlined to God. She gives him and his camels water, and he gives her a golden earring and two heavy gold bracelets.

As the servant and Rebekah talk further, she reveals that she is the granddaughter of Milcah, Sarah's sister-in-law. The servant worships God for guiding him straight to the specific woman Abraham had in mind.

"Praise be to the Lord, the God of my master Abraham, who has not abandoned his kindness and faithfulness to my master. As for me, the Lord has led me on the journey to the house of my master's relatives."

The young woman ran and told her mother's household about these things. (Genesis 24:27–28 NIV)

As you can see, the Bible implies here that Rebekah's mother is the one who runs the household.

These chapters of Genesis are about matriarchy and the Spirit of God moving in the lives of women. The men play important parts, but the protagonists are the women. Even if we assume that the author (or authors) of these scriptures was a man (and the answers to authorship questions are only assumptions at this point), then he went to great pains to include the women's side of the story.

Despite the patriarchy that did exist during this era (as it still does), the Feminine Spirit had Her hand in the Bible's writing. Women are vital to the long history of God's interactions with humankind. Those of us who are feminine readers can look into scripture and see our own faces reflected there.

After Abraham's emissary presents the proposal of marriage to Rebekah's family, he asks that she be allowed to go back with him to Abraham and Isaac.

But her brother and her mother replied, "Let the young woman remain with us ten days or so; then you may go."

But he said to them, "Do not detain me, now that the Lord has granted success to my journey. Send me on my way so I may go to my master."

Then they said, "Let's call the young woman and ask her about it." So they called Rebekah and asked her, "Will you go with this man?"

"I will go," she said. (Genesis 55–57 NIV)

Rebekah clearly has the power to make this decision for herself, and her choice is respected by her family.

They send her on her way with a blessing: "Thou art our sister, be thou the mother of thousands of millions, and let thy seed possess the gate of those which hate them" (Genesis 24:60 KJV). Here we see again references to both abundance and seeds, as we did in the story of Eve. Reading only the first half of the first book of the Bible, we have already found ample evidence of the ultimate triumph of woman over limitation and the curse of Eve.

The narration now moves to Isaac, who is taking a walk in a field, meditating, when he lifts up his eyes and sees the servant returning with Rebekah. In this single sentence (Genesis 24:63), with its familiar words and phrases, we see a perfect example of the Bible being self-referential. First, evening is a transitional time, where one day yields to the next, just as the first chapter of Genesis summarized in its description of the seven days of Creation. Then, Isaac is walking in the out-of-doors in a state of meditation and prayer, which echoes the way in which God walked in Eden, seeking communion with Adam and Eve in the cool of the day. We read in earlier chapters of Genesis that Isaac's father Abraham also spent time meditating in a transitional state, in his case in the doorway of his tent, and like Abraham, Isaac's sight is elevated into another dimension. Finally, Isaac sees, and in Hagar's story as well as the story of Abraham on the mountain, we learned about the significance of both physical and spiritual sight.

NOTE

The importance of eyes and vision will be repeated through-out both the Hebrew and Christian scriptures. Just a few examples include: in Psalms, where we are told that the Divine eye turns toward us when we are in trouble (34:15); the Gospels, when Jesus restores vision to blind eyes (John 9); and the fiery eyes of Jesus in the Book of Revelation (1:14).

And so Isaac sees camels coming toward him. And Rebekah lifts her eyes and sees Isaac. They are both in the timeless, spiritual realm where God communes with human beings.

The Feminine Spirit is present in human love, and this is a love story in which the woman is honored and respected. Rebekah goes with Isaac into Sarah's tent (because this is also a story about matriarchs)—and Isaac loves her and is comforted after his mother's death (Genesis 24:67). The single biblical sentence speaks volumes about the relationship that develops between Rebekah and Isaac.

The scripture says next that *Elohim* blesses Isaac, who is now living in the same place where Hagar encountered God in the desert—Beer-lahai-roi, the "Well of the Living One Who Sees Me."

After their marriage, the couple realizes that Rebekah, like Sarah before her, is "barren." Isaac "entreats" the Living One on Rebekah's behalf (Genesis 25:21)—and Rebekah becomes pregnant with twins. Again and again in these stories, the Spirit makes barren lives fertile.

But Rebekah's pregnancy is not easy. The scripture says that the "children crushed her inmost part" (literal translation). In Robert Altar's translation, he says that the children "clash" within her—and Rebekah asks God directly, "This that, the one, the other . . . why me?"

God answers her: "Two nations are in your womb. And two peoples will be separated from your belly" (25:23, literal translation). The Living One gives Rebekah a prophecy that she will understand and act upon as the twins grow.

The brothers, named Jacob and Esau, may be twins, but as they grow up, their personalities prove to be quite different. Family conflict now enters the story, for Isaac prefers Esau, while Rebekah's favorite is Jacob. The short biblical description captures the situation in a few poignant, bittersweet words (25:28).

Esau, as the first to come out of the womb, is technically the oldest, meaning that he is Isaac's heir. Rebekah, however, has other ideas, and she encourages her favorite son to take back what she believes is his true birthright.

Before the tension between the brothers can go any further, though, famine comes to the land, and the family is forced to move in order to find food. Isaac now follows in his father's footsteps and passes Rebekah off as his sister because he is afraid her beauty could put him in danger with the Philistines, the people who inhabit the land. Once again, the truth is revealed— and like Abraham before him, Isaac is sent on his way unharmed, with his riches increased.

Now, Isaac and his family settle down in a new location, but they have conflicts over water rights with the people of the land. They are forced to continue to move, until at last they find a well they can use without dispute, for no one else has staked a claim to it. Isaac names the well "Rehoboth," which means "broad, open places," because, he says, "The Living One has made a wide, expansive space for us where we can be fruitful in the land" (Genesis 26:22, literal translation).

The same night, the Living One comes to Isaac and says, "I am the *Elohim* of your father Abraham. Do not fear, for I am with you, and I will bless you. I will multiply your seed for the sake of my servant Abraham" (26:24, literal translation).

Seeds again, and water, accompanied by blessing and reassurance and the promise of abundance. The Feminine Spirit is at work.

Although Esau is not the main protagonist in this story, scripture loves to throw in asides here and there, and now we are told that when "Esau was forty years old, he married Judith daughter of Beeri the Hittite, and also Basemath daughter of Elon the Hittite. They were a source of grief to Isaac and Rebekah" (Genesis 26:34 NIV). Again, a few terse words convey much about the emotions and relationships within this biblical family. In short, there's in-law trouble.

In his old age, Isaac continues to prefer Esau, while Jacob is still Rebekah's favorite—and now, Rebekah works out a scheme that will allow Jacob to have the blessing that is entitled to the eldest son. Isaac, who once had such keen spiritual vision, is nearly blind, so Rebekah and her son trick him into thinking that Jacob is Esau. Since Esau is a hairy man, while Jacob is not, Rebekah fastens goatskins to Jacob's hands and the back of his neck, and then sends him to his father with a tasty meal she has prepared.

In doing this, Jacob denies his own identity. Pretending to be Esau in order to gain primogeniture thrusts him into an ongoing deep struggle to regain his spiritual integrity. The blessing of the Living One is not erased—but as with Eve and Adam after they eat from the tree of knowledge of good and evil, there are consequences to human choices and actions. In Jacob's case, he will spend years being deceived, even as he deceived.

When Esau finds out what his brother his done, he is furious and plots Jacob's murder. To protect her son, Rebekah sends Jacob away to live with her relatives.

Family relations are a mess at this point. On top of everything else, Rebekah is still upset with her daughters-in-law. "These Hittite women will be the death of me," she complains to Isaac. "I just hope Jacob doesn't bring home another one as his wife" (Genesis 27:46, paraphrase). To complicate matters further, Esau takes yet another wife, the daughter of Ishmael (the granddaughter of Hagar). If you ever thought that the heroes of the Bible were good, moral people who lived peaceful and orderly lives, by now you should be realizing differently.

Jacob will continue to be embroiled in family conflict in the chapters to come—but first, he is given an amazing vision that has inspired the imaginations of countless artists and poets: a ladder (or staircase) reaching between Earth and Heaven, with angels going up and down it.

And, behold, the Lord stood above it, and said, I am the Lord God of Abraham thy father, and the God of Isaac: the land whereon thou liest, to thee will I give it, and to thy seed; And thy seed shall be as the dust of the earth, and thou shalt spread abroad to the west, and to the east, and to the north, and to the south: and in thee and in thy seed shall all the families of the earth be blessed. And, behold, I am with thee, and will keep thee in all places whither thou goest, and will bring thee again into this land; for I will not leave thee, until I have done that which I have spoken to thee of. (Genesis 28:10–16 KJV)

Jacob's vision has been interpreted in many ways, but one possible perspective sees it as a reflection of cosmic, spiritual time, revealing a living and dynamic unity between the genders. In the Hebrew language "earth" is feminine, and "sky" or "heaven" is masculine, and here we have an image of a ladder—or stairway—that connects the two, allowing God's messengers to go back and forth between them. We also have here, in the words that the Living One speaks to Jacob, yet another reference to the promise of seeds within seeds, alongside both dust and blessing, bringing us back yet again to the Garden of Eden. The men and women in this family have made a royal mess of things, just as Eve and Adam did, but once again, God promises to heal and restore. Creation is unending.

Rachel and Leah

The complicated relationship triangle that emerges now with Rachel, Leah, and Jacob is as compelling as any in the Bible. It's not a just a tale of love at first sight, though it is that. It's also about duplicity, money, sex, jealousy, childbearing, death—and oh yes, mandrakes (an aphrodisiac). Far from being a story about a docile young piece of property who marries Jacob and becomes the mother of two sons, this is a soap opera with strong characters. Timeless elements of love, sacrifice, rebirth, and more love are woven into the drama, revealing the Feminine Spirit at work even within all the messy relationships.

After Jacob's mystical experience, he continues on his travels, which is how he meets Rachel. When he first encounters her, the scripture tells us that she is watching her father's sheep, "for she was a shepherd" (Genesis 29:9). Although Rachel's father later treats her as property, she also clearly has had a role of responsibility and agency. Furthermore, shepherds will become a powerful metaphor for God in the scriptures, as in the Twenty-Third Psalm, which states, "The Living One is my shepherd; I will not be lacking." Later, in the New Testament, shepherds are among the first people to learn of Jesus's birth, and Jesus will identify himself as a shepherd. But the very first biblical shepherd was Rachel, a woman. Although she was a flesh-and-blood real woman, with plenty of flaws, she is also a living metaphor for the Divine, and for some readers, her life of love and sacrifice prefigures Christ's.

As with Rebekah and Isaac, water plays a role in Jacob and Rachel's meeting, giving us still another glimpse of the Feminine Spirit at work. Jacob helps Rachel water her sheep—and in the process, he falls head over heels in love with her. He kisses her and bursts into tears, demonstrating that biblical men are not afraid to express their emotions.

Jacob offers to work for seven years in exchange for Rachel's father's permission to marry her. After the seven years are over, however, Rachel's father tricks him into marrying his oldest daughter, Leah, instead. So Jacob works another seven years and marries Rachel, too. Note the repetition of the number seven, echoing the complete seven days of Creation by *ruah Elohim* in the first chapter of Genesis. Somehow, in the midst of this painful and messy love triangle, the Feminine Spirit is continuing to do the work of Creation.

Rachel and Leah demonstrate both solidarity and competition. They each have reason to be jealous of the other, for Rachel has Jacob's love, but Leah is the one who first bears him children. The two sisters are locked in an ongoing rivalry for Jacob's love and the ability to bear him children. Rachel trades with Leah a night with Jacob in exchange for mandrakes, an aphrodisiac.

They use their maids to conceive more sons with him, which of course complicates matters even more. And yet they also help each other at times, and Leah joins the other women in the household in prayer that Rachel will be able to conceive (which she eventually does).

Caught within a patriarchal system, Rachel and Leah nevertheless are able to step into the foreground of the story as strong and independent characters—but they cannot escape the patriarchy. As with women today, the misogyny within women's own minds—causing us to criticize each other, compete with each other, and support the patriarchy's values—is often the most insidious. In the interactions between these two biblical women we can see a mirror image of the way in which modern women continue to both support each other and tear each other down.

Eventually, Jacob decides it is safe for him to return to his family. He discusses his plan openly with both his wives, even sharing with them a dream he has had, and scripture implies that he is giving them a choice: go with him or remain with their father, Laban. They choose to go with Jacob. In complete agreement with each other, they tell him, "Do we still have any share in the inheritance of our father's estate? Does he not regard us as foreigners? Not only has he sold us, but he has used up what was paid for us. Surely all the wealth that God took away from our father belongs to us and our children. So do whatever God has told you" (Genesis 31:14 NIV). Their father has treated them as though they were property, and the sisters are outspoken in their bitterness.

The family's departure is fraught with additional drama. "When Laban had gone to shear his sheep," scripture tells us, "Rachel stole her father's household gods. Moreover, Jacob deceived Laban the Aramean by not telling him he was running away" (31:19–20 NIV).

Jacob's father-in-law chases after them. When he catches up with Jacob's caravan, he accuses his son-in-law of both lying and theft. Jacob, who does not know that Rachel stole the gods, is offended. "Go ahead," he tells Laban. "Search my tents. You won't find anything" (31:32, paraphrased).

Rachel puts the gods in a saddlebag and sits on it. When her father comes into her tent, she tells him "Let not my lord be angry that I cannot rise before you, for the way of women is upon me" (31:35 ESV).

This deception on Rachel's part can be read two ways. On the one hand, Laban understands her meaning to be that she can't get up because she's menstruating. At the same time, while she is tricking her father so that he goes back home without the household gods, she may also be making a statement about her feelings as a woman caught in a patriarchal society: she has no way of "rising" to plead her case for inheritance, because the societal "way of women" prevents her from speaking or taking action in the way that a man would. According to feminist Bible scholar J. E. Lapsley, Rachel's "subversive action in stealing the [gods] is matched by her equally subversive undermining of male definitions of women and her creation of new meanings out of male-generated language."[1] Along the same lines, author Wendy Zierler writes of Rachel as if she had read her diary:

> Rachel thus emerges from this story as an archetypal feminist writer, who dares to steal across the border of masculine culture, seize control of her cultural inheritance, and make it her own. In this way, the theft of the [household gods] becomes a story of women's potential to use and craft language, holy and mundane, in all of its many meanings, to speak potently—and cause others to listen.[2]

In any case, Rachel succeeds in deceiving her father (for women often take their power in hidden and subversive ways), and the family resumes their journey to Jacob's homeland. Along the way, Jacob encounters messengers from *Elohim*, indicating that the Feminine Spirit is with him. Nevertheless, he is getting increasingly nervous about encountering his brother.

Now comes the turning point in Jacob's life. After decades of in-laws, wives, maids, and children, Jacob spends a night alone, without even his many belongings to comfort him. He has finally set aside all his subter-fuge, all the accretions of property and people he has accumulated to hide his own lack of identity.

And in the night, a mysterious man comes to him and wrestles with him until dawn. With the rising of the sun, the light dispels the darkness, as it did on Day One of Creation, when *ruah Elohim* said, "Let there be light."

The mysterious man gives Jacob a new name—Israel—but he refuses to reveal his own name. Jacob understands, however, that his opponent in the night was God, and he names the place where they wrestled *Peniel*, which means "Face of God." "I have seen *Elohim*, face to face," says Jacob, "and yet my soul was delivered" (Genesis 32:30, literal translation).

Jacob's name change is momentous. *Israel* means "God Strives," referring to Jacob's experience with the mysterious man. This name will reach beyond one individual's life and will now refer to a whole group of people—both women and men—who, like Jacob, will bless and be blessed, deceive and be deceived, go astray and be led back, and wrestle with themselves and with God.

Today the term "Children of Israel" reaches even beyond Jacob's descendants and becomes a metaphor for the person struggling to discover her true, uncom-promised spiritual identity. In the midst of such strug-gles, we seldom recognize who or what we are fighting against—but in the end, like Jacob, we may realize that Spirit was with us all along.

Jacob's story does not end there, nor does Rachel's. Jacob and his brother reconcile. The Breasted One comes to Jacob with another promise of fruitfulness. More babies are indeed born, and in the end, Jacob will have twelve sons (which will become the twelve tribes of Israel). Meanwhile, Leah's sons take a terrible and bloody revenge when their sister Dinah is raped. Then, while they are still journeying, Rachel becomes pregnant with her second child, and they are still on the road when the time comes for her to deliver.

NOTE

The number twelve is another important number that weaves through the Bible's stories. Not only are there twelve tribes of Israel, but Jesus also has twelve disciples, and the number figures prominently in Revelation, the final book of the Bible. Twelve is considered to be a number that symbolizes an inclusive completeness, representing a group of people that includes absolutely everyone, with no one left out.

The labor does not go well. The Bible says that when her pains are at their fiercest, the midwife tells her, "Fear not." These are the words that the Spirit speaks again and again to the Bible's women. As Rachel delivers another son, her birth pangs are not localized, but generic, encompassing. Womanly contractions deliver something new into human consciousness (as we shall see again in the final book of the Bible, the Book of Revelation).

Rachel dies shortly after her baby's birth. The Bible says that her "soul went forth," and here is another example where the Hebrew words carry within them a richness of meaning we miss in our English translations, which say simply that Rachel died. By contrast, the Hebrew term can also have to do with germination and growth, as well as inferences to a water source. Rachel's dying is not the end of a story, for it becomes the fertile ground from which other stories will spring. Rachel is buried beside the road to Bethlehem, linking her to another mother-and-child story, since Bethlehem is where Mary will give birth to Jesus. Ultimately, Rachel's life is part of the long biblical road that leads to Jesus.

Genesis tells about other women, as well as men, and their stories are all important. Throughout the final pages of this book, women continue to be called by name. Despite the patriarchy of their society, they are agents of change. They reflect the fertility and conception, the mothering and the nurturing of the Feminine Spirit. They further the ever-growing work of Creation.

This gathering of women in Genesis is connected with each other by birth, life, death, and birth again, creating an endlessly turning cycle of love, sacrifice, and new life (the same cycle that epitomizes our own lives). And through it all, the Spirit continues to bless, moving on the waters, bringing fruitfulness and light to humankind.

REFERENCE NOTES

1. J. E. Lapsley. "The Voice of Rachel," in *Genesis: A Feminist Companion to the Bible (Second Series)*, edited by Athalya Brenner (Sheffield, UK: Sheffield Academic Press, 1998), page 238.

2. Wendy Zierler. "Contemporary Reflection," in *The Torah: A Woman's Commentary*, edited by Tamara Cohn Eskenazi and Andrea L. Weiss (New York: CCAR Press, 2017).

FIVE

I AM
THAT I AM

And the angel of God, which went before the camp of Israel, removed and went behind them; and the pillar of the cloud went from before their face, and stood behind them.

—Exodus 14:19 KJV.

Spirit—the feminine-masculine *ruah Elohim* of Creation—is very much present in Exodus, the book of the Bible that follows Genesis. Spirit—with another new name, I Am That I Am—is the cause of action throughout the account of deliverance, as both a personal and national Deliverer. The Book of Exodus is a study in the developing understanding of a living, present, all-powerful, all-wise, saving Deity, who remembers, hears, sees, and delivers not only one child, one couple, or two or twelve families, but an entire nation. It is not all sweetness and light. There are many birth pangs—the pain and travail of labor—as well as triumph. But throughout this story, the Spirit of God moving on the face of water is everywhere.

The story of the Exodus of the children of Israel—their "going out" from Egypt led by Moses—begins with remembering, as it repeats the names of the twelve sons of Israel who went to Egypt (Exodus 1:1–5). The beginning of this story, told at the end of Genesis, is one of bitter family betrayal—and ultimate redemption—in which Joseph, the favored son of Israel (Jacob), is sold into slavery in Egypt by his jealous brothers. Joseph, whose name means "he increases," prospers in Egypt, despite his brothers' intention, and when famine forces the brothers to come to him for help, Joseph shows mercy and forgives them. Pharaoh then says to his friend Joseph, "Your father and your brothers have come to you, and the land of Egypt is before you; settle your father and your brothers in the best part of the land. Let them live in Goshen" (Genesis 47:5 KJV.)

NOTE

The word Goshen, a feminine-gendered word, is perhaps from an ancient Egyptian word that meant "flooded land." This portion of Egypt was frequently inundated with water, which left its soil rejuvenated and fertile, pointing us once again toward aspects of the Divine Feminine, the "universal mother," who is, as Umair Haque writes, "the source of renewal, of birth, of creativity, of transformation . . . the Nile River and the first of May . . . the rainforest and the sea . . . the cloud and the rain. . . . She nurtures and nourishes the slumbering seed in the dark soil, with the waters of life. She is the source from which all things flow."[1]

Now, at the beginning of Exodus, the descendants of Joseph and his brothers have lived for 430 years in Egypt, and there is a new king of Egypt who "knew not Joseph" (Exodus 1:8), who does not remember. This single sentence indicates the heartbreaking change in the Israelites' lives. Over the centuries, they have increased in numbers so much that the king fears them—and enslaves them.

Despite their oppression, their birthrate continues to climb, so now Pharaoh, the king, orders that all boy babies be killed by throwing them into the Nile. This attempted ethnic cleansing—the consequence of one people's irrational fear of another—will, after much tribulation, fail. The oppressed will be delivered.

The process of deliverance begins with women.

Women Who Deliver

"To deliver" can mean to save from danger, but it can also mean to give birth. In this story, the word carries both meanings, for two midwives, Shiphrah ("fairness and clarity") and Puah ("beauty and splendor of light"),[2] are the women who save the male babies in defiance of Pharaoh.

The stage has now been set for the birth of Moses:

Now a man of the tribe of Levi married a Levite woman, and she became pregnant and gave birth to a son. When she saw that he was a fine child, she hid him for three months. But when she could hide him no longer, she got a papyrus basket [or ark] for him and coated it with tar and pitch. Then she placed the child in it and put it among the reeds along the bank of the Nile. His sister [whose name we will later learn is Miriam, meaning "well" or "water"] stood at a distance to see what would happen to him.

Then Pharaoh's daughter went down to the Nile to bathe, and her attendants were walking along the riverbank. She saw the basket among the reeds and sent her female slave to get it. She opened it and saw the baby. He was crying, and she felt sorry for him. "This is one of the Hebrew babies," she said.

Then his sister asked Pharaoh's daughter, "Shall I go and get one of the Hebrew women to nurse the baby for you?"

"Yes, go," she answered. So the girl went and got the baby's mother. Pharaoh's daughter said to her, "Take this baby and nurse him for me, and I will pay you." So the woman took the baby and nursed him. When the child grew older, she took him to Pharaoh's daughter and he became her son. She named him Moses, saying, "I drew him out of the water." (Exodus 2:1–8 NIV)

Note that except for Moses and Pharaoh, so far there are only women in this story—midwives, mother, sister, Pharaoh's daughter, and a female slave, all of whom work together to save the child. The dark, threatening, death-giving aspect of water, which was intended by Pharaoh, is transformed into the source of salvation. The mothering Spirit has moved once again on the face of the waters, from delivery out of the womb, to the baby's ark in the river, to the compassion of Pharaoh's daughter and her slave, to the baby's tears, to the name given to Moses. And the women are the ones who make possible the entire story of deliverance that will be told in Exodus.

Adventures in the Wilderness

In less than a sentence after Moses is named as a child, he appears as a grown man, and now the action moves along rapidly. Moses kills an Egyptian who is beating a Hebrew; he flees Pharaoh, who wants him killed; and he ends up in the desert, sitting by a well, where he meets the seven shepherdess daughters of the priest Midian, who have come to draw water for their flock.

Here again we are in both the literal world and the symbolic realm, where references and allusion give the events a deeper meaning, and once again we see the self-referential nature of the Bible. The words from the Bible's first chapter, the spiritual Creation, are repeated over and over—the well as the source of water; the number seven, a sign of the completeness represented by the days of Creation, as well as the blessing and goodness of Creation; the shepherdesses, who, like Rachel before them, foreshadow the Good Shepherd, who is Deity; and now the word "flock," which biblically refers not only to sheep but also to the people who follow God. ("We are God's people," says Psalm 100, "the sheep of his pasture.") The Bible layers meaning upon meaning so densely that the stories of Genesis and Exodus become one narrative, even though they happen in different eras to different individuals.

Moses' encounter with the seven daughters at the well exemplifies another recurring biblical theme:

how men treat women has widespread repercussions at the national and international levels. In this case, male shepherds are harassing the women at the well (Exodus 2:17–22), and Moses rises up in their defense and "waters the flock"—an indication on a local scale of what he will later do on a national scale, when he stands up to Pharaoh and helps the Hebrews escape from slavery. Moses will also spend forty years with these women, and later in the story, the children of Israel will wander in the desert for another forty years.

NOTE

The number forty in the Bible generally symbolizes a period of testing or trial. It will recur several more times in Moses' life, and it is also mentioned in the stories of Jonah, Ezekiel, and Elijah. In the Gospel, Jesus spends forty days and nights in the wilderness alone before he begins his ministry.

In the midst of all these deep and spiritual meanings, the Bible also describes daily existence. The story of the seven daughters at the well ends with Moses marrying one of them, Zipporah (whose name means "bird"). Moses lives with this family in the desert and begins to raise his own family with Zipporah.

But then, the Bible says at the end of the second chapter of Exodus, *Elohim* hears the Israelites' *groaning* (another feminine-case noun, one which we shall see again in the Bible, that calls to mind a woman's labor in childbirth), and She remembers the covenant that was made with Abraham, with Isaac, and with Jacob. *Elohim* is aware of and is concerned for their descendants (says the literal Hebrew translation of Exodus 2:25). The story will soon shift from the personal to the national level.

But first, something will happen to Moses that changes him forever. While he is watching his father-in-law's sheep in the wilderness (where so many significant spiritual events occur in the Bible—and for us, as well, when we are alone) on the mountain of Horeb, he sees a bush that is aflame and yet is not consumed by the fire (Exodus 3:2). The biblical God supersedes what we know scientifically about matter and energy.

NOTE

Horeb, referred to in this chapter in Exodus as "the mountain of Elohim," will be referred to later as Mount Sinai, where Moses receives the Ten Commandments from God.

As in the earlier stories of Hagar and Abraham, an angel appears first—and then God. Out of the burning bush, God calls Moses by name (Exodus 3:4), and Moses responds, "Here am I." He is fully present, both spiritually and geographically.

"The place where you are standing is holy ground," God tells Moses. Note that this holy location is not a building constructed with hands or machinery, not a center of social and political events, but a patch of ground on a remote mountain in the wilderness. Alone with God.

The Breasted One is remembering and reminding as Moses hears: "I am thy God of thy father; the God of Abraham, the God of Isaac, and the God of Jacob" (Exodus 3:6 KJV). Not abstract or distant, this Mothering Presence is visible, palpable. She says of Israel, the nation, "I have seen, I have heard, I know its pain, I have come down to rescue." Moses too has seen, heard, and known the pain of his people, and he will, in a mimetic pattern, come down to rescue them.

But first he asks God, "Suppose I go to the Israelites and say to them, 'The God of your fathers has sent me to you,' and they ask me, 'What is his name?' Then what shall I tell them?" And God answers, "I am who I am. This is what you are to say to the Israelites: 'I AM has sent me to you' " (Exodus 3:13–14 NIV). Another timeless, mimetic moment.

The words God gives as a name have also been translated "I will be who I will be." As Robert Alter comments,

God's response perhaps gives Moses more than he bargained for—not just an identifying divine name . . . but an ontological divine mystery of the most daunting character. Rivers of ink have since flowed in theological reflection and philological analysis of this name.[3]

Had Deity wanted to be known as a male God sitting on a throne, this defining mountaintop moment might have been the time to declare that. But no such declaration was made. Instead, God gives Moses a name that turns us to the very nature of being itself. "This is my name forever," says God, "the name you shall call me from generation to generation" (Exodus 3:15 NIV).

I Am Who I Am instructs Moses to tell the Israelites that the God of their ancestors has sent him and "now, let us go three days into the wilderness, that we may sacrifice to our God" (3:18 KJV). The designation of three days signals a return to the third day of Creation in chapter 1 of Genesis. The ensuing events in Egypt and the parting of the Red Sea will signify Creation and the *ruah Elohim*, Spirit God, moving on the waters. Events are moving into another dimension.

More good news comes with the reminder that God provides—"ye shall not go out empty" (3:21 KJV)—and that God's concern is inclusive of physical as well as spiritual needs. The Hebrews need not leave Egypt emptyhanded. From Abraham to Hagar to Rachel and Leah and now to the Israelites, for every injunction to leave, there is given provision for the journey.

Moses doubts his own ability to carry God's message to the people, however, and asks, "What if they don't believe me?" (Genesis 4:1). God's response is another question: "What is that in your hand?"

Moses has a staff in his hand (he is, after all, a shepherd on a mountainside), and God next commands him to throw the staff down on the ground. When Moses obeys, the staff turns into a snake. The snake—a reference to the serpent in the Garden of Eden—turns back into a staff when Moses picks it up again. The serpent was an illusion. (As perhaps it was in Eden as well.)

The narrative in Exodus will describe the people's deliverance from the serpent of Eden; it will displace the misty creation of Genesis 2 with the tangible absoluteness of Genesis 1. The theme of power over the serpent—over illusion—continues through the Bible and culminates in Revelation, when the woman is pursued by a serpent (Revelation 12:3).

In case the power of this sign wasn't enough to convince Moses of the illusory nature of his fears, I Am Who I Am next tells Moses to put his hand inside his cloak—and when he takes it out again, it is covered with leprosy. He puts the hand back inside his cloak, and this time when he pulls it out, it is healed, free of disease. From Exodus to the Psalms to the Prophets to the Gospels, health and wholeness are conditions that God provides. The I AM on Mount Horeb, whose name shall be forever, has power over human flesh (as is also the case with human conception in earlier chapters).

NOTE

"I Am Who I Am heals you," says Exodus 15:26. "For I will restore you to health and I will heal all your wounds," declares Yahweh in Jeremiah 30:17; "then your light shall break open like dawn, and your healing will speedily spring up" (Isaiah 58:8, literal translation). These are just a few of the verses in the Bible that promise us health and healing.

Chimerical leprosy as a symbol of a body not in harmony with God also reappears throughout the Bible, including later in Exodus when Moses' sister Miriam is stricken with the disease, in the Book of Numbers when Naaman an army commander is healed through the help of young servant girl, and in the Gospels when the lepers come to Jesus for healing. Each time, God restores the person with leprosy to wholeness and health.

Remembering

Remembering is more than important in the Bible. It is essential to how the spiritual story is revealed throughout scripture, from beginning to end. Remembering is referred to both explicitly and implicitly.

The celebration of Passover is also a form of remembering—a script of the living drama that took place when Pharaoh at first refused to let the Hebrews go. Passover is not just about the past, however, nor is the Bible's remembering focused backward only; it is also about the here and now, as well as the future, addressing the consequences of personal and political action.

The story of the plagues visited upon Pharaoh and his people, as a result of his refusal to release the Israelites, indicates the destruction of any power or belief antagonistic to spiritual Creation. John D. Currid, in his book *Ancient Egypt and the Old Testament,* outlines the plagues as "De-Creation." Plague nine, for example, where darkness prevails over light, is the reverse of Day One of Creation, when Light is created out of darkness.[4]

The Passover meal also contains elements with symbolic value that transcend clock time: lamb, unleavened bread, and bitter herbs. In the Gospels, the Passover meal will be a significant event that marks the end of Jesus' life on earth (which Christians refer to as the Last Supper).

At last, Pharaoh lets the children of Israel leave Egypt—but then he changes his mind. He and his army catch up with them at the Red Sea. As the Israelites see them coming, they are terrified, but Moses tells them, "I AM will fight for you, while you keep silent" (Exodus 14:14). Moses stretches his hand over the sea—and the people escape, walking on dry land between the two walls of water. In Genesis 1, on the third day of Creation, the dry land appears, but only after the waters have been gathered together, just as they are again gathered together here for the children of Israel. Chronological time and simultaneous, cosmic time meet—and the sea parts. Moses and the people are acting in unity with *ruah Elohim*, the Breasted One, the Existing One, the I Will Be Who I Will Be. In this remembrance and reenactment of the spiritual Creation in Genesis, the people live and are free. No oppressors are left to follow them.

Mothering and Fathering

Now the people are in the wilderness, where they must deal with the I Am directly and daily. The first way that they do that is with a celebration led by the women, who in some way knew that salvation would come as they left Egypt, bringing their tambourines (or drums) with them. The women had prophetic vision.

Then Miriam the prophet, Aaron's sister, took a tambourine and led all the women as they played their tambourines and danced. And Miriam sang this song: "Sing to the Lord, for he has triumphed gloriously; he has hurled both horse and rider into the sea." (Exodus 15:20–21 NLT)

But life is not always easy in the wilderness, as the people soon discover. After they travel three days, they still have found no water to replenish the supplies they brought with them from Egypt. They at last come to an oasis—only to discover that the water there is too bitter to drink.

Bitterness is another recurring theme throughout the Bible, and the root word leads to the name Miriam. Biblical bitterness signifies more than an unpleasant taste but rather refers as well to an emotional state of disappointment or deprivation. The juxtaposition of joy and bitterness often reappears in the Bible—as it does in life.

NOTE

The word marah, translated as "bitterness," is used here as well as later in the Book of Ruth, when Naomi, widowed and with her two sons dead, says, "Call me not Naomi, call me Marah." One translation of Mary (who is the mother of Jesus in the Gospels) is "bitter sea," referring to the sorrow she endures as she watches her son be crucified.

Chapter 19 of Exodus further expands the qualities of the many-named God: "You have seen what I did to the Egyptians, how I bore you on eagle's wings and brought you to Me" (verse 4 TNK). In this verse, in the masculine-gendered eagle with feminine-gendered wings, we see the way in which Mother-Father God has been defined throughout scripture, from the Feminine Spirit moving on the waters of Creation, to the feminine protection of the Ark, to the I AM, the I Will Be Who I Will Be beyond gender. God is the One who does all things—unlimited, impossible to confine, immediate, present. In this Mothering and Fathering, in this movement of protection and definition of eternal, forever consciousness, preparation is made for the presentation of the Ten Commandments to the daughters and sons borne on eagle's wings.

Protection and Prohibition

Some people have the notion that the Commandments are a set of outdated prohibitions carved onto stone by a vengeful, angry male God and then handed to His appointed male spokesman. But that would be an impoverished mistake, a paltry view of what can be seen within their true context, laid on the ground that has been lain for the Mother and Father and All Being of God as the Primal Cause.

Here is how the Commandments come to consciousness:

On the third day, as morning dawned, there was thunder, and lightning, and a dense cloud upon the mountain, and a very loud blast of the horn, and all the people who were in the camp trembled. (Exodus 19:6 TNK)

The third day again. Then, in chapter 20, God says, "I am the Lord your God, who brought you out of the land of Egypt, out of the house of slavery. You shall have no other gods before Me" (verses 2–3 NASB). The "Me" speaking here is no longer a tribal God for only one family. This "Me" is Spirit—the One who made, makes, and does all things. The people's experiences have led them to a new understanding of the nurturing, caring, providing, ever-present nature of Spirit, who has led them to this point. And now the people are reminded of God's nature through the Commandments. Just as God defined and separated each aspect of Creation, there is no escaping here the call to remember who is who and what is what.

The Commandments also contain reminders of the three realms of spiritual Creation: "You shall make no image of what is in the heavens above or in the earth below or the waters beneath the earth" (Exodus 20:1–17). There is also a reminder of the seventh day of Creation with the commandment to "remember the sabbath and keep it holy" (verse 8).

Viewed not as prohibitions but as protections, the Commandments spare women and men the consequences of murder, theft, and adultery; they alert them to the ravages of envy; and they keep the people from being assimilated into lands where other "gods" are served. They remind the people not to depend on the authority of a king or judge but on their individual responses to Deity, the community, and self. These Commandments are the Israelites' organizing principles, the specific ways in which their relationship to Mother-Father God can be remembered and lived in their daily lives. Law, seated in individual behavior, protects both the individual and community.

God never states that living in harmony with the Commandments is easy—but doing so is part of the way out of slavery into the Promised Land. Slavery is not only a corrupt social state; it is also internal, emotional, and spiritual. We can be in slavery to murder, theft, adultery, envy—and it takes humility to allow the Commandments to set us free.

Shekinah

When Moses is on the mountain of God, the Bible tells us that "the glory of the Lord abode upon Mount Sinai, and then covered it six days: and the seventh day he called unto Moses out of the midst of the cloud. And

Moses was in the cloud forty days and forty nights" (Exodus 24:16 KJV).

Glory and *cloud* are significant recurring themes throughout the Bible, though the "cloud" may obscure the exact outline of the "glory" from both the reader as well as the people below at the foot of the mountain. These words in the Bible, however, point to the indwelling Presence of the Feminine Spirit.

In the ancient rabbinic literature that supplements and comments on the Hebrew scripture, the Feminine Spirit is referred to as *Shekinah*. The word is derived from *shakhan*, meaning "to dwell, reside, abide," but it also implies light and splendor. It is thought to be the form that Spirit takes throughout scripture whenever it speaks of light, as well as whenever the Spirit dwells as Soul with human life. According to some sources, the Shekinah can appear as a manifestation in light and sound to human senses.[5]

Medieval Jewish Bible scholars believed that when the children of Israel endured the agonies of slavery and the hardships of the wilderness, they did not do so alone, because Shekinah, the feminine aspect of God, dwelled alongside them. These thirteenth-century mystics portrayed the feminine Shekinah as a loving mother who suffers with her children and is manifested, literally and physically, through a woman's menstruation and conception of children.[6] In their book *The Divine*

Feminine, Andrew Harvey and Anne Baring write that Shekinah, as She is described in the thirteenth-century Jewish mystical text called the Zohar, exists within the dance of the Godhead, revealed through:

> the mystery of the relationship between the female and male aspects of the godhead expressed as Mother and Father, and their emanation through all levels of creation as Daughter and Son. The essential conception of this mystical tradition expresses itself as an image of worlds within worlds. Divine Spirit . . . beyond form or conception is the light at the center, the heart, and moves outward as creative sound (word), thought and energy, bringing into being successive spheres, realms, veils, or dimensions imagined as veils or robes that clothe and hide the hidden source yet at the same time transmit its radiant light.[7]

This is the cloud that leads the Israelites by day—and it is the pillar of fire that leads them through the night. They do not move without its leading. Eventually, this glory, the Feminine Spirit, will find its home in the Tabernacle that the people will work together to build.

The Book of Exodus begins with the Hebrews suffering in slavery and oppression. Their journey out of slavery, out of Egypt, ends with the reminder of the feminine aspect of God at the very center of their worship—with a female prophet, part of the story from the beginning, leading the way on dry land.

REFERENCE NOTES

1. Umair Haque. "(Why) The Universal Mother is the Antidote to the Authoritarian Father," *Eudaimonia*, January 16, 2019, https://eand.co/why-aoc-short-circuits-the-conservative-mind-2bd6baa-3d7a2.

2. Abarim Publications' Biblical Name Vault, "Puah," http://www.abarim-publications.com/Meaning/Puah.html#.XEjeki2ZNBw.

3. Robert Alter. *The Five Books of Moses: A Translation with Commentary* (New York: Norton, 2008), page 321.

4. You can read more about Currid's ideas regarding Creation and De-Creation in his book *Ancient Egypt and the Old Testament* (Ada, MI: Baker, 2010), page 115.

5. Kaufmann Kohler and Ludwig Blau. "Shekinah," *Jewish Encyclopedia*, http://www.jewishencyclopedia.com/articles/13537-shekinah.

6. To read more about this, see "The Shechinah: A Supernal Mother," by Sharon Koren, online at https://www.myjewishlearning.com/article/the-shechinah-a-supernal-mother/.

7. Andrew Harvey and Anne Baring, eds. *The Divine Feminine: Exploring the Feminine Face of God Around the World* (Newbury Port, MA: Conari Press, 1996), page 157.

SIX

ROUGH PLACES, PLAIN PLACES

*And they came, both men and women,
as many were willing hearted, and
brought bracelets, and earrings,
and rings, and tablets, all jewels of gold.*

–Exodus 35:22 (KJV)

H ow do we get through the rough places in the Bible?
There are stories in the Bible in which
unspeakable things happen to good or innocent people,
and stories in which the marginal and unnamed are

treated horrendously. These are passages so heavy with prescription and proscription that it is hard for the reader to tell at first glance what is going on. Some passages also seem strikingly inconsistent. And some seem hopelessly dated, applicable, it seems, only to a culture thousands of years in the past. There are certainly passages in the Bible many readers today may perceive as antiquated, reflecting opinions, attitudes, and traditions that are not only irrelevant today but may also be offensive. What you think of these sections will have something to do with where you are today in your own conscious path of disentangling opinion from fact.

More often than not, though, the Bible tells how marginal and unnamed people are treated better than kings and princes. And there are places in the text so clear, so inspired, so timely, and so familiar that they seem to contain all the truth you have ever known.

So how do we reconcile these two aspects of scripture? There have been many explanations—and many attempts at explanations—of the rough places. Men and women have founded churches and formed denominations based on their understandings of these passages, as well as on their inspired visions of other biblical texts. But whether the reader finds a satisfying explanation on the first, second, or hundredth reading (should that be the case) is up to her individual sense of revelation as she confronts the scripture in front of her. As time passes, or as the eye and critical faculties become clearer, that sense of revelation may take on even more light, more focus.

Though various options might be considered as a point of departure in interpreting these passages, I am not recommending that you become a Bible scholar as a prerequisite for understanding the Bible. Instead, I am encouraging you to take a personal journey inward, with the Bible as your companion. From this perspective, it is ultimately up to you to find your own explanations for some of these passages of good and evil. Or you may want to avoid them, at least for now, in order to focus on more pleasant biblical sections. The type of relationship with scripture I'm describing has nothing to do with biblical apologetics—defending religious doctrines through systematic arguments and discourse—and everything to do with a personal, inner process toward your own greater consciousness.

But, as we can't always avoid injustice or confusion, let's take just a brief look at a few examples to see if we can find some clarification in the rough places.

Process and the Tabernacle

Few readers would say their favorite section of the Bible is the scripture passage describing the building of the tabernacle in which God dwells (Exodus 25)—but it does give a glimpse into the methodology of some of the Bible and an indication of possible readings.

Quite a few people through the ages have explained the copious instruction for the Tabernacle as a symbolic description of the universe. To those readers, chapter 31, verse 3 of Exodus, "I have filled them with the Spirit of God," echoes chapter 1, verse 2 of Genesis, "And the Spirit of God moved upon the face of the waters." It is an indication that something is going on here in the building of the Tabernacle that relates to Creation.

Others feel even today that these are the actual instructions for building a sanctuary for the Lord, while still others think the instructions reflect the work it takes to develop a spiritual self. Aside from these interpretations, it is clear that the specific detail involved in building the Tabernacle serves as a break in the lives of the people, so that consciousness does not dwell in nostalgia for the irreversible past or a desire to plunge into a rigidly fixed future.

The building of a portable tabernacle, which does not contain God, can be likened to reading the Bible. The Bible is portable—something once quite remarkable that we now take for granted. And Deity may be uncovered not only between the actual pages or when scrolling on an Internet site, but in the very real process of searching, reading, meditating, acting on what is found there—in the weaving and joining and collecting and hammering down of disparate thoughts and ideas. Symbolically, as you read, study, and put into practice what the Bible has to say to you, you are building a tabernacle.

Instructions for building the Tabernacle are given twice and broken up with the story in the middle: the building of the Golden Calf, which is the story of how not to and what not to build. The first set of instructions for building the Tabernacle begins when Moses comes down from dwelling in the clouds, after forty days and nights on the mountain. Amid all the details of construction, Exodus 35:5 states that the Tabernacle is to be built equally by men and women; who does the work will be decided not by gender but by "whosoever is of a willing heart."

The women assemble at the door of the congregation as their mirrors are hammered down to make the laver at the center of the Tabernacle, giving up a merely physical sense of beauty and self in exchange for a spiritual sense of themselves. The passage also indicates that a willingness to work on a project larger than yourself gives you a new and more spiritual character.

The Golden Calf, the Tower of Babel, the Ark, and Solomon's temple are other representations the Bible describes as being built. Some are at God's instruction, built for overall communal benefit. Others are not. Comparing each biblical construction might be of interest to someone building a house, to an architect, to anyone who is interested in learning how to read a story on more than one level, or to anyone seeking to understand patience and the value of process in human life. There is more to the seemingly tedious Tabernacle section than meets the eye at first glance—and what is there can be read at more than one depth of understanding.

Rape, Dismembement, and Murder

The Book of Judges is full of difficult, rough places. One reason for this may be its illustration of women as the movers and shakers of action and central, for good or ill, to biblical events. Historically, many male readers have been ignorant of that understanding, and have instead focused on the political issues at play in the book. And yet, as Mieke Bal points out in her commentary of Judges, "A thorough analysis of this ancient text affects . . . the enterprise of women's history as a whole." She explains:

> The commonplaces about history and women's from it are seriously challenged in this historical book. . . . I will not ignore the claims about why "it is the case" that women are absent or unimportant in biblical history not because I believe it, but because the very dichotomies that are alleged to cause that situation are, in fact, issues within the historiographic text. That is, Judges is about precisely the production, the construction, of those ideas of history.[1]

Taking a brief but closer look at some of Judges' rough places illustrates this approach. In Judges are found most of the things that bother people about the Bible–as well as about human life. The Book of Judges illustrates violent, abhorrent behavior, and much of the violence is against unnamed women. However, it is not an apology for the Bible to say that there is no more or less violence within its pages then there is today on television, in the movies, or on the streets and roads of countless cities and nations. The Bible describes the terrors and joys of human life—as it is, rather than as we *wish* it could be—and in the process it leads our inner thoughts to spiritual identity, exempt from fearful inconsistencies.

A glimpse into the text shows that Judges itself says that all is not sweetness and light:

In those days there was no king in Israel; every man did as he pleased. (Judges 17:6)

The last verse of the Book of Judges, 21:25, repeats this statement.

Returning to the first six verses of the Book of Judges, we read about a war led by Judah and seemingly encouraged by God, in which at least ten thousand people are killed, and a man loses his thumb and big toe. Such dismemberment is not just an example of the gory, uncivilized past rearing its ugly head but continues today in tribal, religious, and state-sponsored wars. But is the point being made here merely that nothing changes? Or does this account warn us also, metaphorically, of the cutting apart, the fragmentation of the extremities of experience?

And what are we to make of the verses in Judges 1:12–15, in which a woman given as a battle prize becomes one of the numbers of women who is granted the good they ask for and more? Achsah, this particular woman, receives not only good, but also a blessing (as Jacob received a blessing and as each of the days of Creation received blessing and the affirmation of goodness), as well as both land and springs of water, symbolizing the Feminine Spirit's life-giving creativity. Even in seemingly unimportant biblical accounts, the Feminine Spirit makes Herself known, calling out for recognition of life-affirming details.

Women's History

Part of Judges, the story and song of Deborah, is thought by some Bible scholars to date from about the same time that Genesis was written. We all know that women's history has been with us as long as there has been human history, and the Bible makes this plain.

But how to interpret that history has not been the province of women until quite recently. Today, you have the option of taking part in the interpretation of this ancient manuscript in the light of today's experiences.

> *Deborah, wife of Lappidoth, was a prophetess; she led Israel at the time. She used to sit under the Palm of Deborah, between Ramah and Bethel in the hill country of Ephraim, and the Israelites would come to her for decisions.* (Judges 4:4–5 TNK)

There are several things hidden within the words of these verses. First, the name Deborah comes from the same root as the Hebrew word for "wilderness," which has to do with a voice speaking. Second, oddly enough, the name Lappidoth (the name of Deborah's husband) is a feminine name in Hebrew meaning "torches" or perhaps "firebrand" or "lightning flashes." (Several scholars say that the mention of a husband is not a proper translation; given the meaning of the two names combined, hinting at a partnership between "speech" and "lightning," what are we to understand about the Voice bursting into light in the wilderness?) Third, the fact that Deborah sits under the tree that stands between Ramah and Bethlehem ties her to geographical locations with symbolic meanings: Ramah is where Rachel weeps for her children, and Bethel is where Jacob builds an altar to the Spirit that renames him Israel. There Deborah is, geographically placed within cosmic, simultaneous time, between symbols of remembrance

of both male and female, as well as sorrow and joy—
and transformation.

Even today, in our supposedly more enlightened
age, society often accuses women of being "too threatening." And yet the Bible gives no indication that the
patriarchy of Deborah's day was threatened in any way
by her authority. The prophetess is a commander-in-
chief with an entire nation, people, and army at her
disposal, as well as the power of God's Voice underlining her decisions. Remembering that Deborah is part of
a woman's heritage today reminds us that women lead
in the name of the biblical God—and that women cannot be legitimately compartmentalized, marginalized,
or stereotyped.

The Bible account next tells us that Deborah sum-
mons her general, Barak, and says to him, "The Lord
God of Israel has commanded: Go, march up to Mount
Tabor, and take with you ten thousand men of Naphtali
and Zebulon. And I will draw Sisera, Jabin's army commander, with his chariots and his troops, toward you
up to the Wadi Kison; and I will deliver him into your
hands" (Judges 4:6–7 TNK).

Mimetic relationship is illustrated by Deborah's
prophecy that "the Lord will deliver Sisera into the
hands of a woman" when later, a woman, Jael, invites
the enemy Sisera into her tent—and drives a stake
through his head. The scene described in chapter
5, verses 28 through 30, with Sisera's mother at the

window, painfully reminds us that for every victor there is a vanquished—and shows us yet another instance when the woman's experience is embedded within a bloody tale of war and violence.

But now, before those events occur, Barak answers Deborah, "If you will go with me, I will go; if not I will not go" (verse 8, TNK). He needs her. Did Barak know better than to go without Deborah? Or is a female leader necessary for final victory?

Deborah's answer perhaps indicates her awareness of the patriarchy's attitudes regarding women's uselessness in war: "Very well, I will go with you . . . but there will be no glory for you since the Lord will give the enemy Sisera into the hands of a woman" (verse 9, paraphrase).

The whole of Judges 5 is called Deborah's song, although Barak also speaks or sings the verse. As you read this chapter, remember that a female voice is speaking. Read the whole song aloud to get the full import of women's strength and place in prophetic authority, as well as in national and international events. When phrases from Deborah's song reappear in the Psalms of David, we see again the force and permanence of women's history.

After Deborah's victory, "the land had rest for forty years" (5:31). The number forty is, as we have already seen, significant in the Bible. Usually, it refers to a time of testing, but in this case, the meaning is reversed: a

woman leader brings a period of peace rather than trials and hardship.

Deborah sets a standard. Who wouldn't want a
woman commander-in-chief if it could mean a period
of restoration and harmony? As both a practical and
spiritual guide to life, the Bible certainly does not
relegate women to the kitchen or to any other pro-
scribed position.

Jephthah's Daughter

The story of the unnamed daughter of Jephthah is one
of the Bible's roughest places. It is one of those biblical
accounts that people point to as proof that the Bible is
anti-woman. But even here, there is more than meets
the eye.

Jephthah, the Bible says, is the son of a prostitute
and Gilead. His half-brothers, Gilead's legitimate sons,
drive Jephthah out of the family, saying that he is the
son of an outsider. Later, though, the brothers come
back to him and ask him to lead them in a fight against
the Ammonites. Jephthah does so on the condition that
if the Lord delivers the Ammonites to him, then he will
become the commander over them all. So Jephthah says
to God, "If you deliver the Ammonites into my hands,
then whoever comes out of the door of my house to meet
me on my safe return shall be the Lord's and shall be
offered by me as a burnt offering" (11:29–31 TNK).

The grim result is that when Jephthah gets what he asks for, it is his only child, his daughter, who comes to greet him, forcing him to change his mind or bring her to sacrifice. He doesn't change his mind, and he carries out the vow he made to his idea of God. Unlike Abraham and Isaac, Jephthah's concept of God remains locked in a false concept of Deity. And his daughter—the girl without a name—goes obediently to her death.

Some people have read into this story a foreshadowing of Jesus, who also was "obedient unto death" (Philippians 2:8). They have held up Jephthah's daughter as a model of the submissive, self-sacrificing woman they claim is the Bible's ideal. From this perspective, every woman who yields to a male abuser, too afraid to protest or seek help, is carrying out God's will for women. No wonder some women want to avoid the Bible.

But actually, God is silent in this story. God did not ask that Jephthah make his vow, and there is no indication that the vow persuaded Divine action. Instead, Deity's perspective is never given in this account. In our own world, we may also wish that God would step in and stop certain tragic things from happening. In the same way that life never explains the problem of evil, though, these passages offer no excuse, rationalization, or explanation of what God is thinking and doing. They only give us an account of a man who thought he was obeying his concept of God.

And while there is no excusing or explaining away the horrifying details of this story, many readers have found a far different message in the narrative, one that does not condone women's submission to being violently objectified. Carol P. Christ, for example, writes:

> We read this story not to celebrate Jepthah's terrible act, but to remind ourselves that every father or mother who goes to war or condones war is signifying his or her willingness to sacrifice not one but many beloved daughters, not one, but many beloved sons.[2]

J. Clark Saunders also sees a "subversive sub-text" told through the end of the story, where the scripture records, "And it was a custom in Israel, That the daughters of Israel went yearly to lament the daughter of Jephthah the Gildeadite for four days in a year" (11:40 KJV). Although the girl's name is never recorded, she has not been forgotten. As Saunders points out, the women's annual ritual is done

> to remember a victim of domestic violence, a victim of a patriarchal system, a victim of the idea that one person can be another person's property, a victim of a man's warped ideas about radical devotion to God coming between him and God's will for integrity and compassion in human relationships.[3]

The story ends with this account of women's solidarity in the face of a cruel patriarchy. The ritual of mourning may seem to accomplish little, and we are left with a terrible taste in our mouths. But as we said earlier, *remembering* is vital to the Bible's message. Thousands of years later, we have not forgotten this young woman; her death still shocks and repulses us. Unnamed as she is, she is still *visible*, demanding even now, in the twenty-first century, that we face realities we would rather avoid.

"What shall we do in remembrance of her?" Saunders asks. The answer he offers is this: we can remember Jephthah's daughter

> by making it clear that the system that allowed such a thing to happen is not tolerated in places where we have a say about it, that God's silence in the story cannot be construed as God's approval for what Jephthah did, that no parent has the right to sacrifice a child on an altar of pride or frustration or failed ambition or a misguided sense of honour or unresolved anger. . . . How shall we keep faith with this nameless one? By mourning her. By being outraged at the injustice of her story. By dedicating ourselves to being vigilant about our own attitudes within and society's attitudes without. . . . By ensuring that, though we have forgotten her name, we shall not forget her story.[4]

Ending as the Beginning

Toward the end of Judges is a story that echoes the dismembering narrated at the beginning of the book. In this monstrous story (if taken literally), a man offers a group of lustful men the women in his house as a substitute for a man who is his guest. (Lot did something similar back in Genesis.) The story goes like this:

> *"You are welcome at my house," the old man said. "Let me supply whatever you need. Only don't spend the night in the square." So he took him into his house and fed his donkeys. After they had washed their feet, they had something to eat and drink.*

While they were enjoying themselves, some of the wicked men of the city surrounded the house. Pounding on the door, they shouted to the old man who owned the house, "Bring out the man who came to your house so we can have sex with him."

The owner of the house went outside and said to them, "No, my friends, don't be so vile. Since this man is my guest, don't do this outrageous thing. Look, here is my virgin daughter, and his concubine. I will bring them out to you now, and you can use them and do to them whatever you wish. But as for this man, don't do such an outrageous thing."

But the men would not listen to him. So the man took his concubine and sent her outside to them, and they raped her and abused her throughout the night, and at dawn they let her go. At daybreak the woman went back to the house where her master was staying, fell down at the door and lay there until daylight.

When her master got up in the morning and opened the door of the house and stepped out to continue on his way, there lay his concubine, fallen in the doorway of the house, with her hands on the threshold. He said to her, "Get up; let's go." But there was no answer. Then the man put her on his donkey and set out for home.

When he reached home, he took a knife and cut up his concubine, limb by limb, into twelve parts and sent them into all the areas of Israel. (Judges 19:20–29 NIV)

What is meant by the symbolism of sending parts of a ravished unnamed woman, to the twelve tribes of Israel? Historically, violence toward a scapegoat unifies a group, a community, for good or evil. In this case the text may mean that a call to the twelve tribes to unify is illustrated by twelve parts of the female body.

The Bible makes no comment, neither approving nor condemning the actions of the men in this account. Throughout it, only the men speak; the woman, as is so often the case with rape victims, even today, has no voice at all. Biblical scholar Phyllis Trible writes:

> The betrayal, rape, torture, murder, and dismemberment of an unnamed woman is a story we want to forget but are commanded to speak. It speaks of the horrors of male power, brutality, and triumphalism; of female helplessness, abuse, and annihilation. To hear this story is to inhabit a world of unrelenting terror that refuses to let us pass by on the other side.[5]

Another author, Dierdre Brouer, notes that the men in this account all appear to believe that they are doing the right thing. She writes that "the text makes a powerful rhetorical statement by connecting a key theme throughout Judges with the rape of the concubine: Everyone was doing what was good in their eyes, but evil in God's eyes."[6]

The final verse of chapter 19 is this: "Everyone who saw it was saying to one another, 'Such a thing has never been seen or done, not since the day the Israelites came up out of Egypt. Just imagine! We must do something! So speak up!'" (Judges 19:30 NIV). Perhaps that is ultimately the message we should take away from this account of rape and murder: *We must do something! We must speak up!*

A cycle of violence follows this incident, resulting in the slaughter of many men, women, and children (20:35–48), including most of the inhabitants of a city (21:8–12), and the kidnapping of four hundred young women (21:15–24). This book of the Bible that includes the story of Deborah, a woman who is strong, honored, and independent, ends with several appalling stories illustrating violent misogyny.

It also illustrates the social and religious chaos of the era. The stories' terrible details indicate the extreme disorder that exists, which will be rectified in the biblical passages that follow. With typical Bible paradox, the stories in the next several chapters of the Bible laud, celebrate, and honor specific, named, independent women.

The rough places in the Bible are not easy reading. Even read purely as allegory, rather than literal history, they are nightmarish, like a modern horror movie full of violent sex and bloody gore. And yet we can see in them much that speaks with a brutal honesty to our modern world. They demand that we not gloss over the evil that human beings do—even humans who consider themselves moral, religious people—that we see the dreadful reality of what humans do to each other.

Ultimately, the predominant message may be this: Beware! If you touch a hot stove, you will be burnt. And if you follow the path of society rather than Spirit, you and the world around you will be brutalized.

Plain Places

What if we could be the first full generation of women and men who say, once and for all, that the biblical God loves women; that women are a Divine concept, embodying aspects of Deity; and that Spirit cherishes women, understands women, and helps them wherever they find themselves?

We can start this process by remembering (as the Bible calls us to do). We recall what the biblical God—the Breasted One, the Existing One, the Shield who bears people on eagles' wings—has done for women so far in just the first six books of the Bible:

• Created women as the highest idea of humankind

- Illustrated the dangers to society when women are dominated
- Showed Divine control of biological conception
- Sent angels to powerless, fearful women
- Appeared directly to women's eyes
- Saved women's children
- Gave women husbands who love them
- Provided homes for independent women
- Protected women
- Healed women of physical ills
- Approved women's strength, authority, and leadership
- Appointed women as leaders
- Made women rulers over their own bodies and minds
- Gave women occasion to sing and dance—and to lead the community in celebration
- Anointed women to carry the message of God to all
- Exempted women from criticism on sexual, domestic, and political actions

These are just the most obvious things. As you interact with scripture on your own, you will discover more affirmations of women woven into the descriptions of what seemed to be a patriarchal society.

You may also find that no matter how many times you read a passage, there is always more to be revealed. This is partly because you bring something new within yourself each time you sit down with the Bible—and partly because the Bible has limitless levels of meaning.

The Bible tells us that despite the ugliness and falseness of some aspects of society, we live in an ordered universe, as well as in a dimension beyond even that universe. Given that, what woman—aware, conscious, inspired by the Spirit—would want to settle for a limited, stultifying life of suffering and punishment?

Who would want to be Eve?

REFERENCE NOTES

1. Mieke Bal and Ruth Richardson. *Death and Dissymmetry: The Politics of Coherence in the Book of Judges* (Chicago: University of Chicago Press, 1988), pages 14, 15.

2. Carol P. Christ. "Who Is Jephthah's Daughter? The Cost of War," *Feminism and Religion*, January 13, 2014, https://feminismandreligion.com/2014/01/13/who-is-jepthehs-daughter-by-carol-p-christ/.

3. J. Clark Saunders. "In Remembrance of Her," http://saltsprin-gunitedchurch.org/wp-content/uploads/2016/06/2016-07-03-Sermon.pdf.

4. Ibid.

5. Phyllis Trible. *Texts of Terror: Literary-Feminist Readings of Biblical Narratives* (Minneapolis, MN: Fortress Press, 1984), page 65.

6. Deirdre Brouer. "Voices of Outrage Against Rape: Textual Evidence in Judges 19," *Priscilla Papers* (Winter 2014)28: 24–28.

SEVEN

THE WOMAN ALONE

*So the woman went her way, and did eat,
and her countenance was no more sad.*

–1 Samuel 10:18 KJV

I n the texts we have looked at so far, it is the widow, the orphan, and the powerless woman who carries to earth the story of the Spirit God. Now, as we look at the Book of Ruth and then move into the First Book of Samuel, we see that not only does God provide for the woman alone, but that without these seemingly

173

powerless women, there would be no story of God's provision for earth . . . no completeness and no happy ending. Being a woman alone is not a dead-end street but an open way to happiness, fulfillment, and self-esteem. Or so says the Bible.

Ruth

"Whither thou goest, I will go; and where though lodgest I will lodge: thy people shall be my people, and thy God my God." Ruth speaks this familiar line from the Bible, used often at wedding ceremonies. Many people assume that a woman says this to a man, but in fact Ruth addresses these words to her mother-in-law, Naomi. The association of Ruth's affirmation with marriage and a man-woman relationship has relegated both Ruth and Naomi to nonthreatening, stereotypical roles. When the story is seen this way, a man ultimately rescues the devoted daughter-in-law and her helpless widowed mother-in-law.

In reality, Ruth and Naomi are smart women making smart choices within a male-oriented society. At first blush they may seem powerless, but throughout their story, they are protected, guided, nurtured, and elevated as they know themselves while they clearly, oh-so clearly, assess their opportunities in a patriarchal world. These women are active and decisive. They are able to set goals and achieve them; they take the initiative. And they illustrate women's spiritual power superseding a hopeless condition.

The Book of Ruth is a slim volume. In just four chapters it tells the story of how two women alone make their way in the world. Within the book's seeming simplicity are breathtaking allusions. Sections like this are what make the Bible the Book that it is—inspiration, not mere information.

As you begin the Book of Ruth, you will see again that the story starts out naming men and then, in a few verses, switches to women—and this is where the action begins. Naomi is the central figure. After the family immigrated to Moab, her husband and two sons have died, leaving her with two Moabite daughters-in-law.

Then she arose with her daughters-in-law, that she might return from the country of Moab: for she had heard in the country of Moab how that the Lord had visited his people in giving them bread. (Ruth 1:6 KJV)

NOTE

The Moabites were the descendants of Lot's incestuous relationship with his daughter. Later, Moses died and was buried in the land of Moab.

Naomi was originally from Bethlehem, and now she wants to return there. As Abraham does, Naomi gets up and goes. Abraham acted because he received a direct order from God, and Naomi is also acting because of something she heard—God is visiting the people, as God visited Sarah (Genesis 21:1).

Few things in the Bible are more empowering to any woman than the sight of women finding their way against all odds. The account of Naomi and her daughters-in-law gives us that vision. One daughter-in-law, Orpah, finds her way when she returns to her people; Naomi and her other daughter-in-law, Ruth, find their way when they go to Bethlehem at the time of the barley harvest.

When Ruth makes her decision to accompany Naomi, she says those famous lines: "Wherever you go, I will go" (1:16). The special relationship between Ruth and Naomi becomes even more evident when we look at a literal translation of the Hebrew. The scripture says that Ruth "clung" to Naomi (1:14), which is an allusion to the verse in Genesis, where the same Hebrew word is used to describe the marriage relationship: "For this reason a man leaves his father and his mother, and clings to his wife" (2:24, literal translation). Here, in the Book of Ruth, it is not a man but a woman who leaves her father and mother, and she clings not to her spouse but to another woman. Although Ruth's story has often been viewed as a romance between a man and woman, its focus is sisterhood and loyalty between two women.

In the biblical stories of feminine competition and jealousy, such as Sarah and Hagar, Leah and Rachel, scripture reveals the reality that women do not always support each other; as women, we carry patriarchy and misogyny with us, and it can become the lens through which we look at one another. But the Bible also shows that these divisive and hurtful relationships between women need not be the norm. Ruth and Naomi demonstrate the unconditional love and intimacy that can unite women.

Naomi is a marvelous character. She reenters Bethlehem (which means "house of bread") after years of exile in Moab with her husband and sons. In *The Complete Jewish Bible* translation, she says, "Call me not Naomi, call me Mara: for Shaddai has made my lot very bitter" (Ruth 1:20). Bitterness is a specific and recognizable allusion to the listening townspeople of Bethlehem. The reminders of the parting of the Red Sea, the escape from the Egyptians, and the bitter waters of Mara are all contained within Naomi's statement, for this is a story that has been handed down from parents to children through the generations.

Naomi is a woman who is not afraid to call attention to her problems. She does not suffer in self-sacrificial silence, as women have often been told is their appropriate mode of being, but rather she firmly states how she feels. We will learn that despite her problems, she continues to have faith that the Breasted One is providing—but she makes clear that her life has not been smooth.

You may have similar feelings. Although you know that the Divine One is caring for you, you have also gotten the short end of the stick. That is true for all of us who are women living within the limitations of chronological time—but it is not what the Bible reveals to be reality in cosmic time. Through the ups and downs of consciousness, we—like Naomi—are cared for, but we are not passive recipients of a masculine God's providence. Woman's strength, intelligence, and insight are essential to the story of Divine care in the Book of Ruth.

As women without men in a patriarchal system, Naomi and Ruth must find a way to support themselves. Since it's the time of the barley harvest, Ruth goes to glean the loose grain from a field. The field she chooses belongs to a wealthy relative of her father-in-law named Boaz. When Boaz visits the field and hears of Ruth's loyalty to his kinswoman Naomi, he tells his workers to allow her to glean and even to leave additional grain in her path.

Ruth, like Sarah and Abraham, has left her family. And she too is rewarded. Boaz says to her, "May the Lord reward your work, and your wages be full from the Lord, the God of Israel, under whose wings you have come to seek refuge" (2:12 NASB)—or, in the King

James Version, "under whose wings you have come to trust." Here again we see, as we did in Exodus, the image of the Spirit's feminine wings, but this time it is a daughter of Moab—an immigrant, an "alien"—who has found shelter within the protection of the nurturing Motherhood of God.

Boaz has shown his willingness to help Ruth, but Naomi wants to push things along toward a more definite resolution. She is a fascinating mother-in-law, not only generous, strong, and dramatic, but also clever. Demonstrating her resourcefulness and insight, she advises Ruth to go to the threshing floor on the night Boaz winnows the barley, to wash and prepare herself, and to uncover Boaz's feet and lie next to them while he sleeps.

Ruth follows Naomi's instructions. When Boaz awakes, Ruth asks him to spread his robe over her—a symbolic act of espousal—because Boaz is a "redeeming kinsman"; in other words, he is in the line of men who, by Hebrew law, owe Ruth and Naomi protection. Then, we are told, Naomi says, "Wait, my daughter, until you find out what happens. For the man will not rest until the matter is settled today" (3:18 NIV).

Each verse of this story has something to offer to a woman who feels alienated, adrift, hungry, unloved—as well as to women and men who are seeking to understand the ways in which Divine providence intertwines with our own initiative and courage. Take a look, for example, at the barley harvest as a symbolic allusion to fruitfulness and Divine abundance, themes that we have already seen run through the entire Bible.

NOTE

Use a concordance to look up the words fruit *and* harvest *in the Bible. As you follow the thread of God's abundant providence through scripture, you may also begin to sense how the Breasted One provides for your own individual life.*

Ruth's story concludes with further affirmation of many of the themes we have already seen in scripture: the Spirit's control over human conception, the importance of "remembering"; and most of all, the essential role of women in the story of God's people.

Then the elders and all the people at the gate said, "We are witnesses. May the Lord make the woman who is coming into your home like Rachel and Leah, who together built up the family of Israel. . . ."

So Boaz took Ruth and she became his wife. When he made love to her, the Lord enabled her to conceive, and she gave birth to a son. The women

*said to Naomi: "Praise be to the Lord, who this day
has not left you without a guardian-redeemer. May
he become famous throughout Israel! He will renew
your life and sustain you in your old age. For your
daughter-in-law, who loves you and who is better to
you than seven sons, has given him birth."*

*Then Naomi took the child in her arms and cared
for him. The women living there said, "Naomi has a
son!" And they named him Obed. He was the father
of Jesse, the father of David.* (11,13–17 NIV)

Naomi and Ruth's relationship continues to be so
close that they will apparently share in the rearing of
Ruth's child.

The Book of Ruth, as Bible scholar Orit Avnery
points out,

> touches in many subtle ways upon such enduring
> issues as one's relation to the other—to those who
> are different, marginal, foreign, alien. Its chosen
> heroine is as foreign as they come—a Moabite—and
> its center, Bethlehem, is the home territory of the
> Israelite monarchy. The peaceful [story] is a poten-
> tially explosive text. . . .[1]

The foreigner, the woman alone, becomes part of the
Bible's royal genealogy, the lineage of David.

Hannah

Although Ruth's and Hannah's stories are not consecutive in the Hebrew scripture as they are in the Christian Bible, there is no question that both accounts unfold the narrative of Creation through women.

Hannah's story, like Ruth's, begins with a man who then fades into the landscape of women's needs and desires. Like Rachel before her, Hannah must share her husband (whose name is Elkanah) with another wife; and although she is the beloved wife, she is barren. Like Naomi, Hannah speaks openly of her bitterness (the same bitterness that the women encountered in Exodus after the parting of the sea). And like Hagar, Hannah feels free to express her anguish directly to God.

She was deeply distressed and prayed to the Lord and wept bitterly. And she vowed a vow and said, "O Lord of hosts, if you will indeed look on the affliction of your servant and remember me and not forget your servant, but will give to your servant a son, then I will give him to the Lord all the days of his life, and no razor shall touch his head." (1 Samuel 1:10–11 ESV)

Note the specificity with which Hannah prays, as well as her sense of certainty about her own individual relationship, rights, and access to the Creator.

In verse 11, our translations say that Hannah addressed Deity as "Lord of hosts," and many commentaries will say that "hosts" refers to armies and warfare. That is one possible meaning, a masculine understanding of Hannah's prayer, but as we have already mentioned, the word translated as "Lord" might better be expressed as the "Existing One," or even the "One Ever Coming into Manifestation," while "hosts" can also refer to the entire Creation, as it does in Genesis 2:1. ("Thus the heavens and the earth were finished, and all the host of them.") The Hebrew word used here has another possible feminine-gendered meaning: "a mass of people." So, keeping these understandings in mind, Hannah makes a vow to God as the "Existing One of the Whole Creation"—or the "One Ever Coming into Manifestation for Everyone."

As she continued praying before the Lord, Eli [the priest] observed her mouth. Hannah was speaking in her heart; only her lips moved, and her voice was not heard. Therefore Eli took her to be a drunken woman. And Eli said to her, "How long will you go on being drunk? Put your wine away from you." But Hannah answered, "No, my lord, I am a woman troubled in spirit. I have drunk neither wine nor strong drink, but I have been pouring out my soul before the Lord. Do not regard your servant as a worthless woman, for all along I have been speaking out of my great anxiety and vexation." (1 Samuel 1:12–16 ESV)

Note that when Hannah "talks back" to the priest, she is not censured, ostracized, or cast out of organized religion. In her contradiction of the priest, she establishes silent prayer as a valid way to communicate with the Divine. Hannah, who is remembered as one of the seven women prophets of Israel, is making an important theological statement here, affirming that God communes with us in our inner, private thoughts.

Note also that the term she uses to address the priest—"my lord"—is the same as that which translators have used for God (though the two words are not the same in the Hebrew). Small wonder that God and men have seemed one and the same, or that women have not been seen as Godlike. This confusion is the fault of our translations, however, rather than the original Hebrew.

Eli accepts Hannah's explanation and blesses her. And then "the woman went her way, and did eat, and her countenance was no more sad" (1 Samuel 1:18 KJV). Scripture tells us what happened next between Hannah and her husband:

They rose early in the morning and worshiped before the Lord; then they went back to their house at Ramah. And Elkanah knew Hannah his wife, and the Lord remembered her. And in due time Hannah

*conceived and bore a son, and she called his name
Samuel, for she said, "I have asked for him from the
Lord."* (1:19–20 ESV)

Here is another of the countless places in the Bible
in which the text illustrates the side-by-side creations
of Genesis, chapters 1 and 2—the intersection of cosmic
time and place with chronological time and geographical location. Eugene Peterson, in *The Message*, makes
an interesting note along the same lines in his introduction to the two books of Samuel:

> Four lives dominate the two-volume narrative: Han-
> nah, Samuel, Saul and David. Not one of them can
> be accounted for in terms of cultural conditions or
> psychological dynamics. God is the country in which
> they live.[2]

Hannah, along with the males in these books of the
Bible, inhabits not only time and space but also the
eternal God.

This is evident when Elkanah, like Adam, "knows"
his wife, and the Existing One remembers Hannah,
just as God remembered Rachel. Hannah conceives as
easily and surely as two and two is four. *Knowing* and
remembering are almost a mathematical equation; they
form a spiritual agreement that produces both spiritual
and physical fruitfulness.

Hannah's first child, Samuel, will anoint David, great-grandson of Ruth, great-great-grandson of Naomi, as king of Israel. The line of women through the Bible is unmistakable, not only in a genealogical sense but in a spiritual sense as well. As women, we can join hands with this long chain of women who prophesied, prayed, acted, and lived with the creative Feminine Spirit of the Bible.

Hannah's song of gratitude to the Existing One reveals the strength and inner authority she experiences:

My inner being rejoices in the Existing One; the feminine rays of my being are lifted up in the Living One; I open my mouth wide against those who are hostile to me, because I am glad in the Feminine Spirit's salvation. Nothing, nothing, nothing is as sacred as the Existing One. No one is like You, no rock is like Elohim. . . . The bows of the strong men are shattered, but those who stumble are equipped with strength. . . . The Living One kills and brings to life, descends into the underworld and ascends, grows, dawns. . . . The Existing One raises those who are poor and weak from the dust, and lifts those who are needy and lacking from the garbage heap and the dust, making them dwell with the generous and take possession of a seat of abundance and honor. For the pillars of the Earth belong to the Living One, who placed the world

on them. . . . For not by power shall a man be strong.
Those who strive against the Existing One shall be
shattered with thunder from heaven. The Living One
defends and administers the ends of the earth . . .
and lifts up the feminine rays of inner being of
those who are anointed. (1 Samuel 2:1,2,4,6–8,9,10,
literal translation)

NOTE

*Most English translations use the word "horn" for what can
also be interpreted as the "rays of inner being." The Hebrew
word, which is feminine in gender, might also be considered
to mean "inner strength."*

*Note too that the Hebrew word for "salvation" is femi-
nine. The word carries within it the meanings of deliverance,
prosperity, victory, health, and welfare. And it is the same
word—yeshua—as the name of Jesus in Hebrew.*

This is not tame stuff. Nor is it arrogant bragging.
It is prophecy spilling out of the mouth of a woman.
Hannah's song refers backward in chronological time
to the second account of Creation, where man (the male
human) is made from dust, and then it affirms that the
Living One lifts us from the dust. She contrasts the
masculine and the feminine, and then weaves them

together. Centuries later, another biblical mother, Mary the mother of Jesus, will reach back through chronological time and join hands with Hannah, repeating parts of Hannah's song as her own after she receives the angelic message that she will conceive through the power of the Existing One alone.

And so Hannah sings in cosmic time, joining past and future into a single reality. Women through the ages, biblical and otherwise, join her, connected to each other as they live and move and have their being in the Living God, as well as in each other's hopes and aspirations.

Abigail

The Bible affirms women's prophetic ability (their power to speak truth). In Abigail's story, it even gets her out of a bad marriage. In less than two weeks, Abigail, a beautiful and intelligent woman (according to the Bible account) married to a foolish drunk, becomes a prophet newly married to a gracious, passionate, warrior poet—David, the Lord's anointed and the king of Israel.

In his book *The Life of David,* the poet Robert Pinsky says about the story of David:

> With its emphasis on competition and succession, loyalty and rivalry among men and between sons and fathers, it seems a male story, in the primal way

of ironbound tradition, and yet women play powerful roles. Michal, Abigail, Bathsheba make decisions that determine outcomes.[3]

NOTE

David, the youngest clever son, is anointed king by Samuel (who has grown up in the temple, just as his mother vowed, and has now become the prophet of Israel). The story of David killing the giant Goliath is much like the story of the young Arthur pulling the sword from the stone—the young, overlooked boy proves to have the strength to become king. Both Pinsky's Life of David *and Robert Alter's* The David Story *explicate the life of this complicated Bible hero in depth; those books might be read for a deeper understanding of David.*

Our concern, unlike Pinsky's, is with the women in David's life, particularly Abigail. Other stories in David's life may be more familiar than his marriage to Abigail, including his relationships with Bathsheba and Michal. Nevertheless, Abigail is a romantic high point in David's complicated interactions with the opposite sex. Unlike the other women in his life, she is neither the seducer nor the seduced, nor is she the daughter of a powerful man—and yet she is another of the seven women who are prophets of Israel. Abigail is a smart, political woman living a political life.

When she meets David, he is not yet king. Instead, Saul is king of Israel. Saul both fears and loves David, whom Samuel has already anointed as God's chosen king, and so David and his men are hiding from the king out in the hills.

Abigail enters the story shortly after Samuel's death, while David is mourning his mentor. She is the wife of a very rich man called Nabal, which is also the Hebrew word for fool. According to the scripture, "she was an intelligent and beautiful woman, but her husband was surly and mean in his dealings" (1 Samuel 25:3 NIV). Reading between the lines, we might infer that Abigail is caught in an abusive marriage.

Nabal owns many thousands of goat and sheep, but when David's men come to him, asking for food on David's behalf, Nabal refuses their request. "I've never heard of this David," he says. "Most likely he's someone's runaway servant" (1 Samuel 25:10,11, paraphrase). When his men report to David what happened, he is incensed at Nabal's response. In a fit of machismo, David straps on his sword, tells his men to do the same, and sets off to fight Nabal.

Nabal's servants report to Abigail what is happening.

"David sent messengers from the wilderness to give our master his greetings, but he hurled insults

at them. Yet these men were very good to us. . . .
Now think it over and see what you can do, because
disaster is hanging over our master and his whole
household. He is such a wicked man that no one can
talk to him." (25:14,15,16 NIV)

Notice what's going on here: the men of Nabal's household are asking a woman what she thinks should be
done. They know Abigail, and they know she is intelligent and sensible, while her husband is not; they expect
her to take care of this situation.

Abigail doesn't pause for a second. She doesn't bother
to defend her husband against his servants' complaints,
nor does she run for help. Instead, she confidently takes
matters into her own hands—immediately.

Abigail wasted no time. She quickly gathered 200
loaves of bread, two wineskins full of wine, five sheep
that had been slaughtered, nearly a bushel of roasted
grain, 100 clusters of raisins, and 200 fig cakes. She
packed them on donkeys and said to her servants, "Go
on ahead. I will follow you shortly." But she didn't tell
her husband Nabal what she was doing. As she was
riding her donkey into a mountain ravine, she saw
David and his men coming toward her. (25:18–20 NLT)

Abigail has not only packed a generous picnic feast
without her husband's knowledge, but she has also

moved into spiritual territory and the land of prophecy. The King James Version translates, "Go on ahead," as "I come after you," a phrase that will be echoed in the New Testament in reference to Jesus, who comes after John the Baptist (Acts 19:4), and also in the words Jesus speaks to his followers in the Gospels, telling them to "come after" him (Mark 1:17, Luke 9:23). Furthermore, donkeys are charged with rich biblical symbolism. Both King David and later King Solomon ride donkeys, and donkeys show up again in the Gospels, when before his crucifixion, Jesus enters Jerusalem riding a donkey as palms are thrown before him. Here, in this chapter of 1 Samuel, we have a woman, not a male king, who is riding a donkey, bringing with her an abundance of food. Abigail can be seen as a representation of the Feminine Spirit, who works in our lives with abundant creativity to restore peace and harmony to the world.

Meanwhile, David is still boiling over with self-righteous male wrath. He says to his men:

"A lot of good it did to help this fellow. We protected his flocks in the wilderness, and nothing he owned was lost or stolen. But he has repaid me evil for good. May God strike me and kill me if even one man of his household is still alive tomorrow morning!" (25:20–22 NLT)

The literal translation of "man" in that last sentence is "anyone who pisses against a wall." With this reference to male territory marking, David is being about as crude and macho as it gets. But Abigail diffuses his anger with clever diplomacy.

When Abigail saw David, she quickly got off her donkey and bowed low before him. She fell at his feet and said, "I accept all blame in this matter, my lord. Please listen to what I have to say. I know Nabal is a wicked and ill-tempered man; please don't pay any attention to him. He is a fool, just as his name suggests. But I never even saw the young men you sent. . . . And here is a present that I, your servant, have brought to you and your young men. Please forgive me if I have offended you in any way. The Lord will surely reward you with a lasting dynasty, for you are fighting the Lord's battles. . . . Even when you are chased by those who seek to kill you, your life is safe in the care of the Lord your God, secure in his treasure pouch! But the lives of your enemies will disappear like stones shot from a sling! When the Lord has done all he promised and has made you leader of Israel, don't let this be a blemish on your record. Then your conscience won't have to bear the staggering burden of needless bloodshed and vengeance. And when the Lord has done these great

things for you, please remember me, your servant!"
(25:23–25,27–31 NLT)

Some Bible readers have interpreted Abigail's actions as a demonstration of submission to David's authority, but they can as easily be read as an affirmation of grace and truth more powerful than military violence.

Although her husband was not familiar with David, Abigail obviously knows exactly who he is. Her mention of "stones shot from a sling" is a clever reference to David's feat of courage and strength against Goliath. While clearly stroking his ego, she also turns David's attention from himself and the situation at hand to the Living One. When she speaks of David being "secure in God's treasure pouch"—which can be literally translated as "bound in the bundle of life with the Living One"—we catch another glimpse of spiritual Creation. Finally, Abigail instructs David to *remember* her, just as one of the men being killed on a cross will ask Jesus to *remember* him when Jesus comes into his kingdom (Luke 23:42). Abigail ties David to Eternal Life, Eternal Life to David, and herself to both. She too is "bound in the bundle of life."

Abigail's song, like Miriam's, Deborah's, and Hannah's, carries much wisdom, strength, and prophecy. In response, David acknowledges that Abigail is acting on behalf of the Living One. Far from being threatened by her authority and audacity, he blesses her (as spiritual Creation was blessed) and says that he has "listened to her voice and respected her person" (1 Samuel 25:35). Unlike some of today's male politicians, David both listens to a woman's words and treats her with respect.

Abigail returns home to find her husband drunk and stuffing himself with food. In the morning, when he is sober, she tells him what happened. Nabal, hung over and bloated from overeating, has a heart attack. Ten days later he dies. When David hears the news, he asks Abigail to marry him.

In yet another example of women laying out a path through scripture, Abigail washes the feet of David's servants, as Mary of Bethany (John 12:1–8) and/or an unknown woman (Luke 7:36–50) will wash Jesus' feet—and finally, Jesus will wash the feet of his disciples (John 13:1–17). There is more to this action than merely a traditional Middle-Eastern custom; it carries deep symbolic meaning regarding the nature of the relationship between humans and Deity, and it indicates as well the relationship we are to have with one another. When Jesus took upon himself to wash his followers' feet, he made clear that this relationship of mutual service transcends gender.

In response to David's proposal of marriage, Abigail once more hurries and mounts a donkey—and then again she "comes after" the messengers to join David and become his wife. These phrases underline Abigail's connection to both the past and the future; biblical repetition asks that we pay attention and take notice of what is happening here beyond the literal events, in the realm of the Spirit.

This is not the end of Abigail's story. Later, she is captured by David's enemies, is rescued by him, and has a child with him. She is yet another biblical woman whose life has many adventures.

As for David, his life is full of women. A partial list of women who have relationships of one sort or another with him, besides Abigail (who is his third wife), includes Ahinoam (his first wife), Michal (his second wife), Bathsheba (his eighth named wife), Abishag (who warms him in his old age), two Tamars (his daughter and a granddaughter), and Zerulah (his half-sister). The Bible also mentions David's encounters with various wise women, the witch at Endor, and the women widowed and left fatherless by his warfare as he unified Israel.

Surely all these women must have influenced David. Did David write some of his wonderful poems—full of ideas that speak directly to the hearts of women starving for spiritual sustenance—as they fell from the lips of Abigail, Ahinoam, Michal, or Bathsheba?

REFERENCE NOTES

1. Orit Avnery. "Who Is In and Who Is Out: The Two Voices of Ruth," *Havruta*, Summer 2010: 70–77.

2. Eugene Peterson. *The Message: The Bible in Contemporary Language* (Peabody, MA: NavPress, 2002), page 457.

3. Robert Pinsky. *The Life of David* (New York: Schocken, 2002), page 7.

EIGHT

PSALMS

They that go down to the sea in ships,
that do business in great waters;
these see the works of the Lord,
and his wonders in the deep.

–Psalms 107:23–24 KJV

In the midst of this book's stories and ideas, now is a good time to pause and reflect for a moment. The Book of Psalms give us a timeless break from the Bible's narrative, and there are words here to inspire and comfort every human heart. So take a moment to read and reread the words that follow. Sit with them for a moment before you move on. Allow them to settle quietly into your mind.

Bless the Living One, O my soul.
Living One, my God, You are abundant and great.
You are clothed with splendor and majesty.
Wrapping Yourself with light
as though it were a cloak,
Stretching out the sky like a curtain,
You lay the beams of Your upper chambers
in the waters.
You make the storm clouds Your chariot.
You walk on the wings of the wind.
You make the winds Your messengers,
The fiery flames are Your ministers.
You fixed the Earth on its foundations,
So that it will not tremble or shake for ever and ever.
You covered it with the deep sea as with a garment. . . .
How many are Your deeds, O Living One!
In wisdom You made them all;
The Earth is full of Your wealth. . . .
When You send forth Your breath, You create,
And You renew the face of the Earth.
(Psalm 104:1–6, 24, 30, literal translation)

This psalm (the word means literally "song") is just one of the 150 poem-prayers in the Book of Psalms.

Although we are jumping ahead in the Bible's standard table of contents, many of the psalms in this biblical book are credited to King David, so now seems an appropriate place to spend some time with them before we move on.

Neither history nor religious doctrine, this book of the Bible is simply poetry—written with heartfelt sincerity and without moralizing. As Carleen Mandolfo notes, the Psalms "are an outpouring of metaphor, flashes of allusive images, and syntactic hodge-podges . . . embodied discourses that find their *telos* in the 'truth' of *experience*."[1] This lavish, wide-ranging collection of poetry continues to speak to us—all of us—today, just as it has to humankind in all times and all places. In the words of Bible scholar Nancy L. Declaissé-Walford, "The sentiments expressed in these psalms are not time-, class-, or gender-exclusive; they are the words of every human."[2]

The emotions expressed in the Book of Psalms span the spectrum of human experience: the joy and sorrow, rage and fear, hurt and despair, disillusionment and awe, which humans have always felt within the context of their friendships, their loves, their illnesses, their political crises, their hatred of their enemies, their guilt, and their awareness of the splendor of Creation and the goodness of God. And in the midst of these intimate expressions of human life, we find all the ideas of the entire Bible, woven through this one poetic compilation.

Although there is much we can learn from the Psalms about the Feminine Spirit, these poems are primarily designed for meditation and prayer. They offer us a place to rest our hearts. They put words to the emotions we have all experienced.

> *Why, Lord, do you stand far off?*
> *Why do you hide yourself in times of trouble?*
> (Psalm 10:1 NIV)

The author of this poem dares to say, directly to God's face, a thought that we have all had. The psalmist then goes on to voice rage, resentment, and the longing for vengeance—frankly, with no sugar coating—but after expressing all the ugly and heartfelt bitterness we feel when we have been wrongly treated, the psalm brings us back to these words of hope and comfort:

> *Lord, you know the hopes of the helpless.*
> *Surely you will hear their cries and comfort them.*
> (Psalm 10:17 NLT)

In Kristen M. Swenson's book on the Psalms, she notes that this book of scripture expresses a more "feminine" way of experiencing life, one in which emotions are fully embodied in lives and relationships. Many psalms, Swenson writes, "are voices out of pain, not thoughts on pain or hypothetical ideas about pain management; they represent a sense of self that is not neatly divided body from mind from spirit from community."[3] Although this more wholistic approach to body, spirit, and heart may seem typically feminine in our current society, patriarchy has wounded men's hearts, as well as women's, denying men their right to both feel and express their emotions openly and honestly. The Psalms gives men the opportunity to recover their own feelings.

Who Wrote the Psalms?

The traditional assumption has been that King David wrote eighty of the psalms, while many other psalms are attributed to other men, including Moses, Solomon, and the sons of Korah; some have no attribution provided. The fact is, we do not *know* who wrote these songs of deep emotion and private feelings. This allows us space to ponder a new possibility: that the Psalms reflect both feminine and masculine authors' perspectives. The reader is the loser if the Psalms are read only in a masculine voice.

We *do* know that other women in the Bible composed similar songs—Deborah, Hannah, and others. We also know that women in similar areas and cultures did in fact compose written and recorded words, and the format and metaphors of these are paralleled in several Hebrew praise poems.[4] And we know that male translators have also *assumed* male authors.

The traditions of male scholarship and interpretation have pointed to the strong masculine elements of kingship and military might within the Psalms. These metaphors are there, reflecting the experience of male authors, but more than half of the Psalms is written in first person—and the "I" is frequently described as poor, needy, humble, afflicted, meek, desolate, all words that were more often applied to women's experience than to men's.

In support of the Psalms' female authorship, scripture scholar Helen Efthimiadis-Keith notes that women in the Bible held the roles of prophetesses and wise women, "and it would seem that gender did not affect either their credibility or authority." She goes on to point out the instances in the Bible where women composed and spoke victory and battle poetry, and concludes, "female authorship of certain Psalms/Psalm types is more than possible; to me, it is highly probable."[5]

Feminine Images of God

Another aspect of the Psalms that may point to female authorship has to do with the poetic metaphors used to describe Deity. Although plenty of masculine images describe God in the Psalms, at least as many feminine images also portray the Divine nature. Several psalms (51:11, 104:30, 106:33, and 139:7) use a feminine noun—translated as "Spirit"—to refer to God, and other feminine nouns throughout this book of the Bible describe Divine activity and relationship with humanity: wisdom, law, truth, light, salvation, and blessing—all aspects of the Feminine Spirit we saw in Genesis 1.

One powerful feminine image of God in the Psalms has its roots in Exodus 34, verse 6, where, as God pronounces Divine self-identity, one of the words used derives from a root noun that means, literally, "womb" (although the word has usually been translated into English as "merciful" or "compassionate"). We could say, then, that God loves us with "womb-love," the love of a pregnant mother for her yet-to-be-born child—and references to Divine womb-love can be found over and over in the book of Psalms.

Psalm 131 connects God to the mother-child relationship in a slightly different way:

> *Surely I have behaved and quieted myself,*
> *as a child that is weaned of his mother:*
> *my soul is even as a weaned child.*
> (verse 2 KJV)

The word translated "weaned" comes from a Hebrew root that means "to deal fully with" or "to complete, to ripen, to bring to maturity." By implication, God is Mother here, and the author of the poem is identifying with a baby who is fed and satisfied, asleep in the mother's arms. Alternatively, if we take the traditional translation as "weaned," with our current understanding of what that means, then the metaphor suggests a child who is mature enough to no longer cry for the mother's breast, yet still rests in the security of the mother's presence. In either case, we have powerful images of the calmness and quiet we find in the embrace of the Feminine Spirit. As Helen Efthimidiadis writes, "God no longer needs to be perceived as a volatile, manipulative father. God may now be understood and experienced as a mother who weans her child, setting down its foot firmly in a first step on the pathway to growth and development."[6]

Another psalm gives Deity the role of midwife. In the words of Eugene Peterson's paraphrase: "And to think you were midwife at my birth, setting me at my mother's breasts! When I left the womb you cradled me; since the moment of birth you've been my God" (Psalm 22:9–10 MSG).

NOTE

The Talmud, the recorded teachings of Jewish rabbis from the first century through the seventh centuries CE, says that

Still another feminine metaphor for God that's found in the Psalms is that of "refuge," which is often imagined as being found under the wings of God.

> *Keep me as the apple of the eye;*
> *Hide me under the shadow of thy wings.*
> (Psalm 17:8 KJV)

> *Let me take refuge in the shelter of Your wings.*
> (Psalm 61:4 NASB)

As we've already seen, the Divine wings are a feminine image. Not only is the Hebrew word feminine in gender, but protective wings bring to mind the image of a mother bird caring for her young, keeping them warm and safe from predators.

NOTE

Jesus, who knew the Psalms well, applies the image of feminine wings to himself when he says to Jerusalem, "How often I have wanted to gather your children together as a hen protects her chicks beneath her wings, but you wouldn't let me" (Matthew 23:37 NLT). Generations of male translators may have been uncomfortable recognizing the Feminine Spirit, but clearly Jesus has no problem claiming feminine identity.

Wisdom is yet another feminine image in the Psalms. The concept of Wisdom as a woman was central to the ancient Hebrews' thinking about God. Outside of the Psalms, Wisdom is portrayed as a Divine consort, a companion, a child, and as a feminine counterpart to the Existing One, but within the Book of Psalms (and later, in the Book of Proverbs) she is the Feminine Spirit, rather than a separate Being from the Living One. In the Psalms, we hear the voice of Woman Wisdom, the Feminine Spirit, calling us all—regardless of gender—to follow Her path to intimacy with the Living One.

A look at three specific psalms will give us a wider understanding of the way in which the Feminine Spirit sings Her song through the words of the Psalms.

Psalm Ninety

This psalm overflows with references to the Feminine Spirit, starting with verse 2:

Before the mountains were born,
before you gave birth to the earth and the world,
from beginning to end, you are God. (NLT)

The literal translation of the Hebrew indicates that God writhes with birth pangs as She gives birth to both the Earth's land and the inhabited world. (Deuteronomy 32:18 contains similar language when it says, "You have forgotten the God who writhed in labor with you.")

So why have so many readers of the Bible overlooked this obvious reference to the Feminine Spirit? Because English translations have minimized the feminine physicality of this image, using phrases such as "brought forth" or "formed." Some more modern versions, such as the New Living Translation quoted above, go so far as to say "you birthed," but even that downplays the power and anguish of a mother's labor. Eugene Boring suggests that language indicating the Existing One might be compared to an "earth mother" may have "sounded too much like Canaanite or Greek fertility goddesses to the male translators"—and so they took it upon themselves to curtail the richness of this feminine imagery.[7]

The psalm goes on to reference the second chapter of Genesis, where God creates the dust-man. The poet then compares cosmic time to chronological time, acknowledging the pain of living outside the synchronous time found in the first chapter of Genesis, before concluding, "Teach us to count our days that we may come to You with a heart of wisdom" (verse 12). Wisdom, as we've already pointed out, is a feminine concept, so the poet is claiming here the companionship of the Feminine Spirit as the anecdote to the despair and difficulty we encounter so often in chronological time. One commentary on the Psalms notes in reference to this verse: "If 'wisdom' means the art of living, then the ability here asked of God to say yes to life and to live that yes (in the midst of the many things that deserve a no) is Wisdom's art of living par excellence."[8]

Psalm 90 ends with these words of hope in God:

Satisfy us in the morning with Your kindness
that we may sing and be glad all our days.
Make us glad in the midst of
the age that weighs us down,
the years we see misery and sadness.
Let Your servants see Your work
and Your splendor in their children.
Let the delight of the Lord God be firm
in the work we do with our hands,
be firm in the work we do with our hands.
(14–17, literal translation)

Psalm Ninety-One

Women's experience sings out again in the very next psalm, where we find both the Breasted One and the womb-like refuge of the Feminine Spirit.

> *The one who dwells in the secret hiding place*
> *of the Most High*
> *Will abide in the shelter of Shaddai.*
> (verse 1, literal translation)

And then we have verse 4:

> *The Living One will cover you with feathery wings,*
> *And under those wings you will take refuge.*

Note that the Hebrew words for feathers and wings are both feminine, and once again we have the image of the Feminine Spirit as a mother bird.

Side by side with these feminine metaphors is a more military reference, comparing Divine faithfulness (feminine gendered) to a "shield and buckler," but the imagery may not be quite as masculine as the English translations make it seem; the Hebrew word translated as "buckler" (a type of shield for battle) in the King James Version is actually a feminine word meaning "something that surrounds a person."

The rest of the psalm describes the perils and terrors of warfare and ends with this comforting promise:

When you call to me, I will answer you.
I will be with you when you are in trouble.
I will save you and honor you.
(verse 15 GWT)

Psalm Ninety Two

In verse 12 of this psalm, the righteous are compared to both the palm tree and the cedar of Lebanon, two parallel metaphors—one feminine and one masculine. In the Bible, the palm tree is a recurring symbol of life-giving water, the water of Creation. In Exodus, we read that immediately after crossing the Red Sea, the Israelites came to a place with twelve springs of water and seventy palm trees (note the significant numbers indicating the spiritual realm). Then, in the Book of Judges, Deborah sat under a palm tree as she acted as a judge for Israel (4:5). The same Hebrew word—*Tamar*—is also used as a name for three significant biblical women: Jacob's daughter-in-law, David's daughter, and David's granddaughter. Later in the Bible, in the Song of Songs, a palm tree is a metaphor for a beautiful and beloved woman. Throughout the Bible, the palm tree is associated with water, with fertility, with the feminine. Meanwhile, the cedars of Lebanon are connected with majesty and strength, masculine attributes of kingship. Together, the palm tree and the cedar of Lebanon are powerful conjoined images of the fruitfulness and endurance of the people of God.

Rough Places in the Psalms

The Psalms are filled with words of comfort; they also sing forth the beauty of Creation; they give voice to sorrow and lamentation—and they express anger, rage, and the longing for vengeance against the authors' enemies. In Psalm 109, for example, the author wishes that an enemy's wife would become a widow. Psalm 58 expresses the terrible desire that enemies will have still-born children (verse 8). These are frank expressions of the writers' angry and bitter emotions, with no moralizing offered. They make us squirm with their ugliness and violence.

Efthimiadis-Keith comments:

These Psalms are so real as to belie the romantic piety of much of modern-day Christianity. For instance, the "I" expresses her/himself in emotional language that contrasts starkly with the negative perception of emotion that persists in the West today. Were the Psalmist to be an ordinary churchgoer, s/he would be chastised for her/his emotionalism and seeming disrespect for God. And yet, this is what makes the Psalms so real and so accessible; just as it is this aspect that clarifies the very deep personal nature of the psalmist's relationship with God and draws the reader closer into the same.[9]

What do these angry psalms tell us, as women and men, about how we are to relate to the Living One? Perhaps that we are to bring everything to God, without reservation, without trying to hide or disguise emotions that are considered "bad." As we commune with God, as the psalmists did, we allow our human experience to pour out. God's love is large enough to contain it all—all our joy, tranquility, sadness, gratitude, exultation, rage. We do not have to censor our feelings on God's behalf—and the Feminine Spirit has the strength to calm our angry hearts.

God's Love and Compassion

Throughout the scriptures we have examined so far, we have seen over and over the concern God has for women. With the Psalms' focus on justice, these prayer songs either explicitly or implicitly express the Spirit's care for marginalized, unprotected women. And over and over they affirm that God nurtures us, protects us, and loves us.

Read the Psalms as they were written—by people who felt what you feel, thought what you think, and turned to God in every circumstance. Within these beautiful words, you will find the nurturing, ever-present Spirit of all Creation, the ever-presence of life.

Listen, O daughter, give attention and incline your ear:
Forget your people and your father's house. . . .
The King's daughter is all glorious within;
Her clothing is interwoven with gold.
(Psalm 45:10,13 NASB)

The Lord is my shepherd; I have all that I need.
He lets me rest in green meadows;
he leads me beside peaceful streams.
He renews my strength.
He guides me along right paths,
bringing honor to his name.
Even when I walk through the darkest valley,
I will not be afraid, for you are close beside me.
Your rod and your staff protect and comfort me.
You prepare a feast for me
in the presence of my enemies.
You honor me by anointing my head with oil.
My cup overflows with blessings.
Surely your goodness and unfailing love will pursue me
all the days of my life,
and I will live in the house of the Lord forever.
(Psalm 23 NLT)

REFERENCE NOTES

1. Carleen Mandolfo. "Discourse of Resistance: Feminist Studies on the Psalter and Book of Lamentations," in *Feminist Interpretation of the Hebrew Bible in Retrospect: 1. Biblical Books,* Susanne Scholz, ed. (Phoenix, AZ: Sheffield, 2013), page 206.

2. Nancy L. Declaissé-Walford. "Psalms," in *Women's Bible Commentary,* Carol Ann Newsom, Sharon H. Ringe, and Jacqueline E. Lapsley, eds. (Louisville, KY: Westminster John Knox, 2012), page 224.

3. Kristin M. Swenson. *Living Through Pain: Psalms and the Search for Wholeness* (Waco, TX: Baylor University Press, 2005), page 11.

4. Sarah Palmer. "Recovering Female Authors of the Bible," *Studia Antiqua* 15.1, Spring 2016: 14–26.

5. H. Efthimiadis-Keith. "Is There a Place for Women in the Theology of the Psalms—Part II," *Old Testament Essays* 17/2(2004): 190–207.

6. Helen Efthimiadis. "Is There a Place for Women in the Theology of the Psalms," *Old Testament Essays* 12/1(1999): 33–56.

7. M. Eugene Boring. "Psalm 90—Reinterpreting Tradition," *Midstream* 40/1-2 (Jan-Apr 2001): 123.

8. Frank-Lothar Hossfield, Enrich Zenger, Linda M. Maloney, Klaus Baltzer. *Psalms 2: A Commentary on Psalms 51–100* (Minneapolis, MN: Fortress Press, 2005), page 423.

9. H Efthimiadis-Keith. "Is There a Place for Women in the Theology of the Psalms—Part II," *Old Testament Essays* 17/2(2004): 197.

NINE

KINGS, QUEENS, WIDOWS, & PROPHETS

And when the queen of Sheba heard of the fame
of Solomon concerning the name of the Lord,
she came to prove him with hard questions.

−1 Kings 10:1 KJV

The Bible belongs to women. Its stories contain women's perspectives and issues, and its messages are directed at women.

And yet for many women, the traditional understanding of the Bible's stories required that they adapt themselves to a masculine worldview. Bible scholar Yvonne Sherwood describes the process as being like a lefthanded person living in world made for righthanded people.[1] But Sherwood also believes that women have another option: just as men have "read" their own interests and emotions into scripture, women can do the same. None of us need look at scripture through the eyes of the patriarchy. We are each called to look at scripture for ourselves.

In the biblical stories that follow the narrative of King David's life, women continue to be visible and, in some cases, center stage. Freed from a masculine lens, women can find themselves in scripture's brief, matter-of-fact accounts. And both women and men can continue to encounter within the Bible's pages the nourishing and nurturing Feminine Spirit.

The Queen of Sheba

The Queen of Sheba makes an international diplomatic mission to Solomon, David's son by Bathsheba. She appears in a mere thirteen Bible verses, but volumes of speculation and commentary have been written about her; the power of her personality shines through those few sentences and grips our imagination. The story of Solomon and the queen is one that transcends time and culture.

One thing that's evident in the biblical account is that the queen's meeting with King Solomon was an equal exchange between reigning monarchs. Somehow, though, as Jacob Lassner points out in his book, *Demonizing the Queen of Sheba*, male commentators through the ages have turned her into a demonic force seeking to dissolve gender barriers.[2]

This is quite a leap but not an unusual one. Male commentators have often held one of only two perspectives on the women in the Bible, seeing them as either mothers or harlots. These men looked at biblical women through the lens of their own belief that women are "not man" but something "other"—and potentially dangerous.

According to the biblical account, the Queen of Sheba, who had heard of King Solomon's reputation for great wisdom, traveled with a caravan of riches to his court, where she tested him with deep theological questions. "She communed with him of all that was in her heart," the scripture says (1 Kings 10:2 KJV). King Solomon sat in conversation with the queen and gave her "all her desire," after which she returned to her own land.

Since many male commentators assumed women could be either mothers or objects of sexual desire, and since the Bible says nothing to indicate that Sheba is a mother, many artists and storytellers have portrayed the queen as a seductress who entered into a sexual relationship with Solomon. The Bible does not say this, though. Instead, the biblical record indicates that Sheba's wealth and beauty do not define her, nor does she use them to beguile or manipulate Solomon. Although the queen is clearly impressed with Solomon, and she is eager to learn from him about the God of Israel, their interaction is one of mutual courtesy between equals. Many centuries later, in the Gospels, Jesus speaks of Sheba with obvious respect for her wisdom (Matthew 12:42).

NOTE

The Queen of Sheba is one of the few women to appear in the sacred texts of Jews, Christians, and Muslims—the Hebrew scriptures, the New Testament, and the Qu'ran. Many folktales have risen around her story as well, adding details to the relatively sparse scriptural description. Until recently, Western artistic portrayals of the Queen of Sheba often painted her with white skin. In fact, however, since she was likely from the region that is modern-day Yemen, she would have had brown skin. Here, as so often happens, sexism meets racism.

In a distant land, the Queen of Sheba had heard about Solomon's understanding of the Living One, and she journeyed far to learn and expand her own understanding. Naomi Lucks writes in her book, *Queen of Sheba*:

> The Queen of Sheba stands as an example for all women who want to leave home to explore the world, ask intelligent questions of it, and return home with more than they could ever imagine.[3]

Sheba's journey may also represent the search—of both women and men—for insight into the meaning of life, a journey that can require that we leave our comfortable "homelands" behind, venture courageously into new and unknown territory, and be openminded enough to learn from those who may be very different from ourselves.

Elijah

Both as an individual and as a representative of key themes, Elijah is the archetypal male prophet of the Hebrew scriptures. His identity—in fact, his very name—is interwoven with Deity; in Hebrew, his name is a combination of *Elohim* and *Yahweh*, meaning "the Living One is God." No journey through biblical consciousness is complete without visiting with him. As you do so, you'll be in good company, for, according to the Gospel scriptures, both Moses and Jesus spent time talking with Elijah (Matthew 17:1–13, Luke 9:28–36, Mark 9:2–13).

In his own day, however, people weren't too fond of Elijah—mostly because he spoke uncomfortable truths to them, but also, perhaps, because he could be harsh and impatient. The Bible says he was a "sojourner," a settler in Gilead; in other words, Elijah was an immigrant.

Scripture tells us that after Elijah had riled the people of Israel, the Living One gave Elijah a message that said basically: "Go hide out for a while until people aren't as angry with you" (1 Kings 17:3). Sometimes, it is better to retreat from conflict.

But once again there is also more meaning here than meets the eye in our English translations. The noun form of the Hebrew word translated as "hide," *seter*, is used to refer to the womb as a secret place, a place of shelter (as in Psalm 139:15). The Psalm also uses the same word to refer to the sheltering wings of the Feminine Spirit, as in Psalm 17:8: "hide (*satar*) me in the shadow of Your wings."

God's instructions are both spiritual and practical. Alongside the spiritual implications are specific geographical direction: Elijah was to hide beside the brook of *Cherith*. Remember, names in scripture are significant and can often shed additional light on a passage. Cherith means "a cutting," a ravine cut into the earth by some geological force, such as an earthquake or erosion. A similar word in Hebrew refers to marital divorce. And so the implication here is that Elijah is to separate himself, temporarily, from the political intrigue and conflict of his day—and hide himself within the life-giving womb of the Divine, beside the flowing waters of Creation. God tells Elijah that his needs will be provided for in this place: he will drink from the water and he will be fed by birds.

> *So he went and did according unto the word of the Lord: for he went and dwelt by the brook Cherith. And the ravens brought him bread and flesh in the morning, and bread and flesh in the evening; and he drank of the brook.* (1 Kings 17:5–6 KJV)

NOTE

Throughout its pages, the Hebrew Bible communicates God's concern for human hunger and thirst, both physically and spiritually. In the Christian scriptures as well, in the Gospel accounts, Jesus provides a meal of bread and fish to crowds of people, and later, he says, "I am the bread of life; whoever comes to me shall not hunger, and whoever believes in me shall never thirst" (John 6:35 ESV). In the next chapter of John, the author tells us explicitly: "By this he meant the Spirit" (7:39).

The external sources of refreshment and nourishment we are given are never intended to be permanent, however, and this is what happens to Elijah: the brook dries up, and God sends him on to the next step in his journey. This time he is to go a city called Zarephath (from a Hebrew word that has to do with refining metal), where he will meet a widow who will be his next source of sustenance.

Again, God has chosen a woman, someone who is marginalized and so poor herself that she cannot imagine how she will be able to provide for one more hungry mouth. When Elijah asks her to bring him food and water, she replies that she cannot feed herself and her son, let alone Elijah.

At first glance, this seems like a story about one more arrogant man expecting a woman to wait on him and supply his needs. But it can be read at another level as well: in Elijah's interaction with the widow woman, they are reenacting the spiritual Creation in the first chapter of Genesis—and here it is the woman who is playing God's role as provider. Rather than being a story of women's subjugation, this is a story of a woman's empowerment.

The woman herself, however, is looking through the patriarchal lens, and as a result, she sees only her own lack and scarcity. Elijah understands the woman's concern, and he's willing to coach her in her role. "Fear not," he says to her (1 Kings 17:13). Here again is the injunction to a woman to "Fear not." When a woman is faced with complexity, denial, or need, as was also true of Hagar beside the unseen spring of water in the desert, the first biblical command is to fear not.

Elijah's next instruction to the woman indicates that as she demonstrates hospitality—giving what she has to a stranger—her own needs will be met.

This is what the Living One says: "The jar of flour will not run out and the level in the jug of oil will not go down until the day the Living One gives rain to the Earth's face." She went away and followed Elijah's instructions. Her household ate for days. The jar of flour did not run out and the level in the jug of oil did not go down, just as the Living One spoke through Elijah. (1 Kings 17:14–16, literal translation)

The mention of oil here is another clue to a deeper meaning, for throughout the Bible oil is a symbol of prophecy and anointing. (Take a look in a concordance to find these references.) The Hebrew word was also used as a metaphor for fruitfulness, richness, and joy. God is not providing the woman, her household, and Elijah with mere dry bread, just enough to get by; the Feminine Spirit is also sharing with them Her enormous, joyful abundance.

The story continues: the woman's son gets sick—and dies. Grief-stricken, the woman blames Elijah; after all, he is the new element in her life that upset the status quo. Elijah prays to the Living One for the boy, and he is brought back to life. No harm has come to the woman because of her hospitality to Elijah. Instead, she has been blessed, and her son is alive, giving physical earthly evidence of the Living One's presence in daily life.

The story of Elijah and the widow has traditionally been read as a story about a male prophet, a difficult and rather cranky holy man, with a slightly clueless woman in the background—but that reading is a projection of an ages-old mindset. An alternate reading is to see that Elijah is the stranger in this story, and the woman is the holy one who provides shelter, food, and water to a man in need.

Methodist minister Quynh-Hoa Nguyen writes about her experience speaking with a Vietnamese woman who read this biblical story from a feminine perspective:

In her experience of sociopolitical and economic vulnerability, she does not encounter Elijah as a miracle worker or a hero of the country who is divinely empowered to reverse the hopeless situation created by the society in which marginal people live. Rather, she remembers the poor widow as

God's never-ending provision for those socially and financially marginalized. In her memory, the widow remains as one who turns a desperate situation into hope and fulfillment. . . . [T]he widow represents empowerment in marginality in the sense that she is socially and financially vulnerable, but she is able to carry God's mission. She appears to have nothing to give, but she eventually can empower the prophet even in her dire circumstances.[4]

At the end of the story, the widow says to Elijah, "Now I know that you are a man of God and that the word of the Lord from your mouth is the truth" (17:24 NIV). As a prophet, Elijah is called to speak Divine truth, but the society of his day, including the king, has rejected him. It takes a woman, a widow, to recognize his truth and sustain him on his mission. Again and again in the Bible, women are the prophetic agents of change.

That theme—the powerless woman recognizing Spirit—is repeated throughout the Bible. The widow is another in the long, long chain of biblical women who recognize, affirm, and set the seal on the activities of *ruah Elohim*.

Jezebel

Elijah's next encounter with a woman is a far different sort of story; it seems to be in almost deliberate contrast to the account of the widow woman. In fact, Jezebel in many ways is the polar opposite of the biblical women we have met so far. As a queen, she is proud and powerful, not marginalized in the least; she is confidant, even arrogant, and never fearful.

Jezebel, a Phoenician princess who worships Baal, a fertility god, marries Israel's King Ahab—and then she becomes the power behind the throne. She instigates the spread of her religion, which does not acknowledge the Living One. This is not merely a matter of interfaith misunderstanding, for the worship of Baal, with its ritual sex and temple prostitutes, subjugated and objectified women in a way that the Hebrews had never tolerated. Under his wife's influence, King Ahab endorses these rituals. Jezebel brings 450 priests of Baal from her homeland and orders the deaths of many of Israel's prophets.

A three-year drought comes to the land, indicating that the waters of Creation have withdrawn from Israel. Baal's prophets cannot make it rain, no matter how hard they try, for water is Spirit's Word, an essential element of spiritual Creation. As we have seen in earlier scriptures, the *ruah Elohim* moves on the face of the waters, giving birth to a unified and unfolding Creation.

To settle the question of which deity is supreme—the Living One or Baal—Elijah calls for a contest on Mount

Carmel. Whichever deity can set fire to a sacrificial bull will be proven to be the true God. Elijah lets the 450 Baal prophets take their turn first.

> *Then they called on the name of Baal from morning until noontime, shouting, "O Baal, answer us!" But there was no reply of any kind. Then they danced, hobbling around the altar they had made. About noontime Elijah began mocking them. "You'll have to shout louder," he scoffed, "for surely he is a god! Perhaps he is daydreaming, or is relieving himself. Or maybe he is away on a trip, or is asleep and needs to be wakened!"*
>
> *So they shouted louder, and following their normal custom, they cut themselves with knives and swords until the blood gushed out. They raved all afternoon until the time of the evening sacrifice, but still there was no sound, no reply, no response.*
> (1 Kings 18:26–28 NLT)

Now it's Elijah's turn.

> *Elijah took twelve stones, one for each of the tribes descended from Jacob, to whom the word of the Lord had come, saying, "Your name shall be Israel." With the stones he built an altar in the name of the Lord, and he dug a trench around it large enough to hold*

two seahs of seed. He arranged the wood, cut the bull into pieces and laid it on the wood. Then he said to them, "Fill four large jars with water and pour it on the offering and on the wood."

"Do it again," he said, and they did it again.

"Do it a third time," he ordered, and they did it the third time. The water ran down around the altar and even filled the trench. (1 Kings 18:31–35 NIV)

The narrative has now placed us firmly in the realm of Creation. Not only is water present, but the word "seed" is also specified in Elijah's directions. Note also the mention of both the number three—the day of Creation when the waters are gathered together and the Earth brings forth fruit with its seed—and the number four—the day of Creation when Light is made specifically for the Earth.

Now, when Elijah prays, fire flashes down from heaven. He says to King Abab, "Go get something to eat and drink, for I hear a mighty rainstorm coming!" (verse 41, NLT).

So Ahab went to eat and drink. But Elijah climbed to the top of Mount Carmel and bowed low to the ground and prayed with his face between his knees. Then he said to his servant, "Go and look out toward the sea."

The servant went and looked, then returned to Elijah and said, "I didn't see anything."

Seven times Elijah told him to go and look. Finally the seventh time, his servant told him, "I saw a little cloud about the size of a man's hand rising from the sea."

Then Elijah shouted, "Hurry to Ahab and tell him, 'Climb into your chariot and go back home. If you don't hurry, the rain will stop you!'"

And soon the sky was black with clouds. A heavy wind brought a terrific rainstorm, and Ahab left quickly for Jezreel. Then the Lord gave special strength to Elijah. He tucked his cloak into his belt and ran ahead of Ahab's chariot all the way to the entrance of Jezreel. (1 Kings 18:42–46 NLT)

As we saw in the story of the great Flood in Genesis, the waters of Creation can be dangerous to those who lack the integral reflection of the Living One. The same rain that brings refreshment and new fertility also has the potential for destruction, as Elijah warns Ahab.

But for Elijah, rain brings amazing energy and strength. After his servant's seven repetitions of looking for rain—indicating the wholeness and completeness of Creation—the rainstorm arrives, and Elijah runs a distance of about twenty miles to the "entrance of Jezreel." In Hebrew, *Jezreel* means "God sows seed."

The drought is over, the lifegiving water of Creation has been restored to Israel, and the fruitfulness of the Feminine Spirit is revealed.

The action now shifts to Jezebel, who is far from happy about the turn of events. The scripture gives us a glimpse of the power she has over her husband, as well as the cruelty she demonstrates as she orders the deaths of innocent people. Meanwhile, Elijah is equally ruthless in his slaughter of his enemies.

In the end, Elijah is victorious, and Ahab is dead. A new man, Jehu, takes the throne (with Elijah's help), and Jezebel, aware that her fate is sealed, calmly prepares herself for her death. She paints her eyes with kohl, styles her hair, and watches for Jehu's arrival from an upper window of the palace.

Jezebel dies a horrific, bloody death. Thrown out of her window by her own servants, she is trampled by horses and then her body is ripped apart and eaten by dogs. Scripture indicates that her entire identity has been dismembered, so that nothing remains of the woman who was Jezebel.

And yet she has never been forgotten. If you do a search using Thesaurus.com, you'll find that the word *Jezebel* is synonymous with "floozy," "harlot," "hooker," and "slut." An Internet search of her name brings up Urban Dictionary definitions, historical references, and images of sultry seductresses—as well as references on some conservative Christian sites to the "spirit of

Jezebel" as a term for the "obsessive sensuality, hatred of male authority, and family-destroying false teachings in the church and society at large." Many readers have understood that when Jezebel put on makeup and styled her hair, preparing to meet her death, she was revealing her vanity and corrupt sexuality—but an alternative reading sees Jezebel as a proud and courageous woman insisting on her right to go to her grizzly death with dignity. What are we to make of those readings?

The Bible *does* refer to Jezebel as a "harlot," but not because she is sexually immoral. In fact, the biblical record indicates she was a loyal and supportive wife. According to the scriptural understanding of "harlotry," however, she was unfaithful to the Living One. The Bible condemns her—but for her cruelty and ruthlessness, not for her sexuality. Jezebel ignored the biblical mandate of hospitality. She violated the law of kindness to strangers, and she made the fatal mistake of entering into a vicious power struggle with Elijah, a messenger of God who was as fiercely determined as she was. (We will run into Jezebel's name again at the end of the Bible, in the Book of Revelation.)

As for Elijah, he emerges triumphant from his struggle with Jezebel, and he continues to play an important role in Israel's politics. An angel sustains him in the wilderness; he gains a follower named Elisha; and he makes many prophecies to the leaders of Israel. His many encounters with women—and theirs with him—are central to his activity. When we read about him, we see that he is here, there, and everywhere. Fiery and flawed, determined and emotional—and very human—Elijah's life points us toward a deeper understanding of the ways in which masculine and feminine can both complement and conflict with one another.

And at the end of his life, Elijah does not die. Instead, the Bible says, the Living One lifts him up (2 Kings 2:1, literal translation).

NOTE

In the Gospels, we hear about Elijah again, when he and Moses have a conversation with Jesus on the Mount of Transfiguration. New Testament scholars have also noted many parallels between Elijah and Jesus: both rebuke the religious leaders for turning away from the true Living One; Elijah multiplies food for a starving widow and her son when she is willing to share what she has, while Jesus multiplies food for a crowd of people when a young boy is willing to share his own small lunch; both have control over the weather (Elijah prophesies that rain will cease, and then prophesies when the rain will return, while Jesus calms the storm at sea); both are ministered to by angels while in the wilderness; and both are taken up into heaven while their followers watch.

But first, before he leaves this world, Elijah has an exchange with his friend Elisha that parallels Naomi's conversation with Ruth:

> *Elijah said to Elisha, "Stay here; the Lord has sent me to Bethel." But Elisha said, "As surely as the Lord lives and as you live, I will not leave you." So they went down to Bethel.*
>
> *The company of the prophets at Bethel came out to Elisha and asked, "Do you know that the Lord is going to take your master from you today?"*
>
> *"Yes, I know," Elisha replied, "so be quiet."*
>
> *Then Elijah said to him, "Stay here, Elisha; the Lord has sent me to Jericho."*
>
> *And he replied, "As surely as the Lord lives and as you live, I will not leave you." So they went to Jericho.*
>
> *The company of the prophets at Jericho went up to Elisha and asked him, "Do you know that the Lord is going to take your master from you today?"*
>
> *"Yes, I know," he replied, "so be quiet."*
>
> *Then Elijah said to him, "Stay here; the Lord has sent me to the Jordan."*
>
> *And he replied, "As surely as the Lord lives and as you live, I will not leave you." So the two of them walked on.* (2 Kings 2:2–6 NIV)

In the words of the King James Version, this is what follows next: "And it came to pass, when the Lord would take up Elijah into a whirlwind, that Elijah went with Elisha from Gilgal."

Like Ruth with Naomi, Elisha insists that he will cling to Elijah, leaving his family, in the same way the Genesis states that a man will cling to his wife. Unlike Ruth, though, Elisha cannot stay with the man he loves so much, and his life will be filled with trials and tribulations as he struggles to make the nation of Israel hear God's truth. Bible scholar Ruth Walfish points out:

> While Elisha is clearly Elijah's successor, and a miracle-worker ordained by God, he cannot effect a real change in society. It is the "Ruths" of this world, in their day-to-day, normative behavior, who seem capable of affecting others, setting off a chain of action that can deeply influence history.[5]

But first, before Elisha continues on without him, Elijah has an appointment to keep with the Living One. The Bible tells us that they come to the River Jordan, and there "Elijah took his cloak, rolled it up and struck the water with it. The water divided to the right and to the left, and the two of them crossed over on dry ground" (2 Kings 2:8 NIV). The story has now moved into another dimension; we have crossed from chronological time into cosmic time, and we are once more in the third day of Creation in the first chapter of Genesis, when *ruah Elohim* separated the seas from the dry land (just as the Israelites were when they escaped from Pharaoh through the divided waters of the Red Sea).

Elijah then disappears in a fiery chariot in the midst of a whirlwind. Since the Hebrew word used here for "whirlwind" is feminine gendered, and the word for "spirit" and "wind" are the same in Hebrew, we might say that Elijah, this most masculine of prophets, was lifted into another dimension by the Feminine Spirit.

But he leaves behind his cloak for Elisha. This cloak played a role earlier in their relationship, when Elisha first followed Elijah, and now it symbolizes the way in which Elisha will inherit Elijah's spirit as a prophet of Israel. The Hebrew word for cloak has another meaning as well, however. It can also mean "glory," a word that is feminine-gendered and carries within it the implication of expansion, of abundance. Like Elijah, Elisha will at times be harsh, angry, and bitter—but nevertheless, the Feminine Spirit works in his life, moving through him, brooding in him to bring forth the life of Creation.

Esther

We are skipping forward now, both in the Bible's traditional table of contents and chronologically, since several centuries separate Esther from Elijah.

Esther is the second of two books in the Bible named for women. Like Ruth, Esther lives among foreigners (Ruth is a Moabite immigrant to Israel, and Esther is a Jewish exile in the kingdom of Persia), and like Ruth, Esther is strong and courageous. While Ruth saves the day for the biological line that leads to King David (and to Jesus), Esther saves the day for the people of Israel as a whole. (Esther also has her own holiday; her story is celebrated each year at Purim.) The account given to us in the Book of Esther is yet another example of how men's treatment of women can have far-reaching repercussions. The name of God is never mentioned in the book, and yet this portion of scripture clearly reveals the movement of the Feminine Spirit.

You would do no disservice to the book's religious importance if you read it as though it were a wonderful short story. It has all the elements needed: a mighty king, a rebellious queen, a scheming and murderous court official, and an orphan princess who lives in a palace. And what a palace! The Bible tells us:

There were white cotton curtains and violet hangings fastened with cords of fine linen and purple to silver rods and marble pillars, and also couches of gold and silver on a mosaic pavement of porphyry, marble, mother-of-pearl, and precious stones.
(Esther 1:6 ESV)

When we first meet Esther, she seems to be a passive model of docile submission to the men in her life. The Hebrew verb meaning "taken" is often applied to her in the first part of her story: she is "taken" in by a foster father; she is "taken" to the king's harem; and she is "taken" before the king. While the queen, Vashti, is bold and rebellious, Esther seems to be meek and obedient (the "good woman," in the traditional understanding).

However, like many women, Esther plays the role men expect of her—in order to get what she wants for her people. Behind her "sweet" façade, she is clever and courageous. As Bible scholar Leah Berkenwald writes, "Vashti refused to obey and paid the price. Esther chose to play the system to get the job done. Regardless of which method you prefer, both women played active roles in their own lives."[6]

The most quoted, and perhaps most significant, line in this book of the Bible is chapter 4, verse 14, where Esther's foster father asks her this question: "Who knows whether you have not come to the kingdom for such a time as this?" (ESV). In the Book of Esther, hatred of women overlaps with hatred of the minority group (in this case, the Jews, who are living in exile in Persia)—and so, within the context of the story, the question relates to our connections to the rest of the human family. What do we owe the larger community around us? What do our lives ask of us?

The Book of Esther shows us that hatred of women or minorities is not acceptable to the Living One, who created all good. The story is replete with references that make clear it is taking place not only in a Middle-Eastern palace-cum-harem but also in spiritual Creation. As you read the ten short chapters, pay attention to these familiar words: *third day, seven days, remembered, abundance, seed, light.*

The Bible is about consciousness, at many levels. The Book of Esther challenges us to be aware of the question we all must answer: *What is my purpose?*

REFERENCE NOTES

1. Yvonne Sherwood. *The Bible and Feminism: Remapping the Field* (Oxford, UK: Oxford University Press, 2017), page 82.

2. Jacob Lassner. *Demonizing the Queen of Sheba: Boundaries of Gender and Culture in Postbiblical Judaism and Medieval Islam* (Chicago: University of Chicago Press, 1993).

3. Naomi Lucks. *Queen of Sheba* (New York: Infobase, 2008), page 95.

4. Quynh-Hoa Nguyen. *Higher Education & Ministry, the United Methodist Church General Board of Higher Education and Ministry*, https://www.gbhem.org/networking/widow-zarephath-story-empowerment-marginality.

5. Ruth Walfish. "Ruth and Elisha: A Comparative Study," *Jewish Bible Quarterly,* 41(3) 2013: 241.

6. Leah Berkenwald. "Vasti Is Not a Failure; Esther Is Not a Bad Feminist," *Jewish Women, Amplified,* February 24, 2010.

TEN

WOMAN WISDOM

Do not forsake wisdom, and she will protect you; love her, and she will watch over you.

–Proverbs 6:7 NIV

Tradition says that the biblical books of Proverbs, Ecclesiastes, and the Song of Songs were written by Solomon, David's son by his wife Bathsheba. Crowned king of Israel when his father became too old and ill to rule, Solomon is famous for his wisdom. His name is from the same Hebrew word as *shalom*, meaning "peace," but with the deeper implied meaning of "whole-ness, fullness, unbrokenness, completeness."

The Bible says that after Solomon becomes king, the Living One comes to him in a dream and tells him, "Ask for whatever you want, and I'll give it to you" (1 Kings 3:5). Solomon's reply has nothing to do with riches. Instead he asks: "Give your servant an inner consciousness (or heart) that hears, so that I will be able to discern the space that lies between what is good and healthy and that which causes misery and harm" (1 Kings 3:9, literal translation). God is pleased with Solomon's request and promises to give him a percep-tive and wise heart.

As a result, Solomon's name has become synony-mous with wisdom. The Bible includes stories that are meant to exemplify this character trait of Solomon's, and it is perhaps because of his reputation for wisdom that the books of Proverbs, Ecclesiastes, and the Song of Songs are attributed to him. Modern biblical scholars question if he was actually the author of these books, but he may have written portions of them, while other authors, including women authors, wrote other parts.

One of the most famous stories about Solomon is the account of two women fighting for possession of the same child—which Solomon suggests cutting in two so each woman gets a part. When one woman responds, "No, let the other woman have him, so long as the child lives," Solomon discerns her to be the true mother. We can read multiple possible interpretations into this account, but what is clear is that Solomon, in his great wisdom, recognizes and elucidates the Feminine Spirit.

The Hebrew word for wisdom—*chokmah*—is a feminine word, and in the writing attributed to Solomon, Wisdom emerges as a living Being. Far more than a quality or characteristic, as we typically think of "wisdom," biblical Wisdom is portrayed as both a woman and as an aspect of the Divine One.

This is not the first time we read in the Bible that Wisdom is equated with the Feminine Spirit. In Exodus, the Living One speaks to Moses about the "wise ones" whom God has filled with the feminine *ruah* of wisdom (28:3). A few chapters later, Moses hears about Bezaleel, whom God has filled with the *ruah Elohim*, which is then explained as being feminine wisdom (Exodus 31:3). In the Book of Deuteronomy, Joshua is also described as being filled with the feminine *ruah* of wisdom (34:9).

In the writings attributed to Solomon, however, Wisdom is fleshed out, described in detail as the Feminine Spirit. She is associated specifically with creativity (both of Creation and human life, as we have already learned is consistently true of *ruah Elohim* and the Breasted One), as well as strategy, good sense, prudence, and competence, all qualities which the Bible describes as being feminine in nature. According to Bible scholar Elizabeth Johnson, Woman Wisdom's "constant effort is to lure human beings into life." She is the creative power of God that is embedded in the world; each created thing, and the Creation as a whole, speaks of the Wisdom of God at its foundation.[1]

Proverbs

Unlike the other books of the Bible that we've looked at so far (with the exception of Psalms), the Book of Proverbs does not contain stories. Instead, it is a collection of wise sayings and poems. Women and womanhood play an important role throughout the book, with numerous word pictures that help us understand deep truths. Not only do we learn in Proverbs about Woman Wisdom, but we are also given an example of Woman Wisdom embodied in a living woman (who is sometimes referred to as the "noble wife").

Woman Wisdom is the specific, illustrative example of feminine incarnation. She is no shrinking violet, and she certainly does not conform to patriarchal expectations. Instead, she is strong and outspoken; she shouts in the streets (1:20), demanding to be heard.

Listen to her voice calling to all people:

To you I am calling.
I send my voice out to humanity. . . .

Listen! For I speak with authority.
Every opening of my lips reveals peace and equity.
All my words are fair and just;
there is nothing crooked or twisted in them. . . .
Feminine purpose is mine,
I am feminine deliverance;
I save you with efficiency, for I am truth.
Courage and strength are mine.
I love all who love.
Look diligently and you will find me. . . .
My fruit is better than gold, even pure gold,
and my fruitfulness is a better choice than silver. . . .
The Living One possesses me from the beginning,
before anything else was made.
I was established for all time from the source. . . .
When there was nothing, not even the abyss,
I writhed in labor;
before the springs grew heavy with water.
Before the mountains were settled,
before the hills, I writhed in birth.
When the countryside was not yet made,
nor any city street,
before the world's first dust,
when the heavens were established, I was there.
When the horizon was drawn on the face of the sea,
when the clouds were fortified,
when deep springs were made mighty,
when the sea's boundaries were drawn . . .

we were joined, a master architect.
Day by day, I was delight, laughing always,
rejoicing in the world, the Earth,
delighting in the children of Adam [the dust-man]. . . .
Happy are those who hear me,
who day by day watch for me at my gates,
who wait at my door.
Find me and you find life,
a life furnished by the delight
and desire of the Living One.
(8:4,6,8,14,17,19,22–31,34,35, literal translation[2])

The words Woman Wisdom uses here are familiar and essential—the heavens, the sea, the Earth, dust, days, fruitfulness, springs of water, mountains, clouds. In her Voice, we clearly hear the Feminine Spirit who is present in the first chapter of Genesis.

In Woman Wisdom, we find insight and truth, justice and peace. She calls out to us not from temples or churches but from places of human interaction, the locations where people gather for business (verses 2 and 3), as well as all the ordinary spaces of human life (verse 1). Like Deborah and Abigail, Wisdom is a prophetess, though a generic one—a woman who speaks the truth while she stands among her people. She is not shy or retiring, and she does not work quietly behind the scenes. Instead, she demands the dominion of her birthright, so that she can take her rightful place as the guiding force in all human affairs. Her leadership creates a just society.

And Wisdom is present at Creation. She gives birth to the world, and then she does not abandon the world but continues to make her home here. She is the creative power of the Living One, and she rejoices in Creation. Her love and joy are present everywhere, unspent.

In Proverbs chapter 31, we hear another woman's voice. The mother of King Lemuel gives "the son of her womb" inspired advice, telling him to avoid sexual immorality, alcohol abuse, and most important, to "speak up for those who cannot speak for themselves; ensure justice for those being crushed. Yes, speak up for the poor and helpless, and see that they get justice" (31:8,9 NLT).

NOTE

No one is certain who King Lemuel is. His name means "belonging to God," and he may be a metaphor for all who belong to the Living One. According to some Jewish traditions, Lemuel is another name for Solomon. If that's the case, then we can surmise that the author of this chapter of Proverbs is Bathsheba, David's wife who was the mother of Solomon.

Lemuel's mother then gives us another image of a woman—the "noble wife." This passage of Proverbs 31 has often been held up as the example of perfect wifehood to which all women should aspire. Many Christian books speak of the "Proverbs 31 woman" as the "godly, submissive wife." Looking at a quick sampling of Evangelical authors, we may read that these verses emphasize "the need for ladies to be concerned about their fitness for their God-given purpose"; that women who make the Proverbs 31 woman their role model will "study their Bibles and give themselves to prayer and fasting"; and that they will "humbly accept correction, submitting to elders, leaders and other spiritual authorities" (who are apparently all male). A more relevant and biblical reading of this passage of scripture, however, reveals a strong, competent, independent, and creative woman.

In verse after verse, Lemuel's mother affirms a woman's true spiritual identity. The woman we see in Proverbs 31 is committed to her relationships; her husband and children depend on her and are blessed by her. (The words "submissive" and "obedient" are never used to describe her relationship with anyone.) She works hard and efficiently, with initiative and creativity. Rather than waiting for a man to come along and give her things, she goes and gets what she needs to do her work—and then she delights in it. She knows how to use her skills to make money, she invests her resources shrewdly, and she's not afraid to try something new. Her strength, generosity, and intelligence are rooted in her knowledge of her spiritual birthright (which includes clothing herself beautifully and creating for herself a lovely place of rest); she understands that her productivity depends on her care for all her resources, including her own physical body and her emotions. As a result, she has what she needs to also reach out to those in need.

Read these verses for yourself, if possible using several translations to capture some of the shades of meaning. If this woman is meant to be our role model, the list of her strengths and behavior can be intimidating—but each detail listed in Proverbs 31 is not meant to describe a specific, single woman who was a paragon of womanly virtue we must all imitate. Instead, these verses shows us a larger picture of the Feminine Spirit embodied in flesh-and-blood. As women and men, the Living One calls us to embody Divine love, courage, wisdom, productivity, and generosity. Each of us does this differently, with our unique talents and individual strengths, but we all have amazing qualities, skills, and resources to offer the world. Lemuel's mother is telling us: "You are strong and wise; you can try new things. You too can contribute to the needs of your world—and at the same time, not be deprived of anything!"

The qualities of the woman in Proverbs 31 can be claimed and reflected by each of us, personally, but we can also read this passage as a description of Woman Wisdom Herself. In verse 10, the King James Version says that the woman's value is "far above rubies"; there's only one other thing that the Bible says is more valuable than rubies, and that's wisdom. (See Proverbs 3:15, Proverbs 20:15, and Job 28:18.) The inference, then, is that the Proverbs 31 woman is equated with Wisdom Herself. Theology professor Robin Branch writes, "The noble wife and Woman Wisdom merge on several levels. Each is practical: each is a faithful guide and a lifelong companion. . . . The noble wife serves as a concrete example of Woman Wisdom."[3]

Lemuel's mother also warns against a woman who is equated with folly and danger, the opposite of Woman Wisdom. Theological scholar Scott Ventureyra explains:

> So, in essence to turn towards Woman Wisdom, which is the embodiment of God, we are granted life and prosperity. This is true because Yahweh is the ultimate true God who controls the world and its order. To choose Woman Folly leads to one's own destruction, since such a god is a false one. This is seen within Proverbs 1:24–27, where to not choose Wisdom, there are dire consequences, where in Proverbs 1:32–33 it leads to death.[4]

The author (or authors) of Proverbs make clear that just as men are not automatically good while women are "bad," women are not automatically good and men bad. Each gender must choose: the fruitfulness of the Feminine Spirit, the blessing of the Living One—or the selfishness that ultimately leads to spiritual, emotional, and physical death.

The Feminine Spirit is vividly presented in the Book of Proverbs. Old Testament scholar Kathleen O'Connor sees Her also in another Bible book credited to Solomon.

The Song of Songs

Specifically, O'Connor connects Woman Wisdom in Proverbs 31 to the woman portrayed in the love poetry found in the Song of Songs. O'Connor points out that in these books, there's a role reversal from the habitual expectations for men and women, with the woman in both biblical books taking the more dominant role. O'Connor goes on to say:

> These connections suggest . . . an additional layer of meaning in connection with the wisdom traditions. If this interpretation is correct, not only is the sexual arena blessed as good in itself, the Song also serves as a metaphor for Wisdom's relationship with human beings. To live with Wisdom, to pursue her and to be pursued by her, is to enter into a love affair set in

a garden of paradise where true human desires will be realized. It is a relationship which itself expresses the harmony and blessedness of the universe.[5]

The eight chapters of the Song of Songs (sometimes also called the Song of Solomon or Canticles) are full of joy, intimacy, physical passion, and sensuousness—the opposite of the relationship of Adam and Eve in the Garden of Eden. Whether we read it literally or take it to be an allegory of God's love for humankind, this book is as sexually explicit as a bodice-ripper paperback. The Song of Songs resounds with physical love.

Curling up in bed with it, lingering over the detailed descriptions and imagery, provides as much juicy eroticism as any popular novel—but more. There is no shame in the book. No sin. No guilt. No Eve. Only kisses, delight, anticipation, and eagerness. The sexes are in complete harmony, just as they were created to be in the first chapter of Genesis, with the woman as the penultimate aspect of Creation. Songs of Songs spills over with the desire that flows between lover and the beloved, affirming that the Bible is not the moralistic, patriarchal text that the ages have pronounced it to be.

Read Song of Songs for yourself. As you do, consider, if you choose, God as your lover—or imagine you and your lover worshipping God as an aspect of physical love. Read it any way you want. No one will be looking over your shoulder. Allow the text to speak directly to you, in whatever way you hear it.

Ecclesiastes

The third book of the Bible traditionally attributed to Solomon is Ecclesiastes. As with Proverbs and the Song of Songs, Bible scholars are not certain who the actual author was; Solomon's name may have been applied to it simply because this book too concerns itself with "wisdom."

NOTE

The Book of Ecclesiastes is also referred to as "Qoheleth," because the author attributes the thoughts he describes to this (perhaps fictional) king of Israel. The word Qoheleth, however, means "someone who addresses an assembly," or "preacher"—and it is feminine in gender. In this book of the Bible, we find a completely human, rather than Divine, perspective. The author's view of life is bleak and pessimistic. Like the Existentialists of philosophy, the author states that life is ultimately meaningless and absurd. He repeats over and over, "Vanity of vanities, all is vanity." The Hebrew word translated as "vanity" in the King James Version literally means "vapor, mist." It implies the futility, emptiness, and fleeting nature of human life. It reminds us of the mist that rose up in the Second Creation, in which Adam and Eve dwelt.

At first glance, Ecclesiastes' depiction of women and sexual relationships seems to stand in sharp contrast to that found in either the Song of Songs or Proverbs. The author's search for "wisdom" is pitted against his fear and hatred of the "snares" of women. The focus seems to be primarily on woman as "folly," as described in portions of Proverbs, warning readers against the dangers of entrapment in her lures.

Not all Bible scholars agree with this reading. Theologian Sinclair Ferguson, for example, believes that Ecclesiastes portrays the division between the sexes. Unlike the Song of Songs, where harmony between the sexes is described so lyrically, Ecclesiastes gives expression to the broken relationship that began in the second chapter of Genesis. Ferguson notes that a woman could easily transpose her own perspective onto Ecclesiastes, in which case, he says, we might read: "I find more bitter than death the man who is an iron fist and whose heart is arrogant and whose feet are steel boots." Among a thousand men, this woman has not found one who is different (a sentiment women have often expressed through the ages).[6]

Another theologian, Dominic Rudman, finds a different interpretation of Ecclesiastes. He points to language in the book that refers to God as "the divine fisherman or fowler catching human beings in his nets,"[7] which parallels the same language used to describe the woman in Ecclesiastes. Rudman believes that the woman represents an inescapable Divine force—not pleasant when we feel we are caught in life's unavoidable pain and difficulties, but not evil either. "The dragnets with which the woman is associated," writes Rudman, "suggest the efficacy of the woman" in her Divine task. She is a huntress, not a temptress.[8]

Rudman concludes that the view of Woman in Ecclesiastes "is at once restricting and liberating."

> Like Man, she is a being controlled by the deity. Yet she is also an extremely powerful semidivine figure. Her weapons are allocated to her by God, and Man has no defense in the face of them. God may pull the strings from heaven, but on earth it is Woman who is the master. In a sense, [this] world view is one in which Eve has ganged up with God against Adam.[9]

If Rudman is correct in his interpretation, then what we see in Ecclesiastes is the voice of the patriarchy rebelling against the power of the Feminine Spirit. It can also be read as an expression of the bitterness we have all felt at times when confronted by the frustrations and losses of life. This is another side of the Feminine Spirit; creation and destruction are linked together, and new life only comes into the world through travail, pain, and brokenness. When we push back against that, the Feminine Spirit can seem hard, relentless, lacking in the compassion we feel we deserve.

NOTE

Western thought, bolstered by a type of Christianity, has often tended to relegate the feminine to one of two categories—the Madonna or the Whore. This way of thinking implies that good women are soothing and kind and pacifying, while the challenging, outspoken woman is outcast. Other religious traditions, however, have represented the truly Feminine as both compassionate and challenging. The Hindu goddess Kali, for instance, is seen as the Great Mother who brings the death of our self-centered view of reality; she liberates her children by destroying all that is unreal. Descriptions of her sound similar to the woman in Ecclesiastes—but her followers regard her with love and trust, rather than bitterness and fear.

Yet another possible interpretation of Ecclesiastes is that it is written as though Solomon were the author in order to point out the contrast between Solomon's great wisdom and his inability to handle his sexuality. Solomon, who is as famous for his thousand wives and concubines as he is for his wisdom, allowed sexual intrigue to damage his governing. If we use this interpretation, the Book of Ecclesiastes points to the danger of allowing exploitive and selfish sex to become a "god," when the sexual relationship was intended to be one of God's blessings, rather than a god in its own right.[10]

Like some of the Psalms, the Book of Ecclesiastes affirms the right to express emotions and ideas honestly, without forcing them to conform to some religious or moral standard. The Living One is big enough to contain our pessimism and despair.

In a reading of Ecclesiastes, though, remember the context of the entire scripture. Despite life's pains, ultimately, the Feminine Spirit brings fruitfulness and blessing and delight.

REFERENCE NOTES

1. Elizabeth A. Johnson. *She Who Is: The Mystery of God in Feminist Theological Discourse* (New York: Crossroad, 1996), page 88.

2. English translations insert the pronoun "he" throughout this passage of scripture, implying that the feminine Wisdom is separate from a masculine Deity, but in the Hebrew, no pronoun is given, and there is nothing to indicate the presence of a masculine God that is somehow distinct from Woman Wisdom.

3. Robin G. Branch. "Women," in *Dictionary of the Old Testament: Wisdom, Poetry and Writings*, Peter Enns and Tremper Longman

III, eds. (Nottingham, England: Inter-Varsity Press, 2008), page 921.

4. Scott Ventureyra. "The Women in the Book of Proverbs: Woman Wisdom Versus Woman Folly," *The American Journal of Biblical Theology* 16(24) June 14, 2015: 13.

5. Kathleen O'Connor. *The Wisdom Literature* (Wilmington, DE: Michael Glazier, 1988), page 82.

6. Sinclair Ferguson. *Pundit's Folly* (Edinburgh: Banner of Truth Trust, 1995), page 35.

7. Dominic Rudman. "Woman as Divine Agent in Ecclesiastes," *Journal of Biblical Literature* 116(3), Autumn 1997: 418.

8. Ibid, page 419.

9. Ibid, page 421.

10. An example of this interpretation is found in "Woman as the Object of Qohelet's Search" by George M. Schwab, *Andrews University Seminary Studies* 39(1), Spring 2001: 73–84.

ELEVEN

THE VOICE
AND JOB

*Hast thou entered into the springs of the sea?
or hast thou walked in the search of the depth?*

—Job 38:16 KJV

"In the land of Uz there lived a man whose name
was Job. This man was blameless and upright; he
feared God and shunned evil." That's how the Book
of Job begins, informing us right from the start who
the central figure in this story will be. More than
any other book in the Bible, this one is written like

a novel, telling a complete story from beginning to end.

This is a tale of a good man who loses everything. He gets little sympathy from his wife, from his friends (who believe that his suffering must be punishment for his sins), or even from God. The story also gives us a fly-on-the-wall glimpse of interactions between Satan and God, which according to some interpretations, reflect the dualism of good and evil. Most commentaries on this book indicate the book's central theme is this: *Why do good people suffer?* At first glance, the answer to that question appears to be found in the conversations between God and Satan, where Job seems to be a pawn in their ongoing contest for power. But what if there's a different way to read this scripture?

NOTE

"Satan" who is described in the Book of Job may not be the devil, in the traditional sense of the word. The Bible does not use "satan" as a proper noun, as we're used to hearing it used. Instead, the word meant simply "an accuser, someone who is opposed to someone or something," in much the same way as a prosecutor in a court of law. Early in the Book of Job, we hear that all the angels have assembled before God, including the one who is acting as an accuser of Job's righteousness, pointing out to God that

Job's morality has very shallow roots. Rather than being a celestial duel for Job's soul, as this account has so often been interpreted, the actual story indicates that it was the satan's job is to pose the questions that will be the central theme of this book.

> *And the Lord said unto Satan, Hast thou considered my servant Job, that there is none like him in the earth, a perfect and an upright man, one that feareth God, and escheweth evil?*
>
> *Then Satan answered the Lord, and said, "Doth Job fear God for nought? . . . But put forth thine hand now, and touch all that he hath, and he will curse thee to thy face."* (1:8,9,11 KJV)

I believe we are missing the point entirely if we understand this scene as a struggle between God and the devil over a man's soul. The story that follows is actually an account of how the Feminine Spirit silences traditional theology—and in the process, restores spiritual Creation to our consciousness.

Job represents all people who think they are doing just fine, judging by life's outward appearances. He's certain he's living a good, moral life, and he takes for granted that he's figured out how things work in life. The loss of material possessions, reputation, and family, however, forces him to confront the God who is beyond human categories of right and wrong. The trigger for Job's crisis is the adversary who "goes to and fro upon the earth" (Job 1:7).

NOTE

If we think of the Book of Job as a novel, the conversations between the satan and God could be merely a narrative device, setting up the action and central theme, while also indicating to readers that the story they are about to read has both earthly and heavenly implications.

But first, the storyteller sets the scene, portraying what life was like for Job before all his calamities. The beginning paragraphs describe a wealthy, successful man who has been blessed with both a large family and material abundance. His adult children seem to be a close-knit group that enjoys getting together on their birthdays.

At this point in the story, before anything else has happened, we get the first hint of a shadow lying across Job's consciousness; we are told that after each family gathering, Job worries that his children may have sinned in their hearts (in their minds, their inner beings), and so he makes sacrifices on their behalf.

Nothing in the story indicates that these birthday celebrations are sinful in any way, and yet Job is so preoccupied with sin—with the rules and mores of his culture—that he makes sacrifices for each of his children's sins "continually" (KJV) or "as his regular custom" (NIV).

The Book of Job can be read as literal events (though many Bible scholars today believe it was intentionally written as fiction to convey spiritual truths). Job's experience can also be understood as something that took place almost entirely within his mind. Three "messengers" come to him, telling him of the terrible tragedies that have befallen his family and property—but are these messengers human beings? Or are they thoughts that come to Job because of the obsessive fears he has harbored for a long time? In Job's own words: "What I always feared has happened to me. What I dreaded has come true" (3:25 NLT). Later, the "three friends" who visit Job, blaming him for his fate and offering him false wisdom about the nature of God, can also be viewed as aspects of Job's own conflicted psyche, rather than actual flesh-and-blood people.

NOTE

There is another possible interpretation of the messengers who bring the evil tidings to Job. In the first chapter, verse 6, we read that the children of God gather to present themselves to the Living One, with the "satan" among them. The Hebrew word used for "children of God" is usually translated into English as "angels." Then, eight verses later, we read that "messengers" bear the bad news to Job—and the Hebrew word used here is more commonly translated elsewhere in the Bible as "angels." If this is the case, that angels are the messengers who come to Job, then his entire tribulation (aside from the boils on his skin) may have been a spiritual test only, rather than an actual series of events.

Job's Trials

However we look at the account—whether as literal fact taking place in the physical world, as pure story, or as psychological or spiritual metaphor—Job exemplifies human suffering in the midst of change and loss. In the story, Satan annihilates Job's family, servants, crops, livestock—everything, except his wife. Next, seemingly with God's permission, Satan "smote Job with sore boils from the sole of his foot unto his crown" (2:7).

There sits Job, crouched in an ash heap, itching at his sores with a piece of shattered pottery, a broken man. And what does his wife say to him? Does she give him words of love and support and sympathy? No, she doesn't. She says, "Are you still holding fast to your integrity? Curse God and die!" (2:9). Job scolds his wife for this seemingly blasphemous advice, and she falls silent.

Job's Wife

For centuries, male interpreters of this scripture have regarded Job's wife as an agent of Satan, following in Eve's footsteps (according to this masculine interpretation) as a temptress luring her man from the way of God. The early Church fathers claimed that the reason Satan doesn't kill Job's wife along with his children is that she is actually one more scourge to cause him pain; the fourth-century theologian Augustine called Job's wife explicitly *diabolic adjutrix* (helpmeet or accomplice of the devil). More than a millennium later, John Calvin, the Protestant reformer, named her as an "instrument of Satan." Many modern male Bible commentators have fallen in line with this way of thinking,[1] insisting that this flawed, if not downright evil, woman is being held up in contrast to Job's total righteousness and innocence.

But once again there is another reading possible here. The words spoken by Job's wife become the background for all that follows. They must have lingered in Job's memory, just as they linger in the reader's. We never hear Job's wife speak again, but, in the words of Bible scholar Holly Henry, "It can be argued that in her silence Job's wife becomes more complex, elusive, and incomprehensible than if she argued further."[2] It may be that Job's wife already knows there is another, better ending to this story.

Jewish scholar Ilana Pardes adds this thought: that in encouraging Job to question his relationship to God, "she does him much good, for this turns out to be the royal road to deepening one's knowledge, to opening one's eyes."[3] As author Miguel Unamuno wrote, "Those who believe they believe in God, but without passion in the heart, without anguish of mind, without uncertainty, without doubt, and even at times without despair, believe only in the God-Idea," rather than the actual Living One.[4] From this perspective, Job's wife is a wisdom-seeker who challenges her husband to look deeper than surface circumstances. She represents the Feminine Spirit confronting narrow, patriarchal assumptions about God and life.

Bible commentator Gerald Janzen expands the words spoken by Job's wife, finding this to be the true meaning of her two simple questions:

Do you still possess your own integrity as an individual? Are you not in danger, through your continued piety, of denying the implications of your own experience. . . ? Are you not in danger of "bad faith" in alienating yourself from yourself by this disgusting display of fawning religiosity? If you really want to keep a grip on your own integrity, you will wake up. . . .[5]

In many ways, Job's wife speaks for Woman Wisdom, the same Wisdom who shouts in the streets in the Book of Proverbs, calling us all to *wake up.*

James Crenshaw explains in his book *Old Testament Wisdom* that the biblical concept of wisdom was that it went beyond mere knowledge in order to make sense of the anomalies in life[6]—all the things that seem unreasonable to our human logic: the complexities in human relationship, as well as the circumstances and ideas that don't seem to fit with the pictures we frame in our heads about what life and God are like. As with many other biblical women before and after her—from Eve to Sarah to Hagar to Deborah, and all the others—Job's wife is outspoken; she feels comfortable asking questions of God; and she points the man in the story to a deeper understanding. She speaks for Wisdom.

She reflects the feminine Voice that will soon speak explicitly in the Book of Job.

Job's Struggle to Understand

The Bible continually illustrates that transformations in people's lives also require a transformation in how they understand and name God. As Abraham was transformed by a new understanding of the Breasted

One, as Moses was transformed by the I AM, the Living One, so will it be with Job. Job is radically changed by his encounter with the God of all Creation—and in the process he comes to himself. He no longer struggles with self-pity, fear, theology, and the male social order. His story is ultimately an exploration of the struggle to understand and acknowledge the feminine nature of the Creator with all its infinite power.

Robert Sacks, in his book *The Book of Job with Commentary*, says that in a certain sense, all the changes that take place in Job begin in the book's first chapter, where Job introduces his preoccupation with wombs, a preoccupation that will continue throughout his story. "Naked came I out of my mother's belly and naked shall I return there," says Job (1:21, Sacks' translation). Sacks further explains:

> Job's perhaps almost thoughtless blurring of the distinction between his own mother and the great mother earth may be seen as a first and naive glimpse into a world larger than the world of man into which he was born. Here as I say, the thought is almost thoughtless. We see it as only a seed, yet we shall see it grow until its roots are sturdy enough to crack the strongest city wall.[7]

In the chapters that follow, Job makes further references to the womb and birth and death. At times, he seems to imply that the womb and death are synonymous. Until the entry of the Voice of God into the text, Job's musings on the womb indicate that he connects it with emptiness and darkness and oblivion, as well as hatred, rage, and contention. The only thing positive he can say about the womb was that there was a certain comfort in a newborn's state of ignorant innocence.

The Voice

After Job's three "friends" have offered him their shallow wisdom and false comfort, finally, out of the darkness of Job's theological wrestling, comes a challenging, provocative Voice. The scripture says that the Living One speaks from a whirlwind. The Hebrew word here means a violent windstorm, but it can also refer to the kind of passionate rage that scatters rational reason to the winds.

"Who is this that darkens my counsel with words without knowledge?" asks the Voice. "Brace yourself like a man; I will question you, and you shall answer me" (38:2–3 NIV). This is the Feminine Spirit speaking, and Her no-nonsense tone is reminiscent of Job's wife. She goes on to confront Job with Her questions:

Where wast thou when I laid the foundations of the earth? declare, if thou hast understanding. Who hath laid the measures thereof, if thou knowest? or who hath stretched the line upon it? Whereupon are the foundations thereof fastened? or who laid the corner stone thereof; When the morning stars sang together, and all the sons of God shouted for joy? Or who shut up the sea with doors, when it brake forth, as if it had issued out of the womb? When I made the cloud the garment thereof, and thick darkness a swaddlingband for it. . . . (38:4–9 KJV)

Later, the Voice also asks, "From whose womb was ice birthed? And the frost of heaven, who was in labor to give birth to it?" (38:29, literal translation). The Voice is describing the primordial Creation of Genesis chapter 1, and She makes clear that it is She who labors to deliver the world—and then wraps it in a baby blanket of cloud and darkness. "Will the faultfinder argue with El Shaddai, the Breasted One?" She asks Job (40:2, literal translation).

The Mother's love, the womb-love of God, shines through these lovely, poetic passages. This strong, infinite Feminine Voice is inviting Job—and us—to drop in with Her for a visit, to look at Creation from Her perspective. In the process, we will be transformed into the feminine-masculine image of God we were intended to be. We catch a glimpse of the equality that the Spirit sees between masculine and feminine when She says: "Has the rain a father? Or who gave birth to the drops of dew?" (38:28, literal translation).

Each day of Creation is reprised in these last chapters of Job: the light, the darkness, the water, the stars, the clouds, the division of dry land from the sea, all Earth's creatures, and finally, humankind. As Sacks writes:

> By the end of the book, the womb or belly has become for Job, and perhaps for the reader, that mighty, turbulent, and often ferocious source out of which there has emerged a world full of life and living creatures, a world larger, stranger, and more violent, but at times curiously more tender, than any man had ever seen. But at all times it is breathtakingly beautiful, and we stand in awe. . . .[8]

This whirling, birthing tempest speaks to Job of a nurturing God who safeguards and cherishes in each being the Divine identity. Job, who once lived in a narrow world of masculine mores and codes, with a self-satisfied yet limited understanding of Deity, sees the bursting forth of Creation.

When the Voice has finished speaking, Job finally answers Her questions: "I know that you can do all things; no purpose of yours can be thwarted. You asked, 'Who is this that obscures my plans without knowledge?' Surely I spoke of things I did not understand, things too wonderful for me to know" (42:1–3 NIV).

And then the Living One rebukes the masculine voices that gave Job such false counsel, saying, "My face burns with anger against you . . . because you have not spoken of Me what is firmly established, as my servant Job has. . . . . Job will intervene on your behalf, and My face will turn back to you, and I won't treat you in the way your senselessness deserves" (42:7,8, literal translation).

Blessing

The story ends with blessing and fruitfulness, as is always the case with the Feminine Spirit. Job's fortunes are restored to him, and more children are born into the family—or it may be that Job simply finds out the truth, that this spiritual test took place only in his mind rather than in the physical world. The fact that Job starts with out with seven sons and three daughters and ends with seven sons and three daughters may indicate that he never actually lost his children. In any case, harmony and joy are restored to Job's world.

But Job is a changed person. We can see this in the fact that he gives his daughters, as well as his sons, an inheritance (42:15). This was not common practice in the biblical world, indicating that Job's understanding of Creation has truly been transformed. Translator Stephen Mitchell comments:

The most curious detail in the epilogue is the mention of Job's daughters. . . . Indeed, they are dignified equally by being given a share of Job's wealth as their inheritance. Each is named, while the seven sons remain anonymous. The names themselves—Dove, Cinnamon, and Eye-Shadow [the literal Hebrew translations of Jemimah, Keziah, and Keren-happuch]—symbolize peace, abundance, and a specifically female kind of grace. . . . There is something enormously satisfying about this prominence of the feminine at the end of Job. The whole yin side of humanity . . . has finally been acknowledged and honored here.[9]

The third daughter's name, Keren-happuch, means literally "Horn of Antimony." Women in the ancient world used antimony, also called "kohl," as eye makeup—but her name holds deeper meaning as well. The word translated as "horn" can mean feminine rays of light and strength. The horn, as a musical instrument, had a central role in the place of worship, and we hear the echo of Hannah's song, when she referred to God as the "Horn of my Salvation."

"And in all the land were no women found so fair as the daughters of Job" (42:15 KJV). "Fair" here means beautiful, both internally and externally, both literally and figuratively. Note that the Bible says nothing about men flocking around these beautiful women; we hear no mention of husbands or dowries, only the detail that these women became wealthy in their own right (since, along with their brothers, they inherited their father's riches). These were women whose names gave them individual and unique identities; they did not need to be defined by men, because they knew they were reflections of the Feminine Spirit.

NOTE

Who wrote the Book of Job? No one really knows. According to Jewish tradition, it was written by Moses, but some scholars believe it was written between the seventh and fourth centuries BCE, long after Moses' death. They assume that it was written by an anonymous Israelite man. But was it? Might it not be just as likely to have been written by an anonymous woman?

The new Job—the one who has seen the treasures of the snow, the way the light parts the darkness, and the animals and plants as they truly are, who has heard the song of the morning stars and the feminine Voice of Creation—establishes the right of women to own property. This is one of the gifts he brings back from the infinite world of Creation. It stands in sharp contrast to the narrow, fear-driven, and masculine theology of his earlier days, when he struggled with the meaning of his life, before he heard the Voice. In the consciousness of the Creator, male and female are equal—and in the story of Job, as in the first chapter of Genesis, "female" is the final idea.

After that, we are told only that Job lived one hundred and forty years. He saw his grandchildren, his great-grandchildren, and their children.

And so Job died old and contented, satisfied with Creation.

REFERENCE NOTES

1. To read more on this, see Holly Henry's "Job's Wife's Name," *College Literature* 18(1) 1991: 28.

2. Ibid.

3. Ilana Pardes. "Wife of Job: Bible," *Jewish Women's Archive, Encyclopedia of Jewish Women*, https://jwa.org/encyclopedia/article/wife-of-job-bible.

4. Miguel Unamuno. *Tragic Sense of Life* (Mineola, NY: Dover, 1976), page 193.

5. Gerald J. Janzen. *Job: Interpretation: A Bible Commentary for Teaching and Preaching* (Atlanta, GA: Knox, 1985), page 50.

6. James L. Crenshaw. *Old Testament Wisdom: An Introduction* (Louisville, KY: Westminster John Knox, 2010), page 4.

7. Robert Sacks. *The Book of Job with Commentary: A Translation*

for Our Time (Tampa, FL: University of South Florida, 2000), page 142.

8. Ibid., page 151.

9. Stephen Mitchell. *The Book of Job* (New York: Northpoint, 1987), page xxx.

TWELVE

CRYING IN THE WILDERNESS

I will say to the north, Give up; and to the south, Keep not back: bring my sons from far and my daughters from the ends of the earth.

—Isaiah 43:6 KJV

We have one more section of the Hebrew scriptures to discuss—the Prophets. The books of the Bible named for these individuals reveal men with different temperaments, different styles of writing, and different ways of speaking of the Divine One. These men rant and rave and hallucinate. They share their dreams and visions with us, and through them we learn more about women and nations, about human nature, and most of all, about the changing and expanding perception of the Living One, the Name of God as it's manifested within human consciousness.

The first five books in this section of the Hebrew Bible are sometimes referred to as the Major Prophets: Isaiah, Jeremiah, Lamentations, Ezekiel, and Daniel. The other twelve books are often called the Minor Prophets, but not because their contents are less important; these twelve books are simply shorter. Any summary of these books will fail to convey the depth of the writing found throughout the Prophets, so consider this chapter to be no more than your introduction into these mysterious and difficult, comforting and harsh passages. You should explore further on your own.

The prophets' writings are not always pleasant. These authors seem to spend their lives telling everyone in graphic terms how horrible things are when *ruah Elohim* is forgotten. They are strange, flawed individuals—and yet the Divine Spirit speaks through them. *Trust your dreams,* these writers tell us. *Your dreams tell you about your life—and about the Living One.*

Isaiah

Who is your husband?

This is one of the questions the prophet Isaiah asks us. The answer he offers is outside the familiar patriarchal responses, which even today still often define a woman in terms of her relationship to a man, and the answer applies to all of us, both women and men. Where traditional Bible interpretation has always asked women to find space in the Bible within masculine pronouns and metaphors, Isaiah offers us all a series of feminine metaphors, some of which apply to the Living One, and some to human beings in our relationship with the Divine.

Isaiah addresses many of his words to "Zion." This name has sometimes been thought to be synonymous with the Nation of Israel, the city of Jerusalem, or the holy mountain where God is said to dwell. The Bible, however, always uses the word "Zion" in a poetic way that gives it a symbolic meaning reaching far wider than the geographical and political significance. Wherever the word is used in the Bible, it speaks to the relationship between God and human beings; it is the place where God dwells within the human community. The Hebrew root is a feminine term for a dry, parched, and lonely wilderness (like the place where Hagar encountered the Living One).

Isaiah is writing during the historical period when the Jews have been deported from their own land to Babylon. They are exiled from their homeland, from their own identity. As we read the Book of Isaiah, we too can identify with Zion, because the Book of Isaiah speaks to all people at all times. When God speaks to Zion through the prophet Isaiah, the Living One speaks to us.

And so, in Isaiah we hear God say:

> *Awake, awake, Zion,*
> *clothe yourself with strength!*
> *Put on your garments of splendor. . . .*
> *Free yourself from the chains on your neck,*
> *Daughter Zion, now a captive.*
> (Isaiah 52:1,2 NIV)

Again and again in the Bible passages we have studied so far, we have seen God come to the exiled woman, the woman who is "barren," unloved, or widowed—who in one way or another is marginalized and oppressed. In Isaiah, this repeated story is stated explicitly:

> *Sing, barren woman,*
> *you who never bore a child;*
> *burst into song, shout for joy,*
> *you who were never in labor;*

because more are the children of the desolate woman
than of her who has a husband,"
says the Lord. . . .
"Do not be afraid; you will not be put to shame.
Do not fear disgrace; you will not be humiliated.
You will forget the shame of your youth
and remember no more
the reproach of your widowhood.
For your Maker is your husband.
(Isaiah 54:1,4,5 NIV)

Whether we are male or female, at the spiritual level, we are married to the Creator. The Living One delights in an intimate relationship with us—and within that relationship, we are fruitful, secure, beloved.

The Book of Isaiah also helps us understand our relationship with the Living One through the metaphor of another intimate human relationship—that of a mother and child. In chapter 42, God groans and gasps like a woman in labor. Just as the Creator birthed the world, the Living One also gives birth to Zion.

NOTE

The imagery in Isaiah 42 is both feminine and masculine, for God is said to be a warrior as well as a mother. In Sarah Dille's book, Mixing Metaphors, *she states that in the ancient world warriors and mothers were often compared to one another. From the perspective of those who lived in these earlier times, both mothers and warriors suffer and bleed; both exert themselves physically and courageously for a cause larger than themselves; both actively engage in changing the world.[1]*

Then in chapter 49, verse 15, God compares Divine love to that of a mother for her baby: "Can a woman forget her suckling baby? Can she have no womb-love for the child who came from her womb?" (literal translation). These words speak to a very physical understanding of God's love. Any women who has nursed a baby knows that she literally cannot forget her baby, because her breasts fill with milk, a reminder that comes from her very flesh. At the sound of her baby's cry, her breasts involuntarily let down milk. This intimately connected love is the way God feels about us. "And even if a woman could forget her child," says the Living One, "I will not forget you."

The sixty-six chapters of the Book of Isaiah also include references to the entire Bible (looking both backward and forward), from spiritual Creation and Adam and Eve . . . to Abraham and Sarah . . . to Moses and the Commandments . . .and to the new Heaven and new Earth in the Book of Revelation, the final book of the New Testament. This book of Isaiah's prophecy is filled with parables, visions, oracles, and multidimensional promises.

Early in the book, in chapter 2, verse 22, Isaiah urges us to stop looking backward at the dust-man of the second Creation story; "Stop focusing on the human with breath in his nostrils," Isaiah writes. "Why should he be given so much importance in your mind?" Instead, enter into a new relationship with the Living One, the Breasted One.

Jeremiah

About a century after Isaiah, another prophet wrote words that continue to both challenge and comfort us today. Jeremiah is credited with writing both the Book of Jeremiah and the Book of Lamentations.

Modern Bible critics have reacted against the violence toward women that is portrayed in the Book of Jeremiah. And yet this book starts with the womb. At the beginning of the first chapter, when God tell Jeremiah that the Living One formed him in the womb, God is identifying as the Primal Mother.

Even before Jeremiah's birth, the Living One tells him, he was already chosen to speak on God's behalf. Jeremiah is a young man, perhaps still a boy, when he gets this message, and he is not particularly excited about being told he's about to become a public speaker.

"Sorry, but I don't know how to do this job," he tells God. "It's too big for me" (1:6, paraphrase).

Take comfort and courage from God's response: "Don't be afraid. I'm with you. I'll rescue you."

Images of birth continue throughout the Book of Jeremiah. The prophet refers again and again (seven times, in fact) to a woman in labor, moaning in agony as she gives birth to her child. These references—revealing the presence of the Feminine Spirit—occur within passages of vehement warning. The message Jeremiah delivers sounds harsh and cruel at first glance, but the prophet is describing the horrifying and all-too-realistic consequences of living a life of greed, violence, and destruction. All aspects of society and the Earth itself suffer (as we too have found in our own time) when humans are ruled by their selfishness.

And yet, even when things are at their worst, Jeremiah affirms that there is still hope. The metaphor of the woman in labor speaks of the Feminine Spirit's enduring message throughout all the scripture we have read so far: She brings fertility, in all its meanings. She uses women in trouble, women in pain, women who have been rejected to bring about something new in to the world, something that lifts humanity a little closer to God. The Feminine Spirit restores, She affirms, She blesses.

"The Living One appeared to me from afar," writes Jeremiah, "saying, 'I love you with everlasting, never-ending, unconditional love—and so I pull you back to

Me with love and kindness. I'll rebuild and heal all that you have lost. You will be a virgin again and go out dancing, shaking your tambourines. You'll plant grapes and make wine. You'll live in My presence. So sing out! Be happy!'" (31:3–7, paraphrase).

Even when we are in despair and darkness, Jeremiah affirms, we are like women who groan and labor in childbirth in order to bring new life into the world.

In the Book of Lamentations, the author (who may also be Jeremiah) continues with a similar theme that focuses on women, now speaking directly to women who are burdened. Comparing Zion to a woman, he addresses the state of widowhood, weeping, loss of lovers, friends who betray, children in captivity to enemies, and faded beauty.

How doth the city sit solitary, that was full of people! How is she become as a widow! She that was great among the nations, and princess among the provinces, how is she become tributary! She weepeth sore in the night, and her tears are on her cheeks: among all her lovers she hath none to comfort her: all her friends have dealt treacherously with her, they are become her enemies . . . her children are gone into captivity before the enemy. And from the daughter of Zion all her beauty is departed: her princes are become like harts that find no pasture, and they are gone without strength before the pursuer. (Lamentations 1:1,2,5,6 KJV)

Lamentations' poems of sorrow honor the destruction of Jerusalem and the exile of the city's people into Babylon—but these words can also be claimed by each of us personally. In this book of the Bible, we acknowledge that we experience the pain of loss; life often makes us weep. Lamentations affirms that sorrow is not only part of the human experience, but that it is also an aspect of our relationship with Divinity. We all have moments in our lives when we feel God has become unknown, our enemy (Lamentation 2:5), but we can bring our complaints, our sense of abandonment and desolation and betrayal to the Living One.

> *I weep and my eyes overflow with tears. No one is near to comfort me, no one to restore my spirit. My children are destitute because the enemy has prevailed.* (1:16 NIV)

> *The hearts of the people cry out to the Lord. You walls of Daughter Zion, let your tears flow like a river day and night; give yourself no relief, your eyes no rest.* (2:18 NIV)

When we are in tears, depressed, overcome with despair, we find in Lamentations an empathetic companion. Reading these passages of scripture helps us understand that we can communicate our distress to

God, that this is an appropriate response to the evil in the world. Like Hagar in the desert, we can cry in bitterness—and be heard.

Male commentators of this book have often blamed the central female figure for the humiliation she suffers. (After all, like Eve, she brought it on herself with her sinfulness, is how that line of thought goes.) Other readers, however, believe the metaphor was intended to expose the male community's sins against the feminine and stimulate repentance.

Lamentations speaks with particular power to women's experience. Rabba Melanie Landau invites women to "enter into the pain these texts evoke," to "use them as an opportunity to explore our own lived experience of this breach of the feminine, and to allow ourselves to be with it inside our own bodies and experiences." She goes on to say:

> The metaphor of the humiliated woman that I once had to fight against because of the pain it evoked in me, becomes a portal for me to connect to my own lived experience. . . . Now our challenge is to be able to move forward without re-wounding that original wound but with feeling, naming, validating, and expressing.[2]

Passages like these verses from Lamentations explicitly express a woman's humiliation, her sense of being abandoned by God, at the mercy of an unjust patriarchal system:

> *I am the one who has seen the humiliation*
> *because of the rod of overflowing arrogance.*
> *I have been driven away*
> *so that I walk in darkness and not in light.*
> *A hand has thrown me down*
> *again and again, all day long.*
> *Flesh and skin grow old and waste away.*
> *My bones—the substance of my very self—*
> *have been broken into pieces. . . .*
> *I dwell in a dark place, like those who are long dead.*
> *I am walled in and I cannot leave;*
> *the fetters I wear are a heavy burden.*
> *Even when I cry, when I cry out for help,*
> *my prayers go nowhere.*
> *He has blocked my way with a high stone wall;*
> *he has made my road crooked. . . .*
> *I have lost my path; I am torn into pieces,*
> *I am desolated, filled with horror. . . .*
> *I have become a laughingstock to all my people; . . .*
> *I am surfeited with bitter tears*
> *and drenched in curses.*
> *My teeth are broken from chewing gravel;*
> *I huddle in ashes.*
> *Peace has rejected my inner self,*

and I have forgotten happiness.
I say, "My endurance has died,
and so has my hope in the Living One."
(3:1–4,6–8,11,14–18, literal translation)

The Book of Lamentations truly gives voice to a woman's darkest hours—but the picture it paints in this long song of sorrow from chapter 3 is followed immediately by lines of hope, which begin with the woman claiming a new name for herself: Ithiel—"God is with me."

I turn my inner being back to this,
and because of this I have hope.
The love and kindness of the Living One
is never finished,
womb-love is never spent.
(3:21–23, literal translation)

The Book of Lamentation is full of the ebb and flow of emotion and experience. For many of us, this is a familiar pattern: we are sunk in despair . . . we climb up out of our depression and feel more optimistic . . . something trips us up, and we sick back into our dark hole . . . and then we repeat the entire cycle again. The final chapter of the Book of Lamentations acknowledges that there is good reason for our bitter feelings—truly terrible things have happened—and yet the affirmation of the Feminine Spirit's womb-love weaves like a golden thread through suffering and feelings of abandonment.

Huldah

The books of the Bible named after prophets are all male names—but we know that in fact there are at least seven female prophets. We have already mentioned Sarah, Miriam, Deborah, Hannah, Abigail, and Esther, and now Huldah makes the seventh.

Like Jeremiah, Huldah is the chosen voice of God. Her story is told twice in almost identical words in two books of the Bible, 2 Kings and 2 Chronicles. The author (or authors) of these accounts makes no mention of Huldah's gender as something extraordinary, indicating that it was an accepted practice for women to be prophets. And Huldah has a seminal and vital role in the history of the Bible itself.

The scrolls that contained what is now considered to be the first books in the Hebrew scriptures were lost—but they are found during the reign of King Josiah. When he reads what they have to say, he's upset, worried that his people have not been following God the way they should. He asks his priests to figure out the meaning of these difficult passages.

The priests go to someone they trust, someone they consider to be an expert in the field of Divine interpretation. They go to Huldah.

Huldah confirms that the words written on the scrolls are indeed the words of God, intended to warn King Josiah and his people. In doing this, Huldah is the first to authenticate a written document that will become part of the Bible. By applying these ancient words to her own time, she also affirms that the Bible should be read in the present tense, within the context of our own lives.

Huldah's hearing and speaking for Divinity causes a turnaround in the thinking, observances, and practices of the entire kingdom—and empowers the king, who "turned to the Lord with all his heart, and with all his soul, and all his might, according to the law of Moses" (2 Kings 23:25 KJV). The Bible clearly sets aside the idea that women can't interpret the Bible. Scripture makes abundantly clear that a woman is fully qualified to understand, interpret, and speak for the Supreme Creator.

NOTE

Huldah is one of the seven women prophets of Israel, and each of these women reflect to us a different saving aspect of ruah Elohim. *Huldah's prophetic place in scripture, however, differs from that of the other women prophets in that she is the only one who unveils God's meaning directly from the text.*

Angry Men?

The men who gave their names to the portion of the Hebrew scriptures known as the Prophets can sometimes seem like a long line of angry men, ranting endlessly about the wrath of God and the sinfulness of His people. Embedded in each of their writings, however, are consistent glimpses of that golden thread of the Feminine Spirit and Creation.

Ezekiel speaks with a harsh, emphatic voice. Like all the other prophets, he hears the voice of God, and it is his task to relay God's message to the people. In fact, he hears the voice of God more often (ninety-three times) than any other prophet, and the way God addresses him as "son of Adam" (or "son of humankind"—or "son of the earth") is unique. This phrasing calls to mind the second chapter of Genesis and the creation of the dust-man.

The modern world might dismiss Ezekiel as a delusional schizophrenic. He experiences could be interpreted to be auditory, visual, and even gustatory hallucinations, but they describe Ezekiel's vision into another realm of understanding. He writes:

> *The Voice said to me, "Son of Adam, eat this God-Is-with-Me scroll that I give to you and fill your womb with it, fill your internal organs with this God-Is-with-Me scroll that I'm giving you." Then I ate it;*

and it was as sweet as honey in my mouth. (3:3, literal interpretation)

Note that Ezekiel uses the same mysterious name used by the woman in Lamentations—Ithiel, "God-Is-with-Me." Note also that Divinity first connects Ezekiel to the Creation story in the second chapter of Genesis, and then addresses him as though he were a woman, capable of filling his "womb" (though interpreted as "belly" in most English translations), with the implication that new life will come from this God-Is-with-Me experience. As psychologist J. D. Laing wrote in reference to Ezekiel, "the cracked mind may let in light which does not enter the minds of many sane people whose minds are closed."[3] Laing went on to say, "Madness need not be all breakdown. It may also be breakthrough. It is potential liberation and renewal. . . ."

With his alternative vision on reality, which steps outside the traditional perspectives on life, Ezekiel can be read in several ways: as a political treatise, as a foreshadowing of the Book of Revelation—or as the expression of women's relationships, hopes, and fears. In chapter 17, the Voice gives Ezekiel a riddle that contains many of the words with which we have become familiar as the fingerprints of the Feminine Spirit, words such as *wings, seeds, fertility, water, abundance,* and *fruitfulness.*

The familiar story of Jonah and the great fish, told in the Book of Jonah, can also be read from the perspective of the first Creation. When Jonah refuses to carry the Divine message to the Ninevites, a foreign people he considers to be enemies, the Living One arranges circumstances so that Jonah is thrown off a ship and into the sea. In effect, Jonah has been plunged back into the water of Creation, the primal abyss. There he is literally swallowed up, and he spends three days in the belly of an enormous fish. Note the reference to the number three, reminding us of the third day of Creation. What's more, the Hebrew word that is traditionally translated as "belly" can also mean womb; once again we are seeing the Feminine Spirit at work. Jonah prays to the Living One, and he is ejected from the fish's innards onto dry land. After this symbolic new birth, Jonah is on his way to becoming a transformed person, and the next time God speaks to him, he obeys (although somewhat grudgingly even now).

NOTE

In the Gospel of Matthew, Jesus compares himself to Jonah. Some teachers of religious law had come to him, asking that he prove his authority with a miraculous sign. Jesus answers, "The only sign I will give them is the sign *of the prophet Jonah. For as Jonah was in the belly of the great fish for three days and three nights, so will the Son of Man be in the heart of the earth for three days and three nights" (Matthew 12:38–40 NLT).*

Jonah also refers to the abundant kindness, the unconditional compassion of the Living One (4:2). As reluctant as he is to bring God's word to a community he considers to be an enemy, Jonah nevertheless recognizes that the Living One is impartial to all people without regard for their nationality or religion. He knows that Divine compassion is as unconditional as womb-love (the literal meaning of the word usually translated "compassion"). In the words of Bible scholar Phyllis Trible, "an organ unique to the female becomes a vehicle pointing to the compassion of God."[4]

The Feminine Spirit is revealed in the Book of Hosea as well, when the Voice of God says:

> *It was I who taught Ephraim to walk, taking them by the arms; but they did not realize it was I who healed them. I led them with cords of human kindness, with ties of love. To them I was like one who lifts a little child to the cheek, and I bent down to feed them.* (Hosea 11:3–4 NIV)

According to Hebrew scholar Helen Schüngel-Strau-mann, the word translated as "cheek" can also mean "breasts," giving us an image of the Feminine Spirit lifting a child into Her arms to nurse.[5]

Again and again in the Bible, including here in the books of the Prophets, the Living One is connected to the physical experiences of womankind. As author Rosemary Radford Ruether argues, "These references occur particularly when the author wishes to describe God's unconditional love and faithfulness to the people despite their sins. They express God's compassion and forgiveness."[6]

In the Prophets, we see the concepts found in the Creation account extending beyond political bound-aries, beyond the limitations of time and space into everlasting, cosmic dimension. From Isaiah to Mala-chi, these seemingly angry men tell us that evil has real and dire consequences—but Divine compassion is as inclusive and never-ending as a mother's love for her children.

NOTE

The Hebrew Bible's table of contents does not follow the same order as does the Christian Old Testament's. While the Old Testament ends with the Prophet Mala-chi, the Hebrew scripture closes with 2 Chronicles (just

2 chapters after the story of Huldah and the implications of her interpretation), leaving the interpretation of scripture to be never ending in its application to all time.

We have traveled through all the Hebrew scriptures now, but there is more to come in the Gospels and the other books of the New Testament. The stories of Jesus of Nazareth, his followers, and the early Church, as the Western world knows, have further and continuing implications for international policy, societal practices, and the well-being of women.

And in these accounts, the Feminine Spirit demands to be seen in Her endless impartial act of Creation.

REFERENCE NOTES

1. Sarah J. Dille. *Mixing Metaphors: God as Mother and Father in Deutero-Isaiah* (London: T&T Clark, 2004).

2. Melanie Landau. "For Tisha B'Av, a Feminist Reading of Lamentations," *Jofa's Torch*, July 22, 2015.

3. R. D. Laing. *The Divided Self: An Existential Study in Sanity and Madness* (London: Penguin, 2010), page 27.

4. Phyllis Trible. *God and Rhetoric of Sexuality* (Minneapolis, MN: Fortress Press, 1986), page 38.

5. Helen Schüngel-Straumann. "God as Mother in Hosea 11" in *A Feminist Companion to the Latter Prophets*, A. Brenner, ed. (Sheffield, UK: FCB, 1995), pages 119–134.

6. Rosemary Radford Ruether. *Sexism and God-Talk: Toward a Feminist Theology: With a New Introduction*, 10th ed. (Boston, MA: Beacon Press, 1993), page 56.

THIRTEEN

THE EYEWITNESSES

*But Mary kept all these things
and pondered them in her heart*

–Luke 2:19 KJV

T he four Gospels—Matthew, Mark, Luke, and John—are reports on Jesus, the human being, and Jesus, the Christ.[1] People have died defending their interpretations of the Gospels; nations have been invaded, and wars fought over their meaning. Women have been subjugated, marriage relations dictated, and still, bottom line, the Gospels and the entire New Testament are the first draft of the history of the man Jesus of Nazareth, Jesus the Christ.

And so, if we are to decide for ourselves what we think about Jesus, we turn first to primary sources, the Gospels, and then the rest of the New Testament, all of which is concerned with the story of Jesus. His life is there, in each book, in one form or another, starting with his biological genealogy found in the first chapter of Matthew, and ending with the Book of Revelation, where the story extends out beyond time and space.

Because the central figure of Christianity is male, does that indicate that women are to be submissive to men? Does it imply that men are superior? Are women left without viable role models for a spiritual path? The answer to these questions is clear in Jesus' life. Again and again, he speaks to women, touches women, makes friends with women; Jesus treats women as equals. While the historical Church has found evidence of patriarchy in the Gospels, and then used that to support its own bias, when we listen to Jesus himself speaking in these narratives, we find nothing there that says women cannot be priests or disciples. What's more, we find repeated the themes in the Hebrew scriptures, connecting the Feminine Spirit with the ever-blossoming splendor and abundance of Creation. The New Testament brings women to the forefront, culminating in the image of woman as the bride, the Holy City, the Feminine Spirit.

The Bible's four versions of Jesus' life, work, and sayings are called the Gospels, a word that means "good news." The authors of the Gospels tell us some (but not all) of the same stories about Jesus, but they write from quite different perspectives. Some of them write as eyewitnesses themselves, while others have compiled reports from eyewitnesses.

NOTE

When the early Church put together the New Testament, they placed the Gospels first, not because they were written first (the book of James was the first to be written, followed by the letters that Paul wrote), but because they told the story that was the foundation for everything in all the books that followed. The Gospel of Mark was written before the other three Gospels and probably dates from around 66–70 CE, while Matthew and Luke were written around 85–90, and John around 90–110. Like the rest of the New Testament, the Gospels were written in Greek. The writers combined oral traditions—stories and sayings that had been circulated for years in the community of Jesus' followers—with written accounts from eyewitnesses who include names we may recognize: Mary mother of Jesus and perhaps Mary of Magdalene and Mary and Martha of Bethany.

Matthew

About three centuries after Jesus' death, the early Church decided to place Matthew's Gospel first of all (though it was not the first written), because Matthew's perspective on the Good News emphasizes that Jesus is the Jews' "Chosen One," and as a result, this Gospel forms a good thematic transition between the Hebrew scriptures and the Christian New Testament. There is no evidence that indicates Matthew thought of himself—or Jesus—as someone who had left his ancestral faith and converted to a new religion. Instead, for the author of Matthew, Jesus is the fulfillment of the Hebrew scriptures, and the narratives in Matthew underline that belief. But this doesn't mean that Matthew thought Jesus was intended only for the Jewish people. In fact, his version of Jesus' story makes clear from the beginning that this is a story that's meant for everyone, including women.

NOTE

The Book of Matthew contains sixty-eight references to the Hebrew scriptures. The author also frequently uses the word "fulfilled" to connect Jesus' life to the past. The Greek word he uses does not refer so much to a prophecy that has come true as it does to the idea that Jesus "makes full" or "completes" the ideas in the Hebrew scriptures.

By beginning his Gospel with a genealogy, a long line of "begats" (forty-two in all), Matthew's version of the Good News places Jesus within the context of human generations, the long genetic chain that reaches far back in time—but unlike most ancient genealogies, Matthew's is not a long list of only males' names; it also includes the names of "foreign" women who saved the genetic line in fascinating ways: Rahab (a Canaanite woman who was a prostitute), Ruth (a woman of Moab), and Bathsheba (the Hittite woman who was one of King David's wives and the mother of Solomon) are all listed as ancestors of Jesus. Also included in the long list of begats is Tamar, a mistreated Jewish woman whose father-in-law, Judah, eventually proclaimed was more righteous than he was.

Matthew lists Mary as the mother of Jesus but makes no mention of his father. Traditionally, this has been explained by the story told in the Book of Luke, where Jesus is explicitly said to have been conceived by the Holy Spirit. What is clear in Matthew is that his genealogy reflects a radically different perspective from that of patriarchy. Not only are four women ancestors included, but Jesus' female parent is also highlighted and brought into the foreground. Mary, the mother of Jesus, says something vitally important to all women: *women are chosen to bring the Divine into the world.* Her story affirms the feminine power to incarnate the biblical story of salvation.

Matthew is the only Gospel author who recounts a trip to Egypt to save the baby Jesus from Herod's murderous intent. The second chapter of Matthew (verses 13–16) is one of the many examples given in the Gospel of the past paralleling the present; it is a reprise of the Genesis story of Joseph, who rescues his brothers, father, and all the people of Israel by bringing them to Egypt. Matthew also links Herod's murder of the baby boys in the region around Bethlehem with the words found in the Book of Jeremiah: "A cry was heard in Ramah—weeping and great mourning. Rachel weeps for her children, refusing to be comforted, for they are dead" (Jeremiah 31:15 and Matthew 2:18).

The Hebrew word *ramah* refers to a geographical place (a town a few miles from Bethlehem), but it is also a feminine-gendered noun meaning "a high place, an exalted position." If we look at this verse in Matthew within the entire context of Jeremiah (which the Matthew author would have known well), we find that this reference to being cast down from a high place into sorrow and loss comes after verses referring to God's promise to lead and restore the "pregnant woman and she who is labor" (verse 8). They will come "with weeping," Jeremiah writes, but God will lead them by "streams of water" (verse 9). He goes on to use phrases such as these: "They will come and shout for joy on the height," "they will be radiant over the bounty of the Living One," "their life will be like a watered garden, and they will never mourn again" (verse 12), and "young women will dance and be glad, young men and old as well. I will turn their mourning into gladness; I will give them comfort and joy instead of sorrow . . . my people will be filled with my bounty, declares the Living One" (verse 14 NIV). And then verse 15, with its terrible sorrow, is followed by:

> *But now this is what the Living One says:*
> *"Don't cry anymore, for your work will be rewarded.*
> *Your children will come back to you*
> *from the enemy's land.*
> *There is hope for your future.*
> *Your children will come again to their own land.*
> (verse 16, literal translation)

And finally, in verse 35, Jeremiah says that the Living One "provides the sun to light the day and the moon and stars to light the night, and . . . stirs the sea into roaring waves." By looking at the context of a verse that refers to babies' deaths and mothers' grief, we suddenly find ourselves in the territory of Genesis chapter 1, where the Feminine Spirit creates light, broods over the sea, waters the Earth, gives bounty to human beings, comforts those who have suffered injustice and loss, and makes all things good.

Matthew also more explicitly and obviously affirms the feminine by telling us stories about the women who follow Jesus. In chapter 9, a woman with a chronic uterine hemorrhage seeks out Jesus—and is healed. Just as the Feminine Spirit in the Hebrew scriptures always brings wholeness and health to women's wombs, we see here that Jesus reaches out to relieve and restore this woman whose intimate, womanly disorder would have made her "unclean" within the culture of the day. A few chapters later, a Canaanite woman assertively argues with Jesus, persuading him to come heal her daughter (chapter 15). Both these women are powerless, societal outcasts; they are women in trouble. But, Matthew tells us, Jesus comes with good news and healing for "the harassed and the helpless" (9:36 NIV).

In Matthew, we also hear Jesus' own voice expressing his identification with the Feminine Spirit. He says to us, "How often I have wanted to gather your children together as a hen protects her chicks beneath her wings, but you wouldn't let me" (23:37 NLT), and he identifies himself with Woman Wisdom: "The Son of Man came eating and drinking, and they say, 'Behold, a gluttonous man and a drunkard, a friend of tax collectors and sinners!' Yet wisdom is vindicated by her deeds" (11:19 NASB).

Women in Jesus' story step out from the shadows onto center stage.[2] In Matthew's account of the crucifixion, we read that Jesus' women followers are there with him (27:5), and after the resurrection, it is women who are the first to see Jesus (chapter 28). Women's stories are like bookends that contain Matthew's account of Jesus' life: they are biologically present in his genealogy and birth, and they witness his death and resurrection.

NOTE

Who wrote the Book of Matthew? The book itself never gives the author's name, and the words "according to Matthew" were not added until sometime in the second century after Christ. Since the early days of the Church, however, the book has been attributed to the Matthew who was one of Jesus' twelve disciples.

Mark

"The Gospel of Mark proclaims good news: the breaking in of God's kingdom, bringing abundant blessings," writes Joanna Dewey, a professor of biblical studies. She goes on to say:

> The Markan Jesus calls disciples to join this new community, to engage in a discipleship of service to

those with less power and status than themselves, and to endure persecution by political authorities who reject God's rule. Most of all, disciples are called to trust the power of God for good. Women are an integral part of Mark's proclamation of good news.[3]

The Book of Mark repeatedly highlights women's role in the Kingdom of God.

In the very first chapter, we have the story of Peter's mother-in-law (verses 29–31). When Jesus find this woman sick with a fever, he heals her—and she immediately gets up and, in the words of the King James Version, "ministered unto them." The word used here in Greek is *diakoneō*—the same word as "deacon," a role of authority in many Christian churches. Another meaning, according to Strong's concordance, is "caring for the needs of others in an *active, practical* way." This is not to indicate that women are meant to be subservient servants. Instead, Peter's mother-in-law is an active member of Jesus' followers.

Mark tells this story to underline one of his important themes: Jesus' healing empowers us to take action on behalf of others—to minister. Later in this Gospel, Jesus says, "Anyone who wants to be first must be the very last, and the servant of all" (9:35 NIV), and then, "Whoever wants to become great among you must be your servant, and whoever wants to be first must be slave of all. For even the Son of Man did not come to be served, but to serve" (10:43–45 NIV). Peter's mother-in-law, who gets up and "serves" Jesus and the others in her home, is exemplifying Jesus. She is a role model for us all.

Mark's author gives us another example of a Jesus-like individual who is willing to serve in ordinary, body-oriented ways: the woman in Bethany who anoints Jesus' head with perfume. When the people who are present at this event criticize the woman, Jesus says, "I tell you the truth, wherever the Good News is preached throughout the world, this woman's deed will be remembered and discussed" (14:9 NLT). Like Miriam, Deborah, and Huldah, this woman is acting as a prophet, manifesting the truth of Jesus as the Christ, the Messiah, the Anointed One.

In chapter 12, Mark again uses a woman to reveal what God asks of us. This time it is a destitute widow who puts two small coins into the Temple's collection box. Jesus tells his disciples, "I tell you the truth, this poor widow has given more than all the others who are making contributions. For they gave a tiny part of their surplus, but she, poor as she is, has given everything she had to live on" (verses 43–44 NLT). By calling attention to this widow, Jesus ensures that she, like the woman in Bethany, has an identity that will never be forgotten, despite Mark's failure to give us her name. Jesus seems to consciously align himself with the Feminine Spirit we see acting all through the Hebrew scriptures, working in the lives of women who are outcast and in trouble, women with wombs and pain and longings.

NOTE

Like the Gospel of Matthew, the Gospel of Mark was written anonymously, but the early Church attributed the book to a man named John Mark. Although John Mark was not one of Jesus' twelve disciples, he was a disciple of Peter, and the earliest Church writers agreed that he recorded the report given to him by Peter, who was an eyewitness to Jesus' life. Modern scholars mostly agree with this, noting that this Gospel reports events and perspectives that only Peter could have given. Most Bible scholars also agree that Mark was used by the authors of both Matthew and Luke, since more than 90 percent of the content of Mark's Gospel appears in Matthew's and more than 50 percent in the Gospel of Luke (although each Gospel has its own unique perspectives and emphases).

When Jesus mother and brothers ask to speak to him (Mark 3:31–34), instead of rushing out to talk to his family, he looks around the circle of people who have gathered around him and says, "Whoever does

God's will is my brother and sister and mother." As Dewey notes,

> This group explicitly includes women . . . a radical claim in its first-century context. . . . Here Jesus replaces the blood kinship group with the family of God . . . a community of relationships of solidarity rather than hierarchy. This new community is open to women independent of their embeddedness in the social unit of their blood kin, where they owe obedience to father or husband.[4]

In Mark's fifth chapter, the author tells the stories of two more females who encounter Jesus. First, Jesus restores life to a young girl, and then Mark includes the same story that was in Matthew concerning the woman with a uterine hemorrhage. Both these women would have been considered "unclean" by their culture (the girl is thought to be corpse, and the woman is in perpetual state of menstruation), and yet Jesus does not hesitate to touch them. No longer isolated, they are each restored to the community.

These stories are also tied together by the number twelve: the girl is twelve years old, and the woman has been bleeding for twelve years. Twelve is an important number in the Bible. In Genesis, there were twelve sons of Jacob who formed the twelve tribes of Israel. Then, in the Gospels, Jesus chooses twelve apostles. According to the Book of Revelation, the kingdom of God has twelve gates guarded by twelve angels. The biblical meaning of twelve has to do with Divine authority, harmony, inclusiveness, and completion; it also has to do with those who are chosen by God.[5] By weaving this number through stories about two "unclean" females, the Gospel of Mark makes clear that women are chosen by God, with Divine authority bestowed upon them. Despite the ways in which society has attempted to wound, negate, and obliterate these women, they are now specific symbols of inclusion, power, and health.

Furthermore, the woman who was bleeding for twelve years has the courage to break through the societal rules that insist she has to be submissive and isolated: she is the one who initiates contact with Jesus, reaching out to touch him and claim her healing without his permission. Not only does Jesus not scold her for her audacity, but he praises her and calls her "daughter" (verse 34).

The same language that Mark uses to describe the woman's bloody condition is used again to describe Jesus' suffering on the cross. As Hisako Kinukawa points out, "Mark dared to identify the woman's suffering with that of Jesus."[6] How might our understanding of menstruation be transformed if we connected it with the life-giving blood of Jesus—a symbol of rebirth and regeneration and a manifestation of the Feminine Spirit?

In the seventh chapter of Mark, the author tells a story about yet another assertive woman who is not afraid to speak up to Jesus, insisting on her daughter's right to be healed despite the fact that they are not Jewish. Mark uses this story to expand the boundaries of Jesus' kingdom even further, making clear that those who are not Jewish are also included. The community that was at the center of the Hebrew scriptures is still there, but now it focuses on the individual—Jesus—who enters into relationship with other individuals. We see him building a new sense of community, a network of connection, service, and active love, which he calls the Kingdom.

Luke

Luke's account is not as focused on the Hebrew scriptures as Matthew's, and it's not as concise as Mark's or as mystical as John's,[7] but it too highlights the role of women in Jesus' story. Luke may have interviewed eyewitnesses (including, in particular, Mary), as well as compiled other reports that already existed. His account is addressed to "Theophilus"; although some Bible interpreters have believed this to be an actual individual, the word means "friend of God"—which includes the vast panorama of people who have pursued friendship with the Divine, from Abraham and Moses all the way to the present day.

Luke repeatedly uses male-female pairings in his narrative, as well as emphasizing holy paradoxes or surprises, incidents that turn out differently from what we might expect. And so, at the beginning of Luke's account, we have the story of both Elizabeth and her husband Zacharias—and the conception of a child, against all biological odds, whose life will intersect with Jesus'. (The name Elizabeth means "God is abundance," and Zacharias means "remembered by God.") Like Sarah, Elizabeth is barren, and now she is past her childbearing years—and as with Sarah and Abraham, God promises the couple that they will have a child. The angel Gabriel (which means "God is my strength") startles Zacharias with the message that his wife is going to have a son, whom they are to name John (meaning "God—the Living One—is kind").

"Zacharias was shaken and overwhelmed with fear" (Luke 1:12 NLT) when he saw the angel, but the angel tells him to not be afraid. The promised child will be a "joy and delight . . . and many will rejoice at his birth, for he will be great in the sight of the Lord," and "he will turn the hearts of the parents to their children and the disobedient to the wisdom of the righteous—to make a people prepared for the Lord" (1:14,15,17 NIV). The word translated as "Lord" here carries the meaning of "one who has the power of deciding, someone in authority."

Events unfold just as Gabriel promises Zacharias: "Soon afterward his wife, Elizabeth, became pregnant and went into seclusion for five months. 'How kind the Lord is!' she exclaimed. 'He has taken away my disgrace of having no children'" (1:24–25 NLT). This is the first of Luke's holy surprises, a reversal of normal human expectation.

This initial story places Jesus' birth within the setting of an extended human family, for Elizabeth has a cousin named Mary. Luke's next story is about Mary: six months after Elizabeth becomes pregnant, Mary receives surprising news of her own from the angel Gabriel. "Rejoice!" he tells her. "You are favored by the Lord's grace and kindness. The Lord is with you" (1:28, literal translation). The word translated in many versions of the Bible as "grace" comes from a Greek word, *charis*, a feminine-gendered noun that carries the meaning of "leaning toward" or "freely giving oneself away," "extending toward."[8] This is a picture of the Feminine Spirit's constant reaching out to Her unlimited Creation.

A virgin who becomes pregnant is another holy suprise. Understandably, "Mary was greatly troubled at his words and wondered what kind of greeting this might be" (1:29 NIV). But the angel says to her what Elijah said to the widow, what the angel said to Hagar, and what Gabriel said to Zacharias. He says what angels—messengers from God in any form, whether as ideas or as living beings—always say to humans across the centuries: "Fear not."

NOTE

Some modern Bible scholars have speculated that the Greek word used for "virgin" might have actually meant simply a "young woman," while other scholars, down through the centuries, have read into Mary's virginity the implication that sex is sinful, to the point that the holy Child of God could not enter the world through the normal means of conception. Other readings are possible, however. As psychologist and author Sidney Callahan wrote, "Mary's virginity and the virgin birth can be interpreted as symbols of her autonomy, signaling her direct relationship to God, unmediated through any hierarchically placed male, spouse or no. Virginity . . . symbolized integrity, an undivided mind and wholly focused heart."[9] As a virgin, Mary, unlike Eve in the second chapter of Genesis, is free from sexual subjugation—and she needs no man to help her encounter the Divine Spirit in the most intimate of ways.

The angel goes on to tell Mary about her cousin Elizabeth's experience and explains: "The Holy Spirit will come on you, and the power of the Most High will overshadow you. So the holy one to be born will be called the Son of God. . . . For no word from God will ever fail" (verses 35, 37 NIV).

Echoing her ancestors, Ruth and Hannah and Abigail, Mary answers, "Behold the handmaid of the Lord; be it unto me according to thy word" (verse 38 KJV). Phillips has an interesting translation of this verse: "I belong to the Lord, body and soul, let it happen as you say." Mary provides us with a model of what it means to say yes to God, to not only let the Divine intervene in unexpected and extraordinary ways in our lives but to also actively, physically participate in the work of God on Earth.

What Mary does next makes so much sense to us as readers that it seems likely that Luke got this story from Mary herself. She goes to visit her cousin Elizabeth. As soon as Elizabeth greets her cousin, she says, "Blessed is the fruit of your womb." The Greek word used here usually refers to a literal fruit, and Elizabeth's words connect this story to the first chapter of Genesis, when Gods speaks seeds and fruit into being.

Imagine what it must have been like for these two women, speculating together for three months about their pregnancies, their children, their futures, and the potential price to them of these two miraculous conceptions. They must have encouraged each other, supported and protected each other, and mused together on the Spirit of Creation.

During her visit with Elizabeth, Mary praises God with a paraphrase of Hannah's song (1 Samuel 2: 1–11):

> *My soul doth magnify the Lord,*
> *And my spirit hath rejoiced in God my Saviour.*
> *For he hath regarded*
> *the low estate of his handmaiden; . . .*
> *As he spake to our fathers, to Abraham,*
> *and to his seed for ever.*
> (1:46–48,55 KJV)

Here, with Mary's pregnancy, we have the full expression, the complete realization, of what we have read over and over in Scripture: when the Divine Spirit speaks, we see life emerge from seeds and wombs. With her song, often referred to as "The Magnificant," Mary joins the ancient tradition of female singers, from Miriam with her tambourine (Exodus 15:2–21) to Deborah (Judges 5:1–31), as well as Hannah, all of whom sang songs of praise and victory for those who have been oppressed and misunderstood.

"The song of Mary is the oldest Advent hymn," preached Dietrich Bonhoeffer, the German theologian killed by the Nazis. He continued:

It is at once the most passionate, the wildest, one might even say the most revolutionary Advent hymn ever sung. . . . These are the tones of the women prophets of the Old Testament that now come to life in Mary's mouth. Swelling with new life by the power of the Spirit and affirmed by her kinswoman Elizabeth, Mary sings a song that proclaims God's gracious, effective compassion.[10]

When Mary mentions her "low estate" in her song, the Greek term used here implies pain, persecution, suffering, and oppression. As theologian Elizabeth Johnson has reminded us, Mary belongs to the poor and unprivileged because she is a "young, female, a member of a people subjected to economic exploitation by powerful rulers and afflicted by outbreaks of violence." Johnson goes on to write:

What begins as praise for divine lovingkindness toward a marginalized and oppressed woman grows to embrace all the poor of the world. The second part of the Magnificat articulates the great biblical theme of reversal, where lowly groups are defended by God while the arrogant end up losers. . . . [Mary] bursts out of the boundaries of male-defined femininity while still every inch a woman. Singing of her joy in God and God's victory over oppression, she becomes not a subjugated but a prophetic woman.[11]

As Luke continues his account, we have yet another pairing of a woman and a man: when Mary and Joseph take Jesus to be circumcised in the Temple, they encounter Simeon and Anna, two older individuals who have been awaiting the coming of the Messiah, God's Anointed One. Anna, like Huldah, is a prophetess. She is also a widow, who has been on her own for many decades, spending her life in the Temple, actively engaged in Divine service. Both Simeon and Anna affirm Jesus' identity.

So far, Luke's story has kept Mary on center stage. Before he turns his focus away from her, Luke writes that Mary carefully and lovingly kept all the events of Jesus' childhood in her heart (2:52). Earlier, Luke also wrote that Mary "kept close" all that happened and "pondered it in her heart" (2:19). These phrases imply another sort of pregnancy going on within Mary; just as she treasured Jesus within her womb before his birth, keeping him safe while his body developed, now she is lovingly gestating within her heart the meaning of his life.

According to Luke, when Jesus is thirty, he begins his teaching and healing by intentionally linking himself to the prophecy in Isaiah:

> *The Spirit of the Lord is on me,*
> *because he has anointed me*
> *to proclaim good news to the poor.*

He has sent me to proclaim freedom for the prisoners
and recovery of sight for the blind,
to set the oppressed free,
to proclaim the year of the Lord's favor. (61:1–2 NIV)

Luke's account makes clear that Jesus is proclaiming his good news to women as well as men. Stories about men and women alternate in this Gospel; in one story, Jesus heals a man; in the next he heals a woman. Jesus' actions in this Gospel reflect the sixth day of Creation in the first chapter of Genesis, where male and female are equal and in harmony.

Again and again throughout Luke's Gospel, we see Jesus recognizing women's dignity. Contrary to patriarchal expectations, he speaks to women in public. On one occasion, he steps forward in a crowd of mourners to talk with a widow whose son has died (Luke 7:11–17). He publicly affirms a woman known as a "sinner" as a role model of love (Luke 8). He cures a woman who has been physically disabled for eighteen years—and when the religious leaders disapprove of him healing her on the Sabbath, he speaks to her as "daughter of Abraham," a term new to the religion of the day, one that recognizes this woman as having equal standing with the male religious authorities (Luke 13:13–16).

In the Gospels, we meet at least two other Marys besides the mother of Jesus— Mary Magdalen and Mary of Bethany. In Hebrew, the name "Mary" is actually the same as Moses's sister—Miriam. It has various meanings, but one of them has to do with the sea. As in Genesis chapter 1, water is the source of life, and new life enters our world through Mary the mother of Jesus, but also through these other two Marys, whose stories are essential to the Gospels. Each in her own way represents the action of the Feminine Spirit.

We are introduced to Mary of Magdalene in Luke, chapter 8, as well as two other women, Joanna and Suzanna, all of whom minister and follow Jesus. From the time of the early Church until today, Mary Magdalen has had a long history at the hands of commentators and novelists, who have cast her in sexualized roles that range from a prostitute to Jesus' lover or wife. By viewing her through this sexualized lens, the patriarchy discredits and disempowers her spiritual authority, as well as all women's.[12] Historian James Carroll writes that in contrast to the many stories that have arisen around Mary Magdalen, the Gospel itself points to a different reality.

> Jesus' attitude toward women with sexual histories was one of the things that set him apart from other teachers of the time. Not only was Jesus remembered as treating women with respect, as equals in his circle; not only did he refuse to reduce them to their sexuality; Jesus was expressly portrayed as a man who loved women, and whom women loved. . . .

There is every reason to believe that, according to his teaching and in his circle, women were uniquely empowered as fully equal.

As Carroll examines the history of the early Church, he finds that "the emphasis on sexuality as the root of all evil served to subordinate all women. . . . Thus the need to disempower the figure of Mary Magdalene, so that her succeeding sisters in the church would not compete with men for power, meshed with the impulse to discredit women generally."[13] Susan Haskins, author of *Mary Magdalene: Myth and Metaphor*, summarizes the plight of this disciple: Mary of Magdalene, a woman of independence and authority who followed Jesus with courage and power, "became the redeemed whore and Christianity's model of repentance, a manageable, controllable figure, and effective weapon and instrument of propaganda against her own sex."[14]

Then, in Luke 10, we find the story of another Mary—Mary of Bethany and her sister Martha, a story that is usually understood to describe Jesus praising Mary for sitting passively at his feet while her poor sister feels impatient and upset as she frantically prepares the meal alone. Bible teacher Mary Stromer Hanson, however, believes that we have misinterpreted this story. Looking at the original Greek, Hanson finds evidence to indicate that Martha is not rushing around getting a meal on the table, but rather that she is overworked and troubled by her involvement in community ministry—and when she says to Jesus, "Don't you care that my sister has left me to serve alone?" (verse 40), she is referring to Mary following Jesus as a traveling disciple. According to this interpretation, the sisters have indeed chosen separate ways to follow Jesus, but neither woman is confined to the traditional roles of housewife and hostess. Instead, both are active participants in Christ's work.[15] In the Gospel of John, we learn more about these sisters (as well as their brother Lazarus), including the fact that people came to Mary to learn about Jesus (John 11:45).

John

The last of the four Gospels is the most mystical, philosophical, and theological. John not only sees Jesus as a human being and friend; he also is deeply aware of Jesus as the eternal Child of God, present at the Creation of the world and continuing to exist for all Eternity.

NOTE

The Book of John is written anonymously, but it has long been attributed to the John who was one of Jesus' disciples and closest friends. The three epistles of John, as well as the Book of Revelation, are traditionally thought to have been written by the same author. John includes stories in his Gospel that are not in the other three. In his understanding of Jesus' identity, he combines Jewish theology with Greek philosophy, and he emphasizes the role of the individual in the Realm of God, which he describes as an intimate, ongoing relationship with Jesus.

In John, we also read Jesus' own answers to questions about his identity:

- "My Father is working (taking productive action), and so am I." (5:17)

- "I am the living bread come down from heaven." (6:51)

- "Let anyone who is thirsty come to me, and drink." (7:37)

- "Before Abraham came into being, I AM." (8:58)

- "I am the Light of the world." (9:5)

- "I am the door." (10:9)

- "I am the good shepherd. The good shepherd gives his life for his sheep. . . . I know my sheep, and my sheep know me." (10:11,14)

- "I and my Father are one." (10:30)

- "I am the resurrection and the life." (11:25)

- "I am the way, the truth, and the life." (14:6)

- "I am the true vine, and my Father is the farmer (the one who works the soil)." (15:1)

The Gospel of John begins by connecting Jesus' story with Creation:

> *In the beginning was the Word*
> *and the Word was with God,*
> *and the Word was God.* (1:1 KJV)

The word translated "beginning" in Greek is a feminine noun referring to the origins of things, the active cause. In other words, we might say, "At the very birth of the world, was the Word." The "Word" here—from the Greek word *logos*—refers to Jesus, and at the same time, it echoes the words of Genesis, where again and again, "God said."

John goes on to say: "All things came into being through Jesus, and apart from him, nothing came into being" (verse 3), and then, "In Jesus was life, and the life was the Light" (verse 4). Here again we see the light of Creation, the light of Creation's Day One.

John continually uses the imagery of birth throughout his Gospel. "I tell you the truth," Jesus states, "unless you are born again, you cannot see the Kingdom of God. . . . No one can enter the Kingdom of God without being born of water and the Spirit" (3:3,5 NLT). Just as the Spirit brooded over the water during Creation, water is also essential to the new birth Jesus describes.

The term "born again" is especially common in Evangelical churches, but there's no physical image of birth connected to it. In the same way storks were once said to bring babies in order to "protect" children from the shocking truth, there's no mother in the born-again scenario. In the Gospel of John, however, this new birth takes place through the crucifixion. Jesus "labors" on the cross, in the same way a mother labors to give birth to a baby.

Speaking of his coming death, Jesus tells his friends, "Whenever a woman is in labor she has pain, because her hour has come; but when she gives birth to the child, she no longer remembers the anguish because of the joy that a child has been born into the world" (16:21 NASB). At his death, water and blood gush from his body, just as blood and water come out of a mother's womb during birth. In the greatest of holy paradoxes, Jesus—according to John—transforms execution and death into birth and new life.

The birthing imagery in the Gospel of John echoes similar imagery throughout the Hebrew scriptures, starting with Creation in Genesis and reappearing in the Book of Job and in Isaiah, as well as in other places. Theologian Murray Rae sees this as an extension of Creation, writing that "the metaphor of travail thus holds together creation and redemption. The work of redemption is not separate from creation; rather it completes that work by providing the conditions for the new life of communion with God."[16]

Christianity has long focused on the death of Christ on the cross, encouraging us to "crucify" our own sinful natures. But what if in addition to identifying with Jesus' death, we also identified with his labor of love on the cross? What might it mean if our lives became pregnant with life, prepared to be broken open in the creative act of birth?

Although it may seem odd to us to think of the male Jesus as a mother, Jesus in the Gospel accounts sees past gender roles. In the Gospel of Matthew (and also in Luke), Jesus compares himself to a mother hen gathering her chicks around her to protect them, and in John, we see Jesus accepting for himself what have often been perceived as women's roles: caring for his friends' physical bodies by washing their feet (13:1–6), serving his friends breakfast (21:1–14), feeding large groups of people (6:1–15), acting as a hostess who prepares and welcomes others into her home (John 14:2), and again and again speaking of himself in terms of abundant sustenance and nurturing (2:1–11; 6:32–58; and see Mark 14:22).

Like the other Gospels, John also includes stories of Jesus' interactions with women. Jesus discusses theology with a Samaritan woman and sends her as his emissary to her people (4:4–42); he refuses to condemn a woman caught in the act of adultery (8:1–11); he talks to Martha and Mary as intimate friends (11:1–44); he makes sure his mother will be cared for when he is no longer there to do so (19:26–27); and after his resurrection from the dead, he appears first to Mary Magdalen and gives her the commission of telling the other disciples.

The Gospel of John also speaks of weddings, both actual and metaphoric. The first mention of this is the wedding at Cana in chapter 2, where Jesus turns water into wine, another echo of the Spirit that moved on the waters at Creation. When Jesus transforms the ordinary water into the finest wine, it's more than a magic trick; it points to the water that is the essential element of Creation and then, through the symbol of wine, underlines the ways in which God and humans can cooperate in Creation. John's account may also be understood to mean that a more spiritual understanding of Creation—as the union of male and female—is taking place at a very traditional, very human wedding.

In the next chapter, John the Baptist refers to Jesus as the "bridegroom" (3:29), and this imagery is another strand that runs through John's symbolism. It connects Jesus to similar metaphors in the Hebrew scriptures (for example, Isaiah 62:5), while at the same time it draws us toward Revelation 21:2, where the Holy City is adorned as a "bride for her husband."

But first, before that culminating moment of union, the Good News must be carried out into the world. In rest of the New Testament, we will read the story of how the Gospel spreads beyond Jesus' immediate circle of friends to the entire world, until it eventually includes the entire universe and infinity.

REFERENCE NOTES

1. Jesus—or Joshua, in Hebrew—means "savior," and Christ means "anointed one" or the "chosen one." The Messiah is another word with the same meaning.

2. Women are clearly visible in all four Gospels—but it would be a mistake to believe that their authors espoused an early version of feminism. Their patriarchal attitudes are also evident, as feminist Bible scholars have often pointed out. However, the Feminine Spirit manages to slip through the cracks, telling Her story through the lives of women in the Gospels, just as She did in the Hebrew scriptures.

3. Joanna Dewey. "Women in the Gospel of Mark," *Word & World* 26(1) Winter 2006, page 22.

4. Ibid., page 23.

5. Del Washburn. *The Original Code in the Bible: Using Science and Mathematics to Reveal God's Fingerprints* (Lanham, MD: Rowman & Littlefield, 1998), page 212.

6. Hisako Kinukawa. *Women and Jesus in Mark: A Japanese Feminist Perspective* (Maryknoll, NY: Orbis, 1994), page 34.

7. Since Luke also wrote the Book of Acts, the sheer quantity of his words is greater than any of the other Gospel authors and even rivals the volume of writing attributed to the Apostle Paul. Luke's Gospel includes more stories about Jesus than the other Gospels, and where the same stories occur in other Gospels, Luke's version is more detailed; some parables only show up in Luke (like the

Good Samaritan and the Prodigal Son).

8. HELPS-Word-studies, Helps Ministries, Inc., © 1987, 2011, https://biblehub.com/greek/5485.htm.

9. Sidney Callahan. "Mary and the Feminist Movement," *America*, December 18, 1993, https://www.americamagazine.org/issue/100/mary-and-feminist-movement.

10. Dietrich Bonhoeffer. *Dietrich Bonhoeffer's Christmas Sermons* (Grand Rapids, MI: Zondervan, 2011), December 17, 1933 entry.

11. Elizabeth Johnson. "Mary, Mary, Quite Contrary," *U.S. Catholic* 68(12) December 2003: 12

12. Duke University Bible scholar Elizabeth Schrader has found evidence in some of the earliest Gospel manuscripts indicating that the role of Mary Magdalen was downplayed by scribes scratching out her name and writing other names instead. Doing this diluted and distorted Mary's original role by making her merely one of many women interacting with Jesus, as opposed to her being a prominent and authoritative figure. (Eric Ferreri, "A Duke Scholar's Research Finds Mary Magdalene Downplayed by New Testament Scribes," *Duke Today,* June 18, 2019, https://today.duke.edu/2019/06/mary-or-martha-duke-scholars-research-finds-mary-magdalene-downplayed-new-testament-scribes.)

13. James Carroll. "Who Was Mary Magdalene?" *Smithsonian* June 2006, https://www.smithsonianmag.com/history/who-was-mary-magdalene-119565482/.

14. Susan Haskins. *Mary Magdalene: Myth and Metaphor* (New York: Riverhead, 1995), page 94.

15. Mary Stromer Hanson. "Mary of Bethany: Her Leadership Uncovered?," paper presented at Society of Biblical Languages conference, "Maria, Mariamne, Miriam: Rediscovering the Marys," November 22, 2015, Atlanta, Georgia, https://stromerhanson.blogspot.com/2015/11/mary-of-bethany-her-leadership-uncovered.html.

16. Murray Rae. "The Travail of God," *International Journal of Systematic Theology* 5(2003): 47–61.

FOURTEEN

SPREADING THE WORD

And I intreat thee also, true yokefellow, help
those women which labored with me in the
gospel ··· whose names are in the books of life.

–*Philippians 4:3 KJV*

The story that was begun in the Gospels continues in
the Book of Acts and then in the Epistles (the letters
and reports) that follow. This portion of the New Testament discusses the teachings and person of Jesus, as well
as events in first-century Christianity, with numerous

references to the Hebrew scriptures. The Feminine Spirit of God continues to manifest Herself, woven into the ideas and stories of the earliest followers of Jesus.

Acts

Luke wrote the Book of Acts, and like the Gospel that bears his name, he addresses his account to Theophilus—friend of God (Acts 1:1). Luke explains that while in his first book he wrote about all that "Jesus began to do and teach," in this book he will resume his story with how women and men, with the help of the Holy Spirit, carried on with Jesus' work.

NOTE

There are eighty-nine references to the Holy Spirit in the New Testament, and nearly half are in the Book of Acts. The first reference in the New Testament is in Matthew 1:18, when the Spirit fills Mary's womb with Jesus.

The story begins after the Resurrection, while Jesus is on earth teaching his followers. Luke records that although the apostles are still hoping for a political leader who will restore Israel's independence, Jesus makes clear to them that this is not his agenda. Instead, he promises that when he is gone, the Holy Spirit will come to them. Then, according to Luke's account, Jesus is lifted up into a cloud. The Greek word used here for "cloud" is a feminine one, and it may be a reference to the same cloud mentioned in the Hebrew scriptures that led the Israelites to the Promised Land. Much of Acts is interwoven with texts from Exodus.

NOTE

Today, when we hear the word "cloud," many of us think of a network of Internet servers, which store data. Metaphorically speaking, the words "cloud" and "cloudy" often have a negative connotation, indicating confusion or sadness. In the Bible, however, clouds indicate the revelation and presence of God, perhaps specifically the Feminine Spirit. The first time the word occurs in the Hebrew scriptures is after the Flood, when God says, "I set my bow in the clouds" (Genesis 9:13). In the Book of Exodus, Moses receives the Ten Commandments from within a cloud on Mount Sinai, and then a "pillar of cloud" guides the Israelites by day through the desert. In the Book of Job, the main character refers to a feminine cloud, while the Voice talks about masculine-gendered clouds in relation to Creation. In the Gospels, as Jesus has a conversation with Moses and Elijah, they are covered with a cloud. On several other occasions throughout the New Testament, clouds are mentioned in connection with Jesus' return to earth.

After Jesus is gone, Mary, the mother of Jesus, in the first recorded meeting of what was to become the Christian Church, meets together with about 120 women and men (the presence of women is specifically mentioned). The people at this meeting include those who have seen and talked with Jesus during the forty days after the Crucifixion. They take care of a practical item first, voting to replace Judas Iscariot, the disciple who betrayed Jesus and then committed suicide, with another man, Matthias. This way there will still be twelve disciples, just as there were twelve tribes of Israel.

In this meeting, there are no disputes over theology. No separation of one group from the others. The men don't gather in one part of the house, while the woman are in another. The scripture specifically states that they are all together.

Later, as the group continues to gather (probably in someone's home), the Holy Spirit comes to them: "Suddenly there came from the [masculine] sky a roaring, exactly like a [feminine] wind [or spirit] that bears, delivers, brings forth" (Acts 2:2, literal translation). According to Luke's account, the crowd gathered there does not see the human form of Jesus, but a "tongue" of flame settles on each one of them. "They were all made complete and full by the Holy Wind and began to speak in other languages, as the Wind gave them speech" (2:4, literal translation).

A Jewish festival is going on, and Greek, Egyptian, and Persian Jews have gathered in Jerusalem to celebrate the holy day. In a reversal of the story of the Tower of Babel in Genesis 11, where language was confounded and dispersed into confusion, here all the visitors to the city understand their own language being spoken, despite the fact that Jesus' followers speak Aramaic. This incident, referred to as the Day of Pentecost, makes the point that we are all one. The language of the Spirit communicates without regard to nationality.

NOTE

In the third century, Church leaders defined the Holy Spirit as the Third Person of the Trinity. Many Christian denominations continue to think along the same lines, even though the word "trinity" is never used in the Bible. However, the Father, Jesus, and the Spirit are mentioned as different aspects of the One—the Living One. In 1 John 5:7, the King James Version states that "there are three that bear record in heaven, the Father, the Word, and the Holy Ghost: and these three are one." However, these words were apparently added by people copying the scriptures at some point over the centuries. In the original version, John writes, "I AM three that bear witness—the Spirit (or breath or wind), the water, the blood—all three in agreement." This has been interpreted by some Bible scholars to be a reference to Pentecost, the baptism of Christ, and the Crucifixion. It might also be understood to be a reference to the water and blood of birth, as the Living One "births" us into the breath of life, through the Feminine Spirit.

Some of the people who hear Jesus' followers talking, however, can't make sense of their words, so they laugh and accuse the group of being drunk. Peter stands up and answers them:

These people are not drunk, as you suppose. It's only nine in the morning! No, this is what was spoken by the prophet Joel: "In the last days, God says, I will pour out my Spirit on all people. Your sons and daughters will prophesy, your young men will see visions, your old men will dream dreams. Even on my servants, both men and women, I will pour out my Spirit in those days, and they will prophesy. . . . And everyone who calls on the name of the Lord will be saved." (Acts 2:15–18,21 NIV)

Peter is quoting a passage from the Hebrew scriptures (Joel 2:28–32), where women are specifically included.

As Luke continues his account, women continue to be essential players in the history of Jesus Christ's followers. Included in the list are:

- Tabitha (or Dorcas), a disciple who dies and is brought back to life by Peter (Acts 9:32–41).

- Rhoda, a young girl, probably Greek, who is a servant in the house of Mary, the mother of Mark. Rhoda hears Peter knocking on the door after his miraculous escape from prison. She is so excited that she runs to tell the others in the house and forgets to open the door for Peter. They laugh at her and accuse her of being crazy, but eventually, they see that Peter is indeed there (Acts 12).

- Lydia, a well-to-do Greek woman with a business that makes purple dye, who is considered to be the first European convert to Christ (Acts 16).

- Damaris, a woman of Athens who may have been a high-status prostitute or a member of the Stoics (which would make her a philosopher), who decides to follow Jesus after listening to a sermon given by the Apostle Paul (Acts 17).

- Priscilla, a Jewish woman, married to Aquila, who is a tentmaker (Acts 18). She and her husband are Paul's friends, and she is considered to be one of the Church's early teachers. Starting at the beginning of the twentieth century, some Bible scholars have suggested that Priscilla might be the author of the Book of Hebrews (which comes later in the New Testament).[1]

The Book of Acts also tells the story of Saul, a fervent fundamentalist Jew who is enraged by the growing group of Jesus' followers. He goes into private homes and drags women and men off to prison (Acts 8:1–2); he also tortures them and puts them to death. But then Saul is transformed. On the way to Damascus, where he plans to capture more of Jesus' followers, he is blinded by a sudden light and hears a voice asking him, "Saul, Saul, why are you persecuting me?" When Saul inquires who is speaking, the voice answers, "I am Jesus who you are persecuting." The voice implies that the women and men Saul has been mistreating are not merely followers of Jesus; they *are* Jesus, both together and individually.

NOTE

Damascus is a city in modern-day Syria, about 135 miles northeast of Jerusalem. The name, which is feminine, means "silent is the sackcloth weaver." In the Bible, sackcloth symbolizes mourning and repentance—so it's interesting that Saul, that most patriarchal and outspoken religious leader, is on his way to a feminine place of silence and repentance.

After his encounter with Jesus on the road to Damascus, Saul becomes Paul, one of the most prominent leaders of the early Church. Still a fiery and passionate man, he now brings that enthusiasm and energy to teaching others about Jesus the Christ. We get a sense of who he is through his "epistles," letters written to the new Christ-communities in various cities, and these now compose a large part of the remaining books in the New Testament.

NOTE

Paul was originally thought to have written thirteen of the epistles included in the New Testament, but today many scholars believe his disciples may have written some of those. It seems definite that Paul wrote the first epistle to the Thessalonians, the epistle to the Galatians, both epistles to the Corinthians, and the epistles to Philemon, Philippians, and Romans. The epistles to the Ephesians and the Colossians, as well as the second epistle to the Thessalonians, may have been written by Paul. The two epistles to Timothy and the epistle to Titus are generally no longer believed to have been written by Paul himself but rather by an unknown author or authors writing fifty or more years later. Finally, the author of Hebrews is now considered to also be unknown. In 1900, Adolf von Harnack, a Lutheran theologian and historian, advanced the idea that Priscilla was a logical candidate for Hebrew's authorship, since she was an intimate associate of Paul and Timothy, and the early Church might have blotted out her name because she was a women. Several modern scholars support this idea.

Paul (and/or his followers) was not the only one to write letters that were circulated through the early Church. The New Testament also contains three epistles attributed to John, one of the twelve disciples, who also wrote one of the Gospels; two epistles written by Peter, another of the twelve disciples; one epistle written by James, who may have been the biological brother of Jesus; and one very short epistle by Jude, who describes himself as "a servant of Jesus Christ and the brother of James."

The Epistles

Verses from several of Paul's epistles have been particularly troublesome to women. Translated and pulled out of their context, these verses have been used to support patriarchy by insisting that women must be submissive, thus subverting the message of Jesus Christ and the Bible as a whole. Today, some women have a violent reaction to even the mention of Paul's name, while others say that to question him would be heresy. Still others, however, have found new meanings in his original words.

When we read the overall content of Paul's letters (rather than pulling out verses here and there), we find him interacting again and again with women as equal partners in the work of Jesus Christ. Paul speaks of women as friends and indicates that they hold positions of active authority in the young Church. He refers to them teaching, prophesying, and praying. Furthermore, if we take a new look at some of Paul's most troublesome passages, we find that he is following in Jesus' footsteps, presenting a radical new way of living where female and male are equal.

The following passage, however, is one of those that can make the skin crawl:

The women are to keep silent in the churches; for they are not permitted to speak, but are to subject themselves, just as the Law also says. If they desire to learn anything, let them ask their own husbands at home; for it is improper for a woman to speak in church. (1 Corinthians 14:34–35 NASB)

As Bible scholars have studied these verses, they've found several clues that indicate Paul did not write them after all; instead, they were added later. The first clue is that in several ancient manuscripts, this paragraph is placed at the very end of the chapter (after what is now verse 40), rather than where it is located in current translations, as though it were a note or an addendum written there by male scribes or Bible interpreters in the years after Paul wrote the epistle. Another clue is that the injunction for women to "keep silent in the churches" directly contradicts Paul's words earlier in this same epistle, when he gives women directions for how they should prophesy and pray in public settings (1 Corinthians 11:4–5). And finally, nowhere else does Paul appeal to "the churches" and "the Law" as a standard of behavior. In fact, in his epistle to the Galatians, he states, "The law was our guardian until Christ came; it protected us until we could be made right with God through faith. And now that the way of faith has come, we no longer need the law as our guardian" (3:24–35 NLT).

In chapter 11 of this same epistle, Paul has a lot to say about "heads." He writes:

> *But I want you to understand that Christ is the head of every man, and the man is the head of a woman, and God is the head of Christ. . . . For man does not originate from woman, but woman from man; for indeed man was not created for the woman's sake, but woman for the man's sake.* (1 Corinthians 11:3,8 NASB)

For centuries, churches have taught that these verses make clear that men have authority over women. Once again, though, we need to take a closer look.

In our culture, we think of a "head" as a position of authority; a head has power over the rest of the organism or community. We're aware that the head (or the brain) governs the body, and so the head of the government would be the president or prime minister, the head of a company would be the CEO, and so on. However, Paul and the rest of his culture did not understand the word in the same way we do today. For one thing, in Paul's day the heart was considered to be the organ that controlled the body, not the head or brain. In other passages, Paul clearly indicates that he sees the heart as that which commands the rest of the body. In addition, the Greek word used here (feminine in gender) could also mean "source" (as in, the head of a river), or simply that which comes first. So if we insert the word "source" into this passage, we have "Christ is the source of every man, and the man is the source of a woman, and God is the source of Christ." This then would refer to the second Genesis account, where the man (Adam) is created first, and then the woman is removed from his side. The verses that follow indicate that this is indeed the correct interpretation:

However, in the Lord, neither is woman independent of man, nor is man independent of woman. For as the woman originates from the man, so also the man has his birth through the woman; and all things originate from God. (11:11,12 NASB)

Another place where Paul seems to indicate women should be submissive to men is found in his epistle to the Ephesians. The King James Version is worded like this:

Wives, submit yourselves unto your own husbands, as unto the Lord. For the husband is the head of the wife, even as Christ is the head of the church: and he is the saviour of the body. Therefore as the church is subject unto Christ, so let the wives be to their own husbands in every thing. (Ephesians 5:22–24).

Using this translation taken out of context, Paul's message to women seems pretty clear. However, here's an alternative, literal translation of these verses:

Wives, be with your own personal husband, separate from all other men. For a man was the source of the woman, as Christ is also the source of the church, he himself being a deliverer of the body.

Furthermore, the men who have quoted this verse from the King James Version often failed to keep reading the verses that come next. In the next verses, Paul writes:

Husbands, love your wives, even as Christ also loved the church, and gave himself for it. . . . So ought men to love their wives as their own bodies. He that loveth his wife loveth himself. For no man ever yet hated his own flesh; but nourisheth and cherisheth it, even as the Lord the church: For we are members of his body, of his flesh, and of his bones. For this cause shall a man leave his father and mother, and shall be joined unto his wife, and they two shall be one flesh . . . let every one of you in particular so love his wife even as himself; and the wife see that she reverence her husband. (5:25,28–31,33 KJV)

Paul is indicating here that the relationship between a woman and man should be one of equal love and respect, under Christ. And this applies not only to the relationships between men and women but to all relationships. "Submit to one another out of reverence for Christ" (verse 21 NIV), Paul writes, echoing Jesus' invitation to us to serve each other (see Mark 10: 42–45).

In verse 32 of this passage, Paul refers to marriage as a "deep, startling, and enormous mystery concerning those who belong to the Lord" (literal translation of the Greek words). Here Paul sees beyond physical marriage, and we catch a glimpse of the spiritual metaphor used in Song of Songs and then again in Revelation, where we are all the bride and God is our husband. A mystery is something that's not easy to understand, a paradox or seeming contradiction. In the Bible, it refers to something that's ordinarily unknowable to human beings, which can be understood only through Divine revelation. In this case, Paul indicates, the marriage of human beings is the embodiment of a profound Divine mystery contained within the meaning of Christ.

Paul also makes use of birth imagery. In his sermon at Athens, he uses words that imply we are in the womb of God: "In God we live, move, and have our being. . . . We are God's offspring" (Acts 17:28). Throughout Paul's epistles, he speaks again and again of the "new creation" (feminine gendered) that is ours through Jesus—and with this imagery, the text connects both Jesus and our present-day lives to the first Genesis account.

And so we can say that Paul had dazzling bursts of clarity. We also have to recognize that there were times when he, like the authors of the Gospels, like so many of us, could not completely free himself from patriarchal assumptions—but he admits that he's still learning.

> *Not that I have already reached the goal or am already fully mature, but I make every effort to take hold of it because I also have been taken hold of by Christ Jesus. . . . I do not consider myself to have taken hold of it. But one thing I do: Forgetting what is behind and reaching forward to what is ahead, I pursue as my goal the prize promised by God's heavenly call in Christ Jesus.*
> (Philippians 3:12–14 HCSB)

Peter, one of the twelve disciples, also wrote two epistles that are included in the New Testament. He is the author of another passage that has been used to biblically support women's inferiority and subjection:

> *Wives, in the same way submit yourselves to your own husbands. . . like Sarah, who obeyed Abraham and called him her lord. You are her daughters if*

you do what is right and do not give way to fear.
(1 Peter 3:1,6)

If you recall, God told Abraham to do whatever Sarah told him to do—so again, these verses are often read out of context, with little attention paid to Peter's entire message. The primary theme of his letter is to encourage readers to transform unjust social systems from within, with gentleness and submission, rather than with violence and open rebellion. He begins by referring to his readers' new relationship with Christ, "known before the [feminine-gendered] conception of the world but finally made visible for your sakes" (1 Peter 1:20, literal translation). He instructs the recipients of his letter:

> *Have sincere love for each other, love one another deeply, from the heart. For you have been born again, not of perishable seed, but of imperishable, through the living and enduring word of God* (1 Peter 1:22–23 NIV)

Notice Peter's references to the now-familiar territory of feminine Creation.

Having clarified what he means by the "word of God," Peter goes on to address the topics of unfair governmental authorities and cruel slave owners—and then husbands who do not understand the "word" he defined earlier. He is not presenting a hierarchical marriage relationship as the normative ideal; instead, he's including it with other unjust social systems. When he says that women should be like Sarah, the reference to the Hebrew text indicates that Peter's women readers, like Sarah, should be able to make decisions for themselves, despite the patriarchy of their culture.

Another verse in this epistle has been used to "prove" that women are "weak":

Husbands, in the same way be considerate as you live with your wives, and treat them with respect as the weaker partner and as heirs with you of the gracious gift of life. (3:7 NIV)

Again, reading this in context, the "weaker partner" is the one who does not understand God's "word"—the loving, creative, life-birthing action of the Feminine Spirit. This means that the weaker partner in chapter 3, verse 1, would in that case be the man. "Weakness" is not the result of gender but is caused by a lack of understanding.[2]

If we take a look at the original word that has traditionally been written in English as "weaker," we can go even a step further. This is the only instance in the New Testament where the Greek word used here, *poieó*, has been translated as having anything to do with weakness. In all other cases, it has to do with something that is being made, formed, accomplished, something that is becoming. So the implication is that those who don't yet understand the "word" are not weak so much as they are still growing, still evolving and developing—and yet at the same time, Peter affirms that these individuals are to be valued and respected as "co-inheritors who share in the grace of life" (literal translation of the final phrase in verse 7).

From the Gospel accounts and the Book of Acts, we know Peter as an often impulsive and outspoken individual. Initially, he and Paul are in conflict. Peter believes that Jesus' message is for the Jews only, while Paul insists that the Good News is for everyone. Later, due to a dream, Peter changes his mind.

We can see in the lives of both these men an evolving understanding of the Living One. The Bible does not portray them as static saints, unchanging in their perfection. Like all human beings, they have their own past histories, lived out in the midst of the values and traditions of their time and place. Each of us—including the individuals who wrote the biblical epistles—are at different states and stages of progress.

At the same time, says the Bible, the full and complete idea of who you are as God created you to be is already established. We need not fear growth or change, for it only leads us closer to our truest identities. As

Habakkuk 2:14 says, one day "the earth shall be filled with the knowledge of the glory of the Lord, as the waters cover the sea"—the whole Earth will finally acknowledge and experience spiritual Creation.

Creation is an open-ended, progressive process—and yet the Church has traditionally looked at these letters, written to specific communities or individuals regarding their unique circumstances, and pronounced them to be the last word throughout Eternity. The inconsistencies that we see in the epistles, however, force us to see their authors as human beings on their own trajectories of growth, rather than as perfected saints. The authors themselves give us no indication that they expected their writings to be considered "inerrant."[3] As Bible scholar F. F. Bruce has written, "Paul would roll over in his grave if he knew we were turning his letters into Torah."[4] Along the same lines, author Rachel Held Evans has pointed out:

> In our rush to find proof texts to support our various positions, we tend to skip past the initial greetings that designate the recipients of the message—*"to the church of God in Corinth," "to the churches in Galatia," "to God's holy people in Ephesus," "to Timothy," "to Titus"*—or those odd little details that remind us that we are essentially listening in on someone else's conversation. . . . *The epistles were never meant to be interpreted and applied as universal*

law. Rather, they provide us with an instructive and inspired glimpse into how Jesus' teachings were lived out by real people, in *real* communities, facing *real* challenges.[5]

NOTE

A verse in 1 Timothy has also been used to support women's subjugation: "I do not permit a woman to teach or to assume authority over a man; she must be quiet" (2:12 NIV). Current experts in ancient Greek suggest that the word "authority" would be better translated as "the misuse of authority," indicating that women did have authority but that they were not to abuse it. In all other instances where the word authentein occurs in ancient Greek, it refers to those who committed violent crimes, including murder and self-destruction.[6] Here again we do not know the specific situation being addressed in this letter to Timothy, but the words are certainly not intended to apply to all women.

As Rachel Held Evans notes, "It is not the details found in the letters that we should seek to imitate, but rather the attitudes."[7] And so, let's pay close attention to the attitude expressed in these verses from the New Testament's epistles:

So in Christ Jesus you are all children of God through faith. . . . There is neither Jew nor Gentile, neither slave nor free, nor is there male and female, for you are all one in Christ Jesus. If you belong to Christ, then you are Abraham's seed, and heirs according to the promise. (Paul's Epistle to the Galatians 3:26,28,29 NIV).

If you really keep the royal law found in Scripture, "Love your neighbor as yourself," you are doing right. (Epistle of James 2:8 NIV)

Most important of all, continue to show deep love for each other, for love covers a multitude of sins. (1 Peter 4:8 NLT)

Let us think of ways to motivate one another to acts of love and good works. (Epistle to the Hebrews 10:24 NLT)

Verses like these clearly indicate the overarching nature of God's "word."

John, in his three short letters, further communicates the same message. In his writing, John, ever the mystic, focuses on what it means to be "born of God"—birthed into being by the Divine—and then defines the nature and importance of love. Finally, he boils all theology down to these two concise statements: "God is love. Whoever lives in love lives in God, and God in them" (1 John 4:16 NIV). This is a summation of the biblical message. It's that simple.

John's second letter (which is only a few paragraphs long, as is his third letter) is addressed to the "chosen lady and her children" (2 John 1:1 NLT). The historically minded have speculated who this woman might have been. In the early years of Christianity, "church" consisted of people gathering together in people's homes, and the leaders of these groups would often have been women. John may have had another, more mystical meaning in mind as well. Perhaps he is speaking to the woman we will meet in the final book of the Bible, Revelations. Or John may be seeing through time to address a still-unknown woman. While the Bible makes some truths definite, other things are left open ended.

The last epistle of the New Testament is Jude's. In his short letter, he starts with Jesus and the abundance of mercy, peace, and love, and then he looks backward in time, reminding us of names and events from the Hebrew scriptures: Adam, Enoch, Egypt, Sodom and Gomorrah, and others. Finally, before we read the Bible's final conflict and resolution, Jude gives us this affirmation:

To him who is able to keep you from stumbling and to present you before his glorious presence without fault and with great joy—to the only God our Savior be glory, majesty, power and authority, through Jesus Christ our Lord, before all ages, now and forevermore! Amen. (verses 24,25 NIV)

REFERENCE NOTES

1. In Ruth Hoppin's book *Priscilla's Letter: Finding the Author of the Epistle to the Hebrews* (Fort Bragg, CA: Lost Coast Press, 2009), she builds a compelling case that the author of the Epistle to the Hebrews was indeed Priscilla. Hoppins maintains that Priscilla "meets every qualification, matches every clue, and looms ubiquitous in every line of investigation," and suggests that the feminine pronoun may have been later altered by a scribe, or that the author deliberately used a neutral pronoun as "a kind of abstraction."

2. We might also keep in mind the perspective that Paul wrote: God's power is "made perfect" in weakness (2 Corinthian 12:9).

3. The "inerrancy" of Scripture is a theological concept that is important to many branches of the modern Christian church. According to this belief, the Bible is without errors. The belief is based on Bible verses such as Isaiah 40:8, "The word of our God stands forever" (NASB); Matthew 24:35, where Jesus says, "Heaven and earth will pass away, but My words will not pass away" (NASB); and 2 Timothy 3:16, "All Scripture is God-breathed and is useful for teaching, rebuking, correcting and training in righteousness" (NIV). However, the authors of these statements nowhere define God's "word" as the Bible we know today. In fact, in some places they clearly define the "word" as meaning something

quite different. New Testament authors were generally referring to the message and person of Jesus. They did not consider their own writing to be "scripture," which would have meant to them the Hebrew writings now contained in Christians' "Old Testament." Not until the late fourth century, three hundred-some years after Luke, Paul, and all the others were writing, did the Church officially add the New Testament's twenty-seven books to our understanding of what is included in the Bible.

4. F. F. Bruce. *The Message of the New Testament* (Grand Rapids, MI: Eerdmans, 1973), page 85.

5. Rachel Held Evans. "For the Sake of the Gospel, Let Women Speak," Rachel Held Evans' blogpost, June 7, 2012, https://rachelheldevans.com/blog/mutuality-let-women-speak.

6. For more on this, see J. K. Gayle's "Authentein: Paul & Timothy Reading the LXX," June 7, 2015, https://bltnotjustasandwich.com/2015/06/07/authentein-paul-timothy-reading-the-lxx/.

7. Evans, ibid.

FIFTEEN

THE SPIRIT AND THE BRIDE

The woman whom you saw is the great city,
which reigns over the kings of the earth.

–*Revelation 17:18* NASB

The Book of Revelation is perhaps the most mysterious book in the Bible. It has been interpreted in a variety of ways—as literal prophecy about a great battle that destroys the Earth and all its inhabitants, as a symbolic description of events that took place in the first-century Roman world, and as an allegory of the archetypal struggle between good and evil.[1] Many of us may be most familiar with the idea that Revelation is a blueprint for the imminent end of the known world.

But what if we were to tighten the focus of the Book of Revelation, away from an immense political and universal diorama, to an intimate look at the struggle for personal spiritual consciousness—*your* spiritual consciousness?

NOTE

The author of Revelation names himself as "John." For many centuries, most Bible scholars believed him to be John the Apostle, one of Jesus' twelve disciples, and they also attributed the Gospel of John to him, as well as the three epistles that bear his name. Modern Bible scholars question whether this assumption is justified—but no one knows for sure. Because of the mystery surrounding Revelation's authorship, it was not officially accepted as scripture until the very end of the fourth century, making it the last book to be added to the "canon" of the New Testament.

Remember, the Bible is the most self-referential of books. It says of itself that it speaks to all people who read or hear it. The Book reveals itself. So if at first glance the symbolism in Revelation seems obscure and overwhelming, we may want to look more deeply. When we do, we might find that the bizarre and graphic imagery can be applied to our own hearts and lives. It mirrors the struggle we each experience to accept individual spiritual revelation and to put that revelation into daily practice.

The book opens with these words:

This is the [feminine] unveiling, the disclosure, the manifestation of Jesus the Chosen One, who God sent to show us, the servants of the Divine, what must immediately come into being, a communication sent by angel to John, a servant. (Revelation 1:1, literal translation)

Note that the revelation—the unveiling of Jesus—is addressed to all servants of God, without limitation as to time or place. This is a book with immediate meaning for all people for all time.

Later in Revelation (22:18–19), there's a stern warning to neither add to nor subtract from the words of this book; the book must be read not selectively but as a whole. Summaries and commentaries alone will not do justice to the force, power, and message of Revelation. Still, with so many scholarly interpretations of Revelation out there, it may seem presumptuous to seek our own meanings.

NOTE

*John's injunction to neither add nor subtract from "this book"
has often been understood to apply to the entire Bible, with
the implication that Revelation concludes the Word of God.
However, when John wrote the Book of Revelation in the final
years of the first century, he was not writing the concluding
pages of the New Testament, since there was no New Testament in existence at that time. His manuscript was entirely
independent of the other twenty-six separate manuscripts
that later came to form the anthology that we know as the
New Testament. Furthermore, Revelation was written around
95 CE, and several other New Testament books were written
after that date. It's likely then, that when John spoke of "this
book," he was referring only to the Book of Revelation.*

Given the nature of Revelation, the best thing you
can do is to read it for yourself and see what it says
to you. For now, as Isaiah says, "Come to the waters"
(55:1)—the same waters on which the Spirit moved in
the first chapter of Genesis. Let's plunge in and see
how and where we find the Feminine Spirit in this final
book of the Bible.

Salutation

John starts his book with a greeting to the "seven
churches of Asia" (Revelation 1:4). Many Bible inter-

preters have believed that John was writing to seven actual churches, in the way that Paul, in his epistles, wrote to the churches at Corinth, Ephesus, and so on. However, there were no known churches at some of the cities that John lists, and it seems more likely that right from the start, John is telling a story that's hidden within metaphors, images, and symbols.

When we hear the word "church," we may imagine a building where Christians gather for religious services. We might also think of the word in terms of a larger organizational structure, as in the "Methodist Church," the "Catholic Church," and so on. But neither of these meanings would have been in John's mind as he wrote his book. The Greek word he uses—*ekklesia*—is a feminine-gendered noun referring to a gathering of people who have been "called out from." In this sense, the word is not limited to any specific location or place; instead, it applies to all of us. Like Moses who was called out from the waters as a baby (Exodus 2:10), we too have been called into life by the Spirit.

The number seven figures prominently throughout the book of Revelation. It has also occurred again and again throughout the entire Bible, starting with Creation, when God rested on the seventh day and hallowed it (Genesis 2:2,3). Seven is a biblical symbol of both perfection and rest. It implies a sense of abundance and completion (see Matthew 18:22). So now we add that meaning to our understanding of *ekklesia*.

John says that this complete and abundant gathering is from Asia, which again seems to thumbtack his message to a specific spot on the map. Asia was a province in the Roman Empire (the name did not yet refer to a continent), but let's assume that every word and image in Revelation contains layers of meaning. In that case, when we look at the meaning of "Asia," we find that it is a feminine word referring to the sunrise. In the book of Luke, Zechariah speaks of Jesus as the "sunrise": "whereby the sunrise shall visit us from on high to give light to those who sit in darkness and in the shadow of death, to guide our feet into the way of peace" (1:78 ESV). Asia was also a Greek goddess, a "light-stepping daughter" of the Ocean, whose job was to look after the earth and water. Did John have any or all of this in mind? We don't know. But he does tell us that he is "in the Spirit"—so perhaps the question is, what did She have in mind?

NOTE

The names of John's seven churches also each have their own meaning.

- *Ephesus: feminine, "that which comes later"*
- *Smyrna: feminine, "myrrh" (a perfume used for both romance and to anoint dead bodies)*

John continues his salutation to the seven churches with these words:

> *Grace and peace to you from him who is, and who was, and who is to come, and from the seven spirits before his throne, and from Jesus Christ, who is the faithful witness, the firstborn from the dead, and the ruler of the kings of the earth.* (1:4,5 NIV)

Whenever we see the word "grace" in the New Testament, we are catching a glimpse of the Feminine Spirit. As we have mentioned before, the Greek word, *charis* or *xaris*, is a feminine term that implies "reaching toward, extending toward, leaning toward." It gives us an image of the Spirit reaching out to us with Her arms outstretched, Her hands full of gifts to give us. She is always leaning toward us to share with us Her abundance; She freely extends Herself to give Herself to us.[2]

The Living One, says John, is also giving us peace. Here the feminine-gendered Greek word *eiréné* means more than merely the absence of strife. It is a positive quality that implies not only rest and well-being but also the sense of "wholeness," with all essential parts joined together in unity.[3]

The vision John is about to describe is filled with darkness and danger, with sharp calls to repentance and warnings against sin. We need to keep in mind, though, that all this is contained within these two feminine words: grace and peace. As we saw with the Voice that spoke to Job, the Feminine Spirit can bring destruction and death—but only to facilitate birth and new life.

Look!

As John moves into the body of his story, he writes: "Look, he is coming with the clouds!" (1:7). As so often happens in the Bible, clouds (feminine gendered) are connected to the manifestation of God, the Divine revelation in the world of the five senses. Notice, though, that John is speaking in the present tense. Jesus' coming is happening *right now.*

John explains that he was "in the spirit" (or perhaps the "Spirit") when a voice like a trumpet speaks to him, telling him to write his vision in a book that he will send to the seven churches. When John turns around to see who is speaking, he sees:

seven golden lampstands, and in the middle of the lampstands someone who looks like a human offspring, wrapped in a garment that reaches to the feet, a golden belt girded across the breast. The head and hair are bright, like white wool, like snow; the eyes are like flame, like fire; feet like burnished bronze, like bronze that glows from the furnace; and a voice that sounds like many waters. The right hand holds seven stars; a sharp, two-edged sword goes forth from the mouth; and the face is like the sun shining in power. (1:12–16, literal translation)

John is so startled that he faints. The shining figure, however, touches John and says that old familiar message, given so often to women: "Do not be afraid." The figure goes on to say, "I am the First and the Last. I am the Living One; I was dead, and now look, I am alive for ever and ever! And I hold the keys of death and Hades [the underworld]" (1:17 NIV).

NOTE

John tells his readers that his vision happened while he was on the Island of Patmos. Why Patmos? It may simply have been where John happened to be, for whatever reason—but even then, it's likely that meaning upon meaning is enclosed in the word. Patmos is one of the islands collectively known as the Sporades, which means "the scattered"; Patmos is the northernmost island of the Dodecanese (literally, "Twelve Islands"). According to tradition, the name "Patmos" comes from the Greek word pateo, meaning "to tread upon," and may have been a reference to a legend that said the sea god stepped out of the water onto the island. Equally likely, "Patmos" may be derived from the word patema, "that which is trodden." The reference may be to grapes that are trodden in preparation for winemaking, but it could also be a reference to refuse, that which is thrown upon the ground because it is considered worthless. What spiritual implications come to your mind from these possible meanings?

The Women in Revelation

Revelation is full of metaphors and mysterious symbolism: living creatures covered with eyes and wings, an open door into heaven, a slaughtered Lamb with seven horns and seven eyes, a pale horse and a black horse, a throne, angels, stars, three rivers, locusts, scorpions, and terrifying dragons. In the midst of this welter of fantastic light and grotesque darkness, feminine images stand out again and again.

These images have been interpreted in many ways. Down through the centuries, people have tried to point to various institutions or groups of people as being the reality behind these feminine symbols. Some modern women see in Revelation a story that endorses sexism and patriarchy, with stereotyped "good women" and "whores," both persecuted and abused. But the "expert" interpretations do not matter. The real questions are: What do you see in these women? Can you see yourself? Can you see the Feminine Spirit, expressing herself through human beings, both female and male? Only you can say.

The first feminine figures we find in Revelation are the seven cities themselves. Each of them also has an "angel" who symbolizes her spiritual identity. In chapters 2 and 3, Jesus addresses these angels, discussing the qualities and characteristics of individual behavior while contrasting the best in human behavior with the worst.

1. The first message, to the church at Ephesus ("that which comes later"), affirms her for intelligently testing all things for herself, showing hard work and patience. But she has left her

first love, either abandoning it or allowing it to weaken in fervor. Unless she changes her thinking, she will be in trouble and bereft. Jesus refers to the "practices of Nicolatians," which he, like Ephesus, hates. Interpretations of this name include the subjugation of women through temple prostitution, the domination of unjust rulers, and the corruption of religious leaders who exercise abusive power over people. If Ephesus returns to her "first works," she will receive the right to eat from the tree of life that was forbidden to Adam and Eve. (Revelation 2:1–7)

2. In the second message, Jesus points out that although Smyrna ("myrhh") is wealthy, she is at the same time stressed and spiritually impoverished. She is a hypocrite, who claims to be one thing while actually being another—and yet Jesus comforts her, telling her not to be afraid. She will suffer testing, pain, and captivity for ten days; biblically, the number ten symbolizes our responsibility to God and others (as in the Ten Commandments), as well as singleness of purpose until the proper time has been completed. "Be faithful unto death," Jesus tells her, "and I will give you a crown of life." (2:8–11)

3. Jesus commends the faithfulness of Pergamum ("fortified tower"), even while she has been

surrounded by evil. He compares her, however, to Balaam, a prophet in the Hebrew scriptures who was pressured by King Balak to curse rather than bless God's people. If she overcomes these tendencies, Jesus will give her a "white stone, and a new name written on the stone, which no one but her will know."[4] (2:12–17)

4. Speaking to the angel at Thyatira ("fort of the fertility goddess"), Jesus commends her hard work, love, faith, service, and perseverance. He recognizes that she is growing in excellence—but he also points out that she "tolerates Jezebel." This is a reference to the woman in the Hebrew scripture who fought for power against Elijah; here, Jesus accuses her of corrupting the true message of the gospel, so that Thyatira accepts ego-driven, idolatrous behaviors. (We will hear more about Jezebel later in Revelation). As you read the destruction that Jesus promises, think of Jezebel and her children symbolically, as internal aspects of your own nature. If Thyatira can hold out against Jezebel, Jesus promises, she will receive power and "the morning star." (2:18–28)

5. Next, Jesus speaks to the angel at Sardis ("the red ones"), telling her to "wake up and strengthen the things that are about to die."

Remember the things she has learned, he tells her; stop sleeping—and she will walk with Jesus, "clothed in white garments," her name written in the book of life. (3:1–6)

6. Jesus tells Philadelphia ("familial love") that he has put an open door in front of her that no one can shut. "I am coming soon," he says, "so hold on tightly to what you have and don't lose your victory garland." Jesus will write on her his "new name," a name we still do not know, but that we discover as we meet Spirit face to face. (3:7–13)

7. Finally, Jesus tells the angel of Laodicea ("people of justice") that she is lukewarm in her devotion and practice, complacent in her material wealth. Like the emperor in the old story, she thinks she is clothed when all the while she is naked. Jesus advises her to replace her riches with his spiritual wealth, to cover her nakedness with his bright garments, and to rub her spiritual eyes with salve so that she can once more see clearly. "Those whom I love, I correct," he tells her, "so turn around, change your direction." (3:14–22)

The next woman we meet in Revelation (in chapter 12) is the "woman clothed with the sun, with the moon under her feet and a crown of twelve stars on her head."

This is a woman of great power and authority, dressed in the very fabric of Creation's light. Like so many of the women we have gotten to know in the pages of the Bible, this woman is pregnant. And like the Feminine Spirit at Creation, like Jesus on the cross, she is birthing new life.

A great red dragon—Eden's serpent grown huge—is waiting to devour the woman's son as soon as it is born. God snatches the child up into heaven, however, and the woman flees into the wilderness. Here again, we have another woman alone and in danger in the wilderness, the place where humans encounter the Living One. God has prepared for the woman a place of sanctuary, however, where she is cared for. Does the woman represent humanity—or the Feminine Spirit? Or both?

War breaks out now, with all the angelic forces pitted against the dragon. The dragon is hurled down to Earth, where he "leads the whole world astray." Is this something that happened long ago, at the beginning of human life on Earth? Is it something that will happen in the future? Or is it something that is happening continuously, right now, in all our inner beings? Time is fluid in the Book of Revelation, with past, present, and future intertwined, as though we are seeing chronology from God's timeless and eternal perspective.

On Earth, the serpent dragon continues to persecute the woman. Again the woman is saved; she is given "two wings of a great eagle, to fly into her place in the wilderness where she is nourished for a time, and times, and a time, from the face of the serpent." Here are the same eagle wings we found in Deuteronomy: "The Living One found the people in the wilderness, in howling confusion and emptiness, and God surrounded them and guarded them as though they were the pupil of the Divine eye. Like an eagle who wakes up her nest to hover over her babies, God's wings spread out to catch them and lift them on the Divine feathers" (Deuteronomy 32:10–11, literal translation).

Revelation tells a fast-paced story that's as dramatic as any technicolor saga. The war between the forces of good and evil continues. Paradoxically, the figure at the center of the "good side" is not a knight in a shining armor wielding a mighty sword but a Lamb. The Greek word is even the diminutive form; in other words, the hero of this story of wrath and warfare is a "lamby." In John's Gospel, when he sees Jesus coming toward him, he says, "Look, the Lamb of God who takes away the sin of the world" (John 1:29). These words connect Jesus to both the sacrifices of the Hebrew scripture and to the innocence and gentleness of a baby animal, an animal that is not a predator but eats only grass.

The next woman we meet is the opposite of the woman clothed in the sun. This woman is dressed in purple and scarlet (the colors of wealth and luxury), and she is riding on a scarlet beast. John writes that the name tattooed on her head is "Babylon the great, the mother of harlots and all the Earth's abominations" (Revelation 17:5).

This woman is the spirit of a seductive culture that says, "Me first," that values personal prestige and material possessions over love and self-sacrifice, the culture that today infiltrates our thoughts so easily through the media, as well as the attitudes of ourselves and nearly everyone around us. In Revelation, the scarlet woman, also referred to as Jezebel, is allied with the anti-Christ—in other words, everything that is not Christ, not love and equality.

Theologian Richard Rohr defines Christ as a wider, more inclusive name than "Jesus" (which refers to the specific incarnation of Christ as a human being) and asks:

What if Christ is a name for the transcendent within of every "thing" in the universe?

What if Christ is a name for the immense spaciousness of all true Love?

What if Christ refers to an infinite horizon that pulls us both from within and pulls us forward, too?

What if Christ is another name for every thing—in its fullness?[5]

If this is what Christ is, then the anti-Christ is everything that breaks and warps people and things out of their Divinely intended shape—everything that hates rather than loves, that destroys rather than creates, that empties rather than fills. The anti-Christ is the masculine version of this force, while Jezebel is the feminine. Each reveals gender that has been twisted, so that it no longer reveals the image of God.

Other symbolism is at work here as well. Babylon and Jerusalem are referred to in Revelation as two forms of civilization that have been spiritually at war with each other throughout all history. Babylon is connected to the Tower of Babel, where communication between humans broke down. It represents confusion and arrogance and oppression. Jerusalem, however, is a vision of peace, wholeness, cooperation, and health. These two forces have been mingled together in the human world since the Garden of Eden, and they will continue to be so until the end of the world. Babylon and Jerusalem also represent two aspects of every human being, at war in each of us—selfishness pitted against love.

New Testament scholar Shanell T. Smith admits that although she is repulsed by the woman Babylon in Revelation, Babylon also calls Smith to confront the reality of her own identity. The woman Babylon carries on her forehead the mark of her sexual objectification and subjugation to men—but at the same time she literally consumes the blood of her victims. We may want to distance ourselves from such ugliness, but Smith reminds us: "I must forever be aware that I benefit from the blood, sweat, and tears that were shed and continue to be shed by the many men and women, so many of them African American, who work at menial tasks to make my . . . life comfortable."[6] Even if we are women or people of color, we may still enjoy a life of privilege; as Smith points out, this means we are both victims of our culture and participants in it. In a world where human greed has consumed our planet's life to the point that the Earth is in serious peril, we are not innocent. According to Smith, the woman Babylon is a warning that we too can be influenced by the destructive forces Babylon represents.

John tells us that the words written on Babylon's head, indicating that she is the mother of prostitutes and all of Earth's abominations, are a "mystery." Why a mystery? Perhaps because evil is fundamentally abstruse—dark, not light. And yet the word "mystery" occurs numerous times throughout the New Testament, and in every other instance, it refers to the identity of Jesus. "The word of God in its fullness," writes Paul, "the mystery that has been kept hidden for ages and generations but is now revealed to God's people . . . the glorious riches of this mystery, which is Christ in you, the hope of glory" (Colossians 1:25–27 NIV).

In Ephesians, Paul speaks again of a mystery: "We declare God's wisdom, a mystery that has been hidden and that God destined for our glory before time began" (2:7 NIV). So what can it mean that Babylon's meaning is also a mystery? Perhaps in all these cases the word is a reminder not to put our ideas into a box. Whether we are speaking of Jesus or Babylon, we are challenged to resist the assumption that we have everything neatly figured out and defined. As the Greek philosopher Epictetus said long ago, "It is impossible for people to learn what they think they already know."

The word "mystery" warns us that the Book of Revelation is not a difficult code to be cracked, as some people have treated it. It is a vast panorama of multiple meanings. Each time we come to it, we discover some new insight.

The End of the Story

Revelation does not end on a negative note; we are not left with the terrible image of Babylon in our minds. Instead, as John's vision draws to a close, we see a "new heaven and a new earth" (21:1). This phrase echoes the prophecy of Isaiah: "Behold, I create new heavens and a new earth: and the former shall not be remembered, nor come into mind" (Isaiah 65:17 KJV). Masculine heaven and feminine earth represent the forever reunion of male and female.

Ruah Elohim is still creating, moving on the face of the waters of history and of all life and all consciousness. As She does so, masculine and feminine are restored to their truest meanings. They are both aspects of the Living One, as they were in the first chapter of Genesis.

At this point, John sees Jerusalem coming "down from God out heaven, prepared as a bride adorned for her husband" (Revelation 21:2 KJV). Feminine and masculine will no longer be divided, one subjugated to the other. Instead, each retaining its own nature, they will be united, joined in love.

Next, John hears a loud voice saying: "Look! God's dwelling is among humanity. God dwells among them and they are God's people" (21:3, literal translation). The battle within our identities between good and evil has ended, and we are restored to the life-giving intimacy with God for which we were created from the beginning of time.

Jerusalem now has "no need of the sun, neither of the moon" (22:3), for it is lit by the glory of God. Once again, we hear the echo of Isaiah's words: "The sun will no more be your light by day, nor will the brightness of the moon shine on you, for the Lord will be your everlasting light, and your God will be your glory" (Isaiah 60:19 NIV). "Glory," in both Hebrew and Greek, is a feminine noun having to do with the brightness of the sun, moon, and stars, as well as splendor, excellence, dignity, grace, majesty, and honor. Creation has returned to the Light that existed before the heavenly bodies were created.

The voice from heaven continues:

> *God will wipe away every eye's teardrop; death will no longer exist, nor will there be any sadness and sorrow, nor crying, nor anguish and pain—for these earlier things have passed away. The One seated on the throne says, "Look! I am making all things new and fresh." . . . There will no longer be any curse.* (21:4,5; 22:3, literal translation)

Everything that was associated with the "curse of Eve" is eradicated. All is restored; all is whole. The struggle is over, and all consciousness has been brought into the Light.

"It is coming into being," Jesus tells John. "I am the Alpha and the Omega, the origin and the fulfillment" (21:6, literal translation). Alpha is the first letter of the Greek alphabet and omega is the last. With these words, time is enclosed within the Divine Being. Present, past, and future are coexistent. They are all now.

One Story

In the beginning of the Bible we read of two Creations. One account (found in Genesis 1) describes Eternity; the other (Genesis 2) records chronological time. Through the rest of the scriptures we see evidence of these two stories, both separate and intersecting. In the midst of human experience, the narratives periodically give way to reveal the Feminine Spirit at work. The mist of the second Creation parts, allowing us to glimpse the eternal, the spiritual. These are not mere abstractions but rather the presence and power of Spirit in the flesh and the daily affairs of all.

In Revelation, the two stories at last become one story. We have reached Eden, but this time without the serpent, without any deceit, without the curse.

"The Spirit and the bride say, 'Come.' And let the one who hears say, 'Come.'" Not only are masculine and feminine united, but all humanity is also knit together with God, our voices joining with the voice of the Living One. The final note of John's vision is this invitation: "Come!"

"And let the one who is thirsty come; let the one who wishes take the water of life without cost" (22:17 NASB). As in the beginning, *ruah Elohim*, the Feminine Spirit, moves on the face of the waters.

REFERENCE NOTES

1. A concise history of interpretations of Revelation can be found in Arthur Wainwright's *Mysterious Apocalypse: Interpreting the Book of Revelation* (Nashville: Abingdon Press, 1993).

2. These meanings are drawn from *HELPS Word-studies*, https://biblehub.com/greek/5485.htm.

3. Ibid.

4. The nineteenth-century theologian George MacDonald (who filled his fiction with images of the Feminine Spirit) wrote of the white stone: "Each of us is growing toward the revelation of our true selves, the white stone given to each person by God, on which the true name is written. . . . Every moment that we are true to our true selves some new shine of the white stone breaks on our inward eyes." In *The White Stone: Selections from George Mac-Donald* (Vestal, NY: Anamchara Books, 2011).

5. Richard Rohr. *The Universal Christ: How a Forgotten Reality Can Change Everything We See, Hope for and Believe* (New York, NY: Convergent Books, 2019), page 5.

6. Shanell T. Smith. *The Woman Babylon and the Marks of Empire: Reading Revelation with a Postcolonial Womanist Hermeneutics of Ambiveilence* (Minneapolis, MN: Augsburg Fortress, 2014), page 12.

AUTHOR'S READING LIST

In addition to the books and articles cited in this book, here are other readings that may interest you, as they did me, supplying additional information and alternative viewpoints:

Robert Alter

The Art of Biblical Narrative was the first book I read that sent me looking at the Bible's entire text, rather than just verses pulled out from their surroundings. Since then, I've read all of Alter's books.

Eric Auerbach

Mimesis, the Representation of Reality in Western Literature does not focus on biblical interpretation (though he does include chapters on the Bible) but rather helps us to understand the ways in which all art and literature reflect the real world. Applying his ideas to the Bible has deepened my understanding of the ways in which story, meaning, and "real life" are interwoven.

Martin Buber

On The Bible: Eighteen Studies reveals Buber's interpretation of scripture as a way of experiencing the Divine Presence in scripture reading—of entering into a dialogue that creates a relationship with God. Buber states in his introductory essay that the reader should approach the Bible "as something entirely unfamiliar" and yet to be "yielded to" with one's entire being.

Denise Lardner Carmody

Biblical Woman: Contemporary Reflections on Spiritual Texts explains the background and context of particular Bible passages and then suggests what they might mean to today's readers who are searching for a deeper understanding of the feminine themes within the Bible.

Marchette Chute

In *The End of the Search,* Chute introduced me to a new way of viewing the Book of Revelation.

David Curzon

The *Gospels in Our Image: An Anthology of Twentieth Century Poetry Based on Biblical Texts* uses poetry to lead us to a deeper perspective on traditional texts. I love this book.

Rene Girard

Violence and the Sacred and *The Scapegoat* are two of my favorite books by Girard. I reread at least one of his books each year. His analysis of what the Crucifixion and Resurrection of Jesus Christ has brought to the world is profound

Wilda C. Gafney

In addition to her book, *Womanist Midrash: A Reintroduction to the Women of the Torah and the Throne,* I recommend *Daughters of Miriam: Women Prophets in Ancient Israel.* Gafney brings out into the light the female prophets that were hiding in the masculine grammar and patriarchal interpretations of the Hebrew scriptures. Wil Gafney is a force who speaks with a knowledge of Hebrew and women.

Gabriel Josipivici

The Book of God: A Response to the Bible is a riveting journey with the children of Israel. It also offers some interesting comments on Saul/Paul.

Frank Kermode

The Genesis of Secrecy: On the Interpretation of Narrative was the first book I read that showed me how to look at biblical text in detail, while seeing the many possible questions in the text.

Judith Plaskow

In *Standing Again at Sinai: Judaism from a Feminist Perspective*, Plaskow suggests that we can bring women's experience to the naming of God, continuing the ongoing process of "God-wrestling that demands of each generation that it search for and speak its own symbols, standing again at Sinai with the consciousness of today."

Jacqueline Rose

Sexuality in the Field of Vision is not about the Bible per se, but it is an intelligent analysis of the ways in which our gender shapes the lens through which we see the world (which I've found applies as well to the ways in which we read the Bible).

Regina Schwartz (editor)

The Book and the Text: The Bible and Literary Theory is another book that helps us discover new ways to read and interact with scripture.

Mitzi J. Smith

I Found God in Me: A Womanist Biblical Hermeneutics Reader is a collection of essays by a range of woman scholars, focusing on "womanist" biblical interpretative theories and theology.

Harriet Beecher Stowe

Women in Sacred History: A Celebration of Women in the Bible was written in 1873, before the current feminist revolution. It includes short biographies of biblical women, revealing some of the spiritual influences that led this eighteenth-century women to also write *Uncle Tom's Cabin*, a best-selling novel that inspired abolitionist activism in the United States. Stowe's work is an interesting example of the way in which women, of any era, interact with scripture's Feminine Spirit.

Delores S. Williams and Katie G. Cannon

Sisters in the Wilderness: The Challenge of Womanist God-Talk draws on the biblical figure of Hagar as a prototype for the struggle of African-American women. First published more than twenty years ago, this was a groundbreaking book for the way that women, especially women of color, continue to interact with scripture.

GLOSSARY OF IMPORTANT WORDS IN THE BIBLE'S ORIGINAL LANGUAGES

Hebrew

adam Originally, in Hebrew this was not a proper noun—the name of a particular person—but rather a word referring to a generic human being (though masculine in gender). The Hebrew root words have to do with "blood," "red," and "of the ground."

anan A masculine noun meaning "cloud." In the Hebrew scriptures, clouds often accompany the manifestation of the Feminine Spirit as glory (see ***kabod*** and ***Shekinah***) and light (as when God guided the Israelites through the desert, going "ahead of them in a pillar of cloud to guide them on their way and by night in a pillar of fire to give them light" (Exodus 13:21 NIV).

aretz A feminine noun meaning "land." In the first chapter of Genesis, as God "speaks" the process of Creation by making distinctions within Reality, the word is used first for land as distinct from the sky (verse 1) and then for land as distinct from water (verse 12). Later in the Bible, the word will come to be used to refer to political lands (similar to modern-day nations), but here at the beginning, we are talking about soil, earth—the generative and nurturing solid matter of our planet.

beer   A feminine noun meaning a "well." Wells have recurring significance in both Hebrew and Christian scriptures, and they are the setting for several dramatic scenes (from Hagar in the wilderness to Jesus' encounter with the Samaritan woman). In a desert region, wells were particularly important for well-being, and symbolically, they represent the Feminine Spirit as a source of spiritual and physical life, health, and prosperity.

chokmah   A feminine-gendered noun meaning "wisdom." The Hebrew word implies skill, prudence, keen judgment, insight, and good sense. When used as an attribute of God—the Feminine Spirit—the word is often personified: she is the Divine Architect in Creation (Proverbs 8:22–31); she builds a palace and spreads a feast for those who will receive her instruction (Proverbs 9:1); and she teaches in public places (Proverbs 1:20; 8:1,5,11,12).

echad An adjective meaning "one." As with English, the Hebrew word can have a range of meanings that extends beyond the numeral, including "unique," "alone," and "united, unified, together."

El Elyon A name of God. *El* is a masculine noun that refers to God (or gods), with the implicate meaning of "strength, power." *Elyon* means "high," "supreme," "highest one"; the root word is the verb *alah*, which means "to go up, to ascend, to climb."

El-roi See above for the meaning of *El*. *Roi* means "seeing." Together, the two words mean "the God who sees me" or "the Strong One who sees me."

El Shaddai See ***El Elyon*** for the meaning of *El*. *Shaddai* has traditionally been translated "Almighty," in both Jewish and Christian translations, with Bible scholars pointing to a possible root word that meant "destroyer, demolisher." More recent scholarship, however, has found that the word can more accurately be translated "breasts." The combined meaning then would be "God is my breast," or "the God with breasts."

Elohim This biblical name for God is actually the plural form of El (see above). Although it is a plural noun, the Hebrew often—but not always—uses a singular verb with it. When used as a singular name for

Deity, translators have considered it to be a "honorific plural," indicating honor and power in the one named. However, the usage of this word is often ambiguous in the original Hebrew; the plural form, followed by a plural verb, sometimes refers to Deity, but it can apparently also refer to angels and other "powers."

emeth   This feminine noun, as well as *emunah*, another feminine noun, is usually translated "faithfulness." It is used in the Hebrew scriptures to indicate God's firmness, stability, truth, steadiness, and reliability

ezer kenegdo   "A suitable helper"; this is the Hebrew term used for Eve's relationship to Adam, and it has traditionally been understood to imply Eve's subordinance to Adam, with the extended implication that women are intended to make men's lives easier by caring for their physical needs. More recent scholarship, however, has pointed out that the word *ezer* is most often used in scripture to refer to God, always referring to powerful acts of rescue and support. In his commentary on Genesis, John Walton has this to say about the word: "It carries no implications regarding the relationship or relative status of the individuals involved. In fact, the noun form of the word found in this verse as used elsewhere refers almost exclusively to God. . . . Nothing suggests a subservient status of the one helping; in fact, the opposite is more likely. Certainly 'helper' cannot be understood as the opposite/complement of 'leader.'"[1] Meanwhile, the word *kenegdo* has a wide range of meanings: "in front of," "opposite," "opposing," "appropriate," "under," "like, as," "corresponding to," "similar." When combined with the word *ezer*, Bible scholar Walter Kaiser interprets the meaning of *kenegdo* in Genesis to indicate that what "God had intended then was to make a 'power' or 'strength' [ezer] for the man who would in every way 'correspond to him' or even 'be his equal'."[2] Carrie Miles notes that in using the words *ezer kenegdo*, "God says that the lonely [human] needs a source of strength on the same level, face-to-face—not a housemaid."[3]

hebel   This masculine-gendered noun is the word used in Ecclesiastes, when the phrase "vanity of vanities, all is vanity" is repeated again and again. The word refers to emptiness, worthlessness, but literally, it means "vapor, breath." Unlike ***ruah***, however (see below), which indicates the breath of life and is connected to the substantial Divine manifestation of **Shekinah**, *hebel* refers to something that is transitory, lifeless, and insubstantial.

kabod   Usually translated as "glory," the feminine noun has to do with God's light and splendor. We might think of this as something airy, insubstantial, ethereal, but that is not the case: "abundance" is contained within the word's meaning, and the root word has to do with weightiness or heaviness; the glory of God is Divine manifestation in a substantial and tangible form, an ample form with heft and weight. This glory is nurturing; Isaiah 66:11 speaks of "sucking the abundance of glory" (literal translation; the New International Version gives this translation: "For you will nurse and be satisfied at her comforting breasts; you will drink deeply and delight in her overflowing abundance"). *Kabod* can also mean "liver," which was considered to be the seat of the emotions (what we refer to as the "heart"). By implication, we can say that God's glory—the Feminine Spirit—resides as if integral to our own flesh.

kanaph   A feminine noun that means "wing." It can also mean "covering" or "garment." In the Bible, the word often implies the sheltering protection of the Feminine Spirit.

lekh lekha   These are the first words that God speaks to Abram, in Genesis 12:1, telling him to leave his country. *Lekh* means "go," and *lekha* means "to you" or "for you." Most translators indicate that *lekha* makes the command more emphatic; we might say, "Get up and go!" or "Get yourself going!" Literally, though, the words mean "go *to* yourself." Rashi, the eleventh-century rabbi and Bible commentator, said that the meaning is: "Go for your own benefit," while other Jewish scholars taught that the phrase means, "Go to yourself." The implication is that Abram's journey covers more than geographical territory; it is also a spiritual journey, an inward quest toward a new way of seeing the world. Understood in that light, these words ask us to venture out past our familiar comfort zones into new encounters with God and others.

malak   A masculine noun usually translated as "angel," the word literally means "messenger," "envoy, ambassador," or "deputy." Although biblical angels sometimes appear as human beings, they may also be anything—a thought, a revelation, an idea—that carries a Divine message or that acts on God's behalf.

memshalah   A feminine noun meaning "rule, government, power, authority." In modern Hebrew, the word usually refers to a political government, but the word first occurs in scripture in reference to the sun and moon ("the sun to rule the day, and the moon to rule the night"; Genesis 1:16). The implication of this original usage is that this feminine form of authority has defined boundaries and is able to share power—and perhaps that the use of authority is not intended to subjugate but rather to give light.

midbar   A masculine noun that refers to the wilderness—uninhabited land. The word also, however, means "speech" or "mouth" (in the sense that a mouth is the organ of speech). The root word is the verb *dabar*, which means "to speak, to answer, to name, or to commune." Throughout the Bible, in both the Hebrew and Christian scriptures, the wilderness is a place of Divine revelation. It is a place where desperate people are drawn, and where they eventually hear God's voice.

or   As a verb, the word means "to give light, to enlighten, to make luminous." As a noun, it is usually feminine in gender, and it refers to both physical and spiritual/intellectual illumination.

qeren   A feminine noun meaning "horn," which includes the following meanings: a ram's horn, an oil flask, a wind instrument, and a hill. Symbolically, the word indicates personal strength and authority, as well as vision and rays of light. The root verb means "to send out rays of light."

qesheth   A feminine noun that usually refers to the "bow" an archer uses to shoot arrows; in Genesis, the word refers to the rainbow that appears in the sky after the Flood. Usually thought to represent a Divine promise to humanity, Ezekiel 1:28 indicates that the rainbow is also connected to the concept of glory and the Divine presence (see **Shekinah** and **kabod**): "As the appearance of the bow that is in the cloud in the day of rain, so was the appearance of the brightness round about. This was the appearance of the likeness of the glory of the Lord" (Ezekiel 1:28 TNK).

racham Usually translated as "to have compassion," the word also refers to the womb, as the place where the fetus is cherished and kept safe. The King James Version translates it (and its various derivatives) as "mercy" thirty-five times, "compassion" seventeen times, "pity" six times, "love" once, and "womb" twenty-four times. Recently, Bible commentators have used the term "womb-love" to refer to Divine love.

ruah A feminine noun that can mean "breath," "wind," "storm," or "spirit." When used with the word ***Elohim*** (see above), it indicates the Feminine Spirit of God who is present at Creation. Derek Kidner writes that *ruah* is a term "for God's ongoing energy, creative and sustaining."[4] Throughout the Hebrew scriptures, She is shown at work in the ongoing process of nurturing and "breathing" life.

satan In the Hebrew scriptures, this was not originally a proper noun (referring to an evil arch-enemy of all that is good, synonymous with "the devil"), but rather a masculine-gendered generic noun meaning literally "adversary, opponent, accuser." A recent article from the Biblical Archeology Society indicates that in the Hebrew Bible, the word refers to "a job description rather than a proper name. From the Accuser's appearances in the Book of Job and Zechariah, it seems that the job entails calling attention to the unworthiness of [human]kind. The Accuser is essentially the prosecuting attorney of the divine court of YHWH, and part of his job includes collecting evidence to prove his cases."[5]

seter   A verb meaning "to hide," "to keep secret," "to keep close." The similar word *sathar* or *cether* is a feminine noun ("hiding place, secret place," "shelter," or "covering"), which can be used to refer to the womb.

shalom   A masculine noun usually translated as "peace," which contains within it a wealth of meaning that includes wellness, completeness, wholeness, safety, friendship, and prosperity. Rabbi Robert I. Kahn describes the differences between the political concept of peace and the Hebrew concept of *shalom*: "One can dictate a peace; shalom is a mutual agreement. Peace is a temporary pact; shalom is a permanent agreement. One can make a peace treaty; shalom is the condition of peace. Peace can be negative, the absence of commotion.

Shalom is positive, the presence of serenity. Peace can be partial; shalom is whole. Peace can be piecemeal; shalom is complete."[6]

sharats This verb means "to breed abundantly" or "to swarm, to teem with life." Throughout the Hebrew scriptures it refers to fertile, abundant physical life.

Shekinah A feminine noun meaning "covering" or "dwelling," the word refers to the feminine manifestation of God. Like the word *Trinity*, the word *Shekinah* does not actually occur in scripture, and yet its reality is implied by the text. The biblical concept of "glory"— ***kabod*** (see above)—is closely connected to *Shekinah*, as are descriptions of cloud and light as forms of Divine manifestation.

shiphah This is the feminine noun the Voice uses in the Book of Job to refer to the Earth's waters; it is usually translated "abundance." The Hebrew words *athereth* (see Jeremiah 33:6, where it refers to peace [***shalom***]) and *yithrath* (see Isaiah 15:7, where it indicates wealth) are also feminine nouns that are translated into English as "abundance."

yeshuah A feminine noun that means "deliverance," "health, welfare" "salvation," "prosperity," and "victory." The root words have to do with capaciousness (a sense of space and freedom), liberation, safety, and rescue. Jesus' Hebrew name would have been pronounced *Yeshuah*.

YHWH   The proper noun that refers to the God of Israel, which is usually translated as "Lord," although sometimes as "Yahweh" or "Jehovah." Because the name was considered too holy to be spoken, the word was often replaced with "Lord," but recent Bible scholarship indicates that the literal meanings include: "Life-Giver," "The One Who Brings into Being," "The Existing One," "The Ever-Living One," "The Becoming One," and "The Existing One Who Brings into Existence All Things That Exist."

Greek

arché   This feminine noun is the word used in John 1:1: "In the beginning was the Word, and the Word was with God, and the Word was God." It means "origin," "beginning point," or "first in priority."

authentein   This word, usually translated as "authority," is used only once in the New Testament, in 1 Timothy 2:12: "But I suffer not a woman to teach, nor to usurp authority over the man, but to be in silence" (KJV). Everywhere else in the Greek scripture the word exousia is used for "authority." Although this single verse has been used to support patriarchal attitudes toward women, modern scholarship suggests that the meaning of *authentein* has been misunderstood. Although it is not used anywhere else in the Bible, it is common in Classical literature, where it refers to murderers, criminal masterminds, and perpetrators of violence.[7] After looking at every known use of the word *authentein* in Greek literature over the centuries from 200 BCE to 200 CE, Bible scholar Leland Wilshire concludes that *authentein* might best be translated as "to instigate violence." In other words, women in Timothy's congregation were to neither teach violence nor instigate it—but the injunction had nothing to do with women's subordination.

charis A feminine noun that is usually translated as "grace" (as in, "the grace of God"), the word's meanings include: "that which gives joy, pleasure, and delight," "loveliness," "undeserved kindness," and "generosity." *Xaris*, another similar Greek word that comes from the same root word, means "leaning toward someone or something in order to share benefit," "reaching toward," "extending oneself."

diakonos A noun that can be either feminine or masculine, it is usually translated as "deacon." We have come to think of this as a formal officer of the Church, but its original meaning was simply "servant" or "minister"—in other words, someone who tends to the needs of others, who works on others' behalf. Servanthood—being humble enough to give our energy and resources to others—is a central concept to Jesus' message, one that he demonstrated when he washed his friends' feet.

doxa   "Glory"; like its Hebrew counterpart, *kabad* (see above), this is a feminine noun that speaks of splendor, brightness, and the manifestation of God.

ekklesia   The feminine noun usually translated as "church" literally means "assembly, congregation, gathering, or meeting." It is formed from two root words that together mean "called out from." Christians have interpreted this to mean "called out from the world," but the word was in use before the Christian Church was established, when it would have indicated simply that people had been called out from their private homes in order to gather in a public space for some purpose.

eiréné   A feminine noun that's translated "peace," the original word meant "quietness," "rest," "harmony," and "prosperity." (See the Hebrew word *shalom*.) The root word *eirō* means "to join, tie together into a whole"—in other words, "wholeness," the state of integration and completeness where all the separate parts are working together as one.

karpos   Usually translated as "fruit," the word can also refer to both children and the consequences of something. In John 15:16, when Jesus says, "I chose you to go and bear fruit," we might also read it to say, "I chose you to bring forth children" (in a spiritual sense).

kephalé   Usually translated as "head," this feminine noun means "the top or uppermost part." Verses in the New Testament that indicate that man is "the head of" women have traditionally been interpreted to indicate that God intends men to hold a superior position of authority over women. Recent scholarship has uncovered other possible meanings of the Greek word. Letha Scanzoni and Nancy Hardesty write that "*kephale* is used almost synonymously with *arche*, 'beginning,' somewhat similar to our use of 'the head-waters of a river' or 'fountain head.'" In Ephesians 5:23, where it says, "Christ is the head of the church, his body," Scanzoni and Hardesty take it to mean that he is the church's "lifegiver," and when Colossians 2:10 calls Christ "the head of all rule and authority," they say, "Head here obviously means 'source.'"[9] This, then, would not indicate that women are Divinely intended to be subordinate to men but rather would be based on the

Creation story in Genesis 2, where woman is created from man's body.

ktisis   A feminine noun meaning "creation," applied only to God (creation of out nothing). It can mean both the Divine act of creating and "everything that is created."

kurios   A masculine noun translated as "Lord," used in reference to Jesus; the root word means "authority."

logos   Translated as "Word" and used in reference to Christ, the word's literal meaning is a "statement or speech that embodies an idea." In this sense, Christ is the Word of God—he embodies God, he communicates God to us. We might also say that Christ is the "and-God-said" in the Genesis 1 Creation story. Christ is God saying, God speaking, God creating through the Word.

pléroó   This verb, meaning "to make full," "to accomplish," "to complete," and "to bring into realization," is the one Matthew uses again and again to refer to Jesus' relationship to the Hebrew scriptures.

poieó   A verb meaning "to make, to construct, to cause, or to shape." In only one instance, 1 Peter 3:7, is it translated to indicate weakness (women's).

tapeinósis   This feminine noun is the word Mary uses to describe herself in the Magnificat, when she refers to her "low estate." Literally, it means "humiliation," "spiritual abasement," "poverty," "lack of social standing," or "depression." With this term, Mary claims for all the desperate, impoverished, and in trouble women whose stories are told in the Bible (and for all of us) that from now on we will be considered blessed and happy (Luke 1:48).

REFERENCE NOTES

1. John H. Walton. *Genesis* (Grand Rapids: Zondervan, 2001), page 176.

2. Walter C. Kaiser, Jr., Peter H. Davids, F. F. Bruce, & Manfred Brauch. *Hard Sayings of the Bible* (InterVarsity Press, 1996), page 94.

3. Carrie A. Miles. "Gender," in *The Oxford Handbook of Christianity and Economic,* Paul Oslington (ed.) (Oxford University Press, 2014), page 608.

4. Derek Kidner. *Genesis* (London: Tyndale Press, 1968), page 45.

5. John Gregory Drummond. "Who Is Satan?" *Biblical Archeology Society: Bible History Daily,* October 31, 2018, https://www.biblicalarchaeology.org/daily/biblical-topics/bible-interpretation/who-is-satan/.

6. Robert I Kahn. *Bible Readings for the Synagogue* (New York: Temple Emanu-El, 1957).

7. Linda L. Belleville. "Teaching and Usurping Authority: 1 Timothy 2:11–15," in *Discovering Biblical Equality: Complementarity without Hierarchy*, Ronald Pierce and Rebecca Merrill Groothius, eds. (Downers Grove, IL: InterVarsity Press, 2004), pages 205–223, 212.

8. Leland Wilshire. *Insights into Two Biblical Passages* (Lanham, MD: University Press of America, 2010), page 38.

9. Letha Scanzoni and Nancy Hardesty. *All We're Meant to Be* (Waco, TX: Word, 1974), pages 30–31, 100.

INDEX

ezer 53

H

Lapsley, J. E. 121

Lassner, Jacob 219

laughter 75, 94, 95, 98

law 62, 91, 144, 179, 205, 233,
    262, 293, 296, 345, 346,
    356, 357

Leah 117–119, 137, 177, 180

Lebanon 212

Lee, Ann 57

Lemuel 249

leprosy 137, 138

lexicon(s) 26, 27

light 28, 33–39, 42, 44–46, 50,
    82, 122, 125, 128, 130, 138,
    139, 145, 146, 151, 155, 157,
    200, 205, 222, 230, 240,
    273, 275, 276, 290, 295,
    307, 327, 328, 342, 366,
    371, 375, 379, 381, 382

Living One 86, 112–117, 186,
    187, 194, 200, 208, 211,
    214, 220–222, 225, 226,
    228, 231, 233, 234, 236,
    240, 244, 245, 247–249,
    251, 253, 259, 266, 268,
    270, 271, 273, 280–288,
    291, 296–298, 307, 316,
    339, 340, 354, 368, 369,

375, 376, 381, 383

Lord (God) 47, 49, 52, 54, 83,
    95, 102, 106, 108, 110, 116,
    120, 140, 143, 144, 152,
    158–160, 175, 178, 180,
    183, 184, 193, 199, 202,
    210, 215, 217, 223, 227, 229,
    231, 235, 236, 263, 283,
    288, 293, 317, 319, 320,
    322, 340, 347–351, 355,
    359, 381

Lot 75, 96, 164

love
    God's 10, 58, 168, 205,
        214, 215, 247, 249, 251,
        254, 272, 284, 286,
        291, 292, 297, 298, 315,
        323, 330, 357, 358, 367,
        377, 378, 381

    human 99, 101, 107, 112,
        117, 118, 125, 164, 169,
        177, 180, 181, 190, 201,
        205, 236, 243, 253,
        258, 266, 284, 298,
        349, 350, 352, 367,
        372, 377

Lucks, Naomi 221

Luger, Stephen 97, 104

Luke (see Gospel of)

mystery 10, 94, 136, 146, 259, 350, 362, 379, 380

N

Nabal 190, 191, 193, 195

Nachmanides 38

name(s)/naming 66, 68, 79, 85, 86, 90, 92, 113, 122, 275, 276, 316, 373, 384

    of God 46, 49, 74, 81, 86, 87, 89, 127, 135, 136, 138, 269, 270, 280

    meaning of 67, 68, 77, 86, 89, 90, 98, 101, 122, 128, 130, 133, 157, 221, 222, 243, 249, 275, 316, 323

Naomi 141, 174–179, 181, 182, 186, 221, 235, 236, 240

Nashville Statement 70

National Coalition Against Domestic Violence 18

New Testament 22, 26, 36, 43, 59, 69, 70, 93, 103, 107, 117, 192, 220, 234, 285, 299, 301–383

Nguyen, Quynh-Hoa 226

Nicolatians 372

Nile, River 129, 130

Noah 67–71

Numbers, Book of 138

numbers, meaning of

    forty 133

    seven 274–276, 365

    ten 372

    three 296, 339, 340

    twelve 314

O

O'Connor, Kathleen 253

oil 215, 225

"The Original Equality of Women" 57

Orpah 176

P

paradox 48, 167, 316, 329, 350, 376

Pardes, Ilana 65, 66, 268

Pascal, Blaise 11

Y

Z

All Shall Be Well

A Modern-Language Version of the Revelation of Julian of Norwich

The fourteenth-century mystic, Julian of Norwich, was intimately acquainted with the Feminine Spirit. She wrote: "Mercy is an act of compassion that expresses God's Motherhood, the Divine Feminine who is tender and loving. . . . God rejoices that He is our Father, and at the same time She rejoices that She is our Mother." Julian goes on to say, "I understood that we can consider God's Motherhood from three perspectives: the first is that the Divine Mother gave birth to us and gave us life; the second is that She shared our lives; and the third is that She works always to keep us safe."

The great spiritual classic by Julian of Norwich is now available in modern, easy-to-comprehend language that stays true to Julian's original meanings. Discover Julian's joyous affirmation of the certainty of Divine love, a love that overcomes all.

Paperback Price: $24.95

Kindle Price: $9.99

Hazelnuts from Julian of Norwich

Meditations on Divine Love

"The Spirit showed me a tiny thing, the size of a hazelnut," wrote the fourteenth-century mystic, Julian of Norwich. In Julian's vision, the fragile and insignificant hazelnut contains all of Creation—and yet it endures "because God loves it."

In Julian's understanding of the Incarnation, we see the Feminine Spirit doing a mother's work in our lives. Julian wrote, "In Mother Christ we are nurtured so that we grow, and in Mother Christ's mercy we are reshaped, restored, reunited with our spiritual essence. . . . This is our Mother's work in all of us."

These prayer-poems, based on *All Shall Be Well: A Modern-Language Version of the Revelation of Julian Norwich*, are an accessible

introduction to Julian's joyous theology of Divine love. "Take this book from my heart to yours," she wrote. "If you forget all the rest, remember this: Love is everything. Love is God."

Paperback Price: $14.95

Kindle Price: $5.99

Reading the Bible the Celtic Way
The Peacock's Tail Feathers

We need to read the Bible in new ways.

The ancient Christian Celts regarded Scripture as a gleaming, multifaceted treasure trove of meaning. In a time when the Bible is often regarded either as irrelevant or as a literal and rigid monolith, we can learn from the Celts' willingness to see beneath the surface of our English translations, venturing out into the endless depths of metaphors and stories.

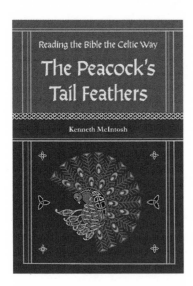

Allow the Christian Celts to lead you on a journey into Scripture, where you will encounter the loving and infinite Mystery in which we live and move and have our being.

Paperback Price: $14.95

Kindle Price: $5.99

The Mother Heart of God

A Modern-Language Version of Hannah Whitall Smith's *God of All Comfort*

Hannah Whitall Smith knew the Feminine Spirit of God. She turned away from a patriarchal notion of God, that looked "upon Him as a stern, unbending Judge, holding us at a distance, and demanding our respectful homage, and critical of our slightest faults." She wrote, "Is it any wonder that our religion, instead of making us comfortable, has made us thoroughly uncomfortable? Who could help being uncomfortable in the presence of such a Judge? But I rejoice to say that that stern Judge is not there. He does not exist.

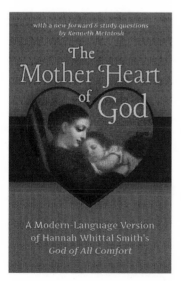

The God who does exist is a God who is like a mother, a God who says to us as plainly as words can say it, 'As a mother comforts, so will I comfort you.'"

This modern-language version of Smith's spiritual classic includes a new introduction by author Kenneth McIntosh, as well as discussion questions.

Paperback Price: $24.95

Kindle Price: $9.99

Lynne Bundesen has written and photographed for publications in the United States, Asia, and Europe. She spent four years in China, the Philippines, and Thailand, covering the fall of Madame Mao and The Gang of Four, the Marcos regime, and the auto-genocide in Cambodia. She is the author of books addressing religious and political issues and a three-time winner of the Angel Religion in Media Award for her syndicated column on women and religion. She has lived in Hong Kong, Thailand, the Philippines, England, France, Sweden, Norway, and currently lives in the U.S.

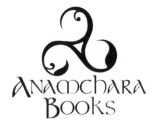

ANAMCHARA
BOOKS

AnamcharaBooks.com